Living Literacy

*The human foundations of speaking,
writing and reading*

MICHAEL ROSE

Hawthorn Press

Published by Hawthorn Press, Hawthorn House, 1 Lansdown Lane, Stroud, Gloucestershire, GL5 1BJ, UK
Tel: (01453) 757040 Fax: (01453) 751138
info@hawthornpress.com
www.hawthornpress.com

Cover photograph by Anna Marshall
Illustrations by Marije Rowling
Cover design by Hawthorn Press, Stroud, Gloucestershire
Design and typesetting by Hawthorn Press, Stroud, Gloucestershire
Printed in the UK by The Cromwell Press, Trowbridge, Wiltshire

Every effort has been made to trace the ownership of all copyrighted material. If any omission has been made, please bring this to the publisher's attention so that proper acknowledgment may be given in future editions.

British Library Cataloguing in Publication Data applied for

ISBN 978-1-903458-52-5

Contents

Foreword

When his servants and friends wanted to stop Don Quixote from undertaking even more madcap adventures they decided to burn his library of books on chivalry. For them, his unbalanced taste for literature had been his undoing. However, this dramatic and preventive action was to no avail as Don Quixote had fully imbibed the medieval stories of knights and valiant quests. His character had been deeply influenced by them, and he continued in his idealistic pursuit of what, in his eyes, was true and good. His literacy had raised questions in him of how he should act in a corrupt world that was decaying around him. Literacy changes us and there is no going back. In recent years the word itself has assumed connotations beyond just reading and writing, and is now used generally to describe the competencies we are thought to need in fulfilling our responsibilities as citizens of the modern world. 'Literacy' in these contexts suggests a way of finding our full potential.

In its more traditional definition literacy is a right that was recognised in the Universal Declaration of Human Rights. It is also the means whereby we achieve those rights, yet is one still denied to a fifth of the world's population. This timely book is being published close to the start of the United Nations' ten-year 'Literacy Decade', from 2003 to 2012. It is hoped that 100 million children not in primary education and 771 million over-15s with no basic literacy skills will be helped to achieve this entitlement. Even in so-called developed countries these skills are still lacking in large segments of the population, and it is the duty of society as a whole to remedy this situation – something that will require a holistic, thoughtful and sensitive approach.

We all recognise that literacy – and engagement, beyond the basics, with life and culture through the written word – is an integral part of our lives and contributes to a sense of identity and self-worth. Where people differ, in an educational sense, is how to get there. This book draws on the Steiner-Waldorf approach, now practised in more than 60 countries, which attempts to imbue the learning and use of literacy with a living quality, rooting it in the child's total experience rather than as mere cognitive icing on the cake. In other words literacy should arise as part of a natural, overall development, which takes full account of 'pre-literate' skills such as physical dexterity, imagination and feeling. Reading and writing skills are part of our human nature and how we acquire them continues to live on in our dispositions regardless of our chronological age. At the same time this book also acknowledges the best in modern literacy teaching, and uses its professional insights to enhance and extend the Steiner method.

Wonder, curiosity and awe are the gifts of childhood, and our attainment of necessary skills should allow us to embrace and sustain them, not lead to their demise. Faced by accelerated technological advances, we have to ask how we can develop in children the inner resources to deal with them; how, in other words, we can keep the human spirit's integrity intact without isolating children from the realities they must inhabit. Courage, insight and inspiration are needed here. Globalisation is a two-edged sword, but literacy has always served to connect people, and now can do so right around the globe.

This book is a call for literacy with attitude: one that is child-focused, and age-appropriate. As is increasingly recognised by governments, educationalists and parents around the world, we need a transformation of educational practice and learning. As Vaclav Havel stated in his 1990 address to the US Congress '…The salvation of this human world lies nowhere else than in the human heart, in the human power to reflect, in human meekness and in human responsibility. Without a global revolution in the sphere of human consciousness, nothing will change for the better in the sphere of our being as humans, and the catastrophe toward which this world is headed – be it ecological, social, demographic, or a general breakdown of civilisation – will be unavoidable.'

The ideas based on Rudolf Steiner's insights are a contribution to this pressing need. They do not supply ready-made answers or fixed formulae but try to look beyond the obvious to seek underlying symptoms and holistic remedies. A truly humane approach must involve dialogue, listening as well as voicing our own views. Through living literacy we educate ourselves in a life-long process, and evolve tools and capacities as befits our particular circumstances, times, environment and ideals. We engage fully with what surrounds us. Nothing in our lives is static, and literacy is not a state but a process which can make our lives infinitely richer and more fulfilling. Don Quixote was unbalanced, unable to match the reality of the world around him with his reading of literature; and this of course is the source of the book's endless humour. But when anchored equally in two worlds at once, that of tangible, physical experience and imaginative, heartfelt sensibility, literacy can relate the child's authentic self to the wider world in a harmonious and dynamic way. 'Only connect….'

Christopher Clouder
Alliance for Childhood

Introduction

Living Literacy – The human foundations of speaking, writing and reading contains a mixture of reflective and practical writing. It is offered equally to parents, teachers, teacher trainers and all who acknowledge literacy's central significance in shaping our world. The questions that the book raises are, I believe, universal ones. The suggestions that it makes for interpreting and addressing these questions in practice have grown out of my own experience as parent, teacher and teacher trainer within the Steiner Waldorf schools movement. This is an international educational movement that has firmly established itself as an independent alternative to mainstream schooling. Its approach to literacy in particular has remained significantly different from standard practice since its inception in 1919.

While much of this book will reflect what is actually thought and done in the Steiner Waldorf schools, it will also cross-reference this with current mainstream principles and practice. In doing so it assumes that both approaches have something to learn from each other. The book also assumes that we all have something to learn from what is, as yet, present only in germinal form – the future. In this it may challenge the 'Waldorf world' as much as any other safe haven.

As a final first word, I want to state that literacy is an ultimately life-changing experience. If this experience is to be positive (and let us not assume this is a foregone conclusion), the ground needs to be prepared well in advance. This book is written, above all, for those who will read it in good time.

*****

To my mother, who first encouraged me to speak and later helped with dotting the i's.

I would like to thank the following people for their help in bringing *Living Literacy* to fruition: Josie Alwyn and Martyn Rawson for their generous early feedback; Tim Byford and Barbara Imrie for providing a more 'mainstream' perspective; Martin Large and Rachel Jenkins at Hawthorn Press for maintaining the dialogue necessary to bring the book through into reality, and my editor Matthew Barton for his invaluable contributions to its final ripening. Finally I wish to express my heartfelt gratitude to the children, parents and teachers at York Steiner School who have given me the inspiration and courage to speak out about things that matter.

Part One: Seeing the Picture

1. The Great Divide

Dear Reader, you are highly privileged. You are literate. You hold the master key to the kingdom of the written word, an ever-extending dominion of the articulate human mind reaching to the boundaries of the world and beyond. You can read records, recipes, poems, narratives, operating manuals, scientific theories, newspapers, candidates' names on ballot sheets, letters from loved ones and the communications of gods and angels. Anything that can be expressed in words is a door you are invited to open.

How you originally got hold of this key called literacy will be different in each case. Most of you will simply have found yourselves holding it. Some will remember having to struggle to possess it. But all of you have it, and for you there is now no personal stigma in facing a world where literacy is the universal ID card – the passport to acceptability.

It is different for others. In a world that has acclaimed universal literacy as its goal, endless droves of young people embark on the established roads to its attainment but increasingly fail to arrive. It is not just the dusty tracks of Africa that are strewn with these failures; they are piling up everywhere, in our own countries, our own cities, our own metalled streets. We really don't have to look far to find people who feel crushed, confused, distracted, deserted and ultimately despairing – and who in many cases have abandoned the quest for literacy completely. For these young souls the written word remains an empty oracle – and they seek their compensations elsewhere.

From the high ground to which you and I still have access, and where many still dwell in security and contentment, not all of this will necessarily seem so urgent and apparent – yet. But when a child we know, maybe even our own, loved child, starts to 'turn off', to lose interest and motivation in whole areas of life, including and perhaps especially school – then we are faced much more immediately with what's going on right now. Down there in the lowlands, in the inner city wastelands, deprivation, dysfunction and alienation are commonplace sociological distinctions. We can look at the rise of illiteracy in that setting and relate it to a more generalised and obvious social and economic malaise, for which literacy alone offers no ready remedy. But why has it started to happen to the rich kids too? What are the common denominators between a boy who drops through the bottom of school into an inner city gang and one who drops to the bottom of the class and is only held from further descent by a more intact relation to home and the security that goes with it?

In the complex tangle of our times three main strands appear to be strangling the life out of literacy, and out of much else besides.

Communication in the home

Many youngsters, rich as well as poor, grow up in homes where both parents work, parental attention has multiple demands, parent relationships are frequently strained and may break down completely, where everything is prone to sudden change – all of it directly or indirectly threatening the basic structures of the child's world. Environmental, social and moral status quo is a thing of the past. What can today's children safely take for granted, draw meaning from, construct a sense of self around? Whether in the background or foreground of their consciousness, children from all walks of life are experiencing a kind of spiritual vacuum, a profound uncertainty under the surface of their lives.

At the core of this uncertainty lurks an experience of emptiness in relation to words. Not only written words, but all words. Words that human beings use to confirm how things are between themselves, and how things are out there in the world. The way a child learns to become a confident citizen of the world is intimately connected with his* experience of language. Language isn't something learned at school, but unfolds at home long before formal teaching begins. Its medium is living human speech. Not for nothing do we describe our native language as 'mother tongue'. It is something we first begin to develop in our mother's womb through listening to her speech in a sound-sphere resounding with the living rhythms of her – and our own – heartbeat.

Where this natural, familiar, living exchange of words is able to continue uninterrupted after birth, with the conscious and sympathetic inclusion of the new arrival, then the foundations for both language and literacy are laid in a healthy way. Where social or economic pressures or temptations insert a wedge between children and their parents and immediate family, and where no proper substitute is found to replace this fundamental 'language community' – which amongst other things is what a human family is – then the trouble starts. Then the mother tongue cannot continue her seamless linguistic mothering of our innate predisposition for language, announced forever and again in the lovely, melodious, universal 'babble' of infancy. Every language the world has ever known is seeded in the sounds and consonance of infant utterance.

---

* I will alternate gender from chapter to chapter to avoid the awkward use of both.

Television

It is deprivation enough for a child to grow up without being surrounded by the constancy of loving conversation. More disturbing still is when false substitutes are put in place that appear to provide a wonderful consolation for a missing experience of community. One of these, perhaps the most significant, has established itself in the corner of most of our living rooms. Even in the poorest quarters of our cities and the remotest rural corners of every country in the world, the television binds our lives together in a new kind of association. The nature of this 'television community' is that its human participants neither face each other, nor speak to each other, nor interact in any other significant way with each other – or with anything much else in the world around them, except occasionally the kettle. What binds this community together is the illusion that it is participating in a shared reality that is both interesting and meaningful. The growth of 'reality TV' coupled with 'interactive' and 'You decide' options give added credibility to the impression that television is an extension of real life in which the viewer has a real role to play. Everything otherwise so difficult to achieve seems suddenly immediately accessible. As adults fall under television's spell, they likewise draw their children into its enchantment.

The television's power isn't merely that it blurs the distinction between fiction and non-fiction – which it does, and which books do as well; it is also – and this is where it differs fundamentally from books – that watching television (and computer images) has a paralysing, anaesthetising effect on both outer and inner human activity, allowing the media's content to pass uncensored and undigested into a person's life of thought and will. Adults are better able to be discerning, to respond critically to what they view, but young children have far fewer critical defences, simply absorbing what they see. It is not yet the case that people watch television 24 hours a day, but it is the case that television's spell is not automatically broken by switching it off. The lingering, malingering effect of prolonged passivity in the thrall of electronic simulation is increasingly recognised as detrimental to health, including 'educational health'. Amongst other things it is now known for a fact that babies do NOT learn to speak through listening to recorded human voices on TV or radio or audio-tape: for them such 'words' are truly empty shells, uninteresting, signifying nothing.

Education

If the dissolution of established social structures and relationships, and the omnipresent influence of electronic media and 'media culture' forms the background to literacy problems in many if not most settings, the third strand to be considered is that of education itself, which sets out to solve such problems. Different countries have different education systems. Some do better and some worse at raising and sustaining literacy levels – and it is certainly not the more developed countries, whose new technologies and ideologies are reflected and integrated into new ways of learning, that always come out on top here. Common sense would suggest that any educational system should be judged on its outcomes, and on this basis we are bound to ask why a remote country like Finland should top the world's educational league tables, and why alternative educational approaches such as that of Steiner and Montessori and indeed home-schooling should increasingly be seen to bring better results than the mainstream options. We should certainly feel encouraged to see beyond the bluff and bluster of all the claims made about education by its professional proponents and political sponsors and look at what is actually happening and at what can and might happen. We should also feel empowered in believing that we can make a personal difference to education's outcomes.

The purpose of this book is to try and establish what really counts, and what really works, in the healthy preparation for literacy, the healthy teaching of literacy and the healthy integration of literacy into the whole of life. The book's central argument is that the single common denominator that can unite these different requirements is the fundamental, rock-bottom, absolute prerequisite that literacy should remain from beginning to end a HUMAN activity, springing and flowing from human needs and purposes and developing through the channels of human relationships. The necessary acquisition of knowledge, the mastery of technique, the interpretation of meaning, the articulation and application of intention – these must be built upon human foundations or they will crumble into sand.

For any of this to make sense we shall need to have a clear understanding of what literacy actually is, exactly what purposes it is able to serve and also – very significantly – what purposes it is able to thwart and disfigure. The first part of the book will therefore investigate the different elements of literacy, how it has evolved in and changed the world, and how it relates to and can affect child development. Then will follow a more practical exploration of how to prepare for the transition from instinctive to conscious language acquisition, in particular through conversation, story, song and play, and from there how to introduce writing and reading formally in a relevant and living way. There will be discussion of children's learning differences and different teaching responses to these, of the nuts and bolts that hold it all together and ways of helping to tighten these up, of different contexts in which literacy properly belongs and the different styles and forms of expression appropriate to them, of other activities that can continue to support literacy, of telling the truth and telling lies, of communication generally and electronic communication in particular. While *Living Literacy* will focus centrally on the adverse influences that threaten the very life and nature of communication itself and the medium of language that first mothered us into this world, it will also attempt to look beyond our current challenges to the possibility of a positive and creative future ahead.

2. What IS Literacy?

Your literacy, dear Reader, has cost you dearly. Like a thief in the night it stole upon you unawares and took away something vital, potent and precious – something you may long for but do not expect to possess in the same way again. Call it, if you like, your innocence: your wide-eyed, childlike openness to life's springing source and the wonders of the world. Perhaps it was not literacy alone that brought about this change, but it was literacy that set the seal upon your loss.

Yet as the fairy folk leave a changeling when they steal a human child, so literacy left you with its own special gift. Along with the wonder, power and significance of this gift comes illusion and danger also. The faculty of literacy relates to a world of reflections, whose laws are different from the laws of nature: neither time, place or circumstance are binding constraints within it; nor is the nature of identity; nor is truth itself. Just as a mirror may be flat, curved or cracked, so the reflections of literacy may reveal, distort or destroy the images they appear to represent. And just as your first sight of yourself in a mirror creates a self-image that was never there before, so literacy changes your experience of your self, and not merely of the world at large.

The last faculty to evolve

Defining literacy as the ability to read and write tells us next to nothing about it. In reality it is among the last, and most complex of our human faculties to evolve. Its processes require a blend of physical, emotional and mental activities, and its character is altogether different from other more instinctive or organic human functions. Certain specific preconditions must obtain before literacy can flower at all, and it must be continually nourished it if is not to destroy the life that engenders it.

Let's consider the example of minimum literacy: the ability to write one's own name. How different this is from the ability to *speak* one's name! Or the ability to draw a self-portrait. Or the ability to build a house in which to live.

Writing one's name involves a co-ordinated pattern of movements – like drawing, house-building and all sorts of other things. What distinguishes it from the bulk of all other activities is not merely the refinement required in hand-eye co-ordination, although this is significant enough to place handwriting a long way up on any child's kinaesthetic (movement-related) learning curve. The crucial distinction that makes writing so difficult for a child to learn is that it bears no obvious relation to the world of ordinary perception and tangible realities. The letter forms that need to be memorised do not really look like anything. The word that is supposed to represent ME doesn't look remotely like me. With a bit of imagination I can make a self-portrait seem perceptually plausible – and a child has oodles of such imagination. But not MICHAEL. That I have to take on trust. And to memorise it I cannot easily make use of the normal range of visual associations that confirm the basic contours of other mental images.

It doesn't get any easier when a child is told that letters 'stand for' sounds. The young child does not hear her name (any more than you or I do normally) as a sequence of separate sounds but as a single entity. And anyway, why on earth should sounds take such strange and specific and statuesque forms? Not to mention the further complication that they may after all take a number of different forms that only an experienced contextual understanding can decipher. Calling it a puzzle is putting it mildly.

Knowing the way literacy has developed historically can help trace the connections that appear missing for today's western child. A later chapter will be devoted to exploring this theme in detail, but some salient points can be made here. One is that writing was not always related to the sounds of speech at all. Nor was it always dissociated from the realm of ordinary visual perception. Nor was it always learned hand-in-hand with reading. It was, however, originally and fundamentally linked with a collective human experience. There was nothing about it, in the beginning, that was remotely abstract or divorced from immediate, shared and credible reality – even where this was the reality of a select few. It was simply a confirmation and a means of preservation of things already known, already lived through, already understood. Today it has all but lost its roots in local, actual and immediate experience and become a medium for generalisation and speculation. This is why it has become so difficult to teach and so difficult to learn.

Reading versus writing

The really challenging demands of modern literacy are linked more with the element of reading than writing. For a medieval scribe who had the sacred task of hand-copying the scriptures, and for whom the slightest copying error would be a blasphemy, the ability to read was actually discouraged. The church hierarchy undoubtedly had its own hierarchical reasons for keeping its scribes illiterate, but there were practical ones too. Scribes who could read were, quite simply, more prone to copying errors. The best scribes were just calligraphers, whose kinaesthetic skills enabled them faithfully and beautifully to copy what they saw before them without having any specific idea of what the words or even letters represented.[1] Obviously they had some general notion of the mystery they were practising, but essentially they were object-drawers for whom words were cult objects amongst other cult objects – visible, but with a hidden significance accessible only to the initiated few.

Reading opens up and inhabits a dimension that is only hinted at in writing. In a sense we could say that writing, as such, gets in the way of reading. What the reader wants to do is to look *through* the writing, through the words, to the meaning that is behind them. The better the reader, the less time she actually spends looking at the words on the page. Just as when you or I meet a friend whom we recognise at a glance, so a good reader recognises words in an instant, without having to study their every feature. All that is required for such a recognition, it seems, are certain basic 'cues', registered fleetingly as direct perceptions, that trigger memories and associations to complete the picture in the 'mind's eye'.

What an extraordinary, sophisticated and speedy activity this is! The key to its success is our human ability to recognise the *identity* and *wholeness* of things, and to distinguish the essential from the inessential as we do so. The drawback of this talent is that it can sometimes get it wrong: it can mistake an inner picture based on memory and imagination for the outer one based on direct perception. Words are misread because their meaning has been wrongly guessed, just as people may be misread because their expressions and gestures have been wrongly interpreted. When a reader does this a lot – as many do – this has to be acknowledged as qualifying her general level of literacy.

In questioning what lies behind such misreading there are two particular aspects to consider. One is how the reader *looks*, the other is how she sees. The first has to do with perception as such, the second with the interpretation of perception. Whichever of these aspects may be playing into the equation, if this manner of looking at words on the page were translated back into a style of writing, the latter would be sloppy and sometimes illegible. Not surprisingly, but not without significance either, sloppy readers and sloppy writers do tend to combine under one hat.

While reading is an activity that necessarily attempts to dissolve the physical products of writing into meaning, it remains the case that good reading needs first to be apprenticed to good writing, and then to remain faithful to its teachings once fluency has been achieved. The essential thing that writing has to teach reading is *respect*. At one level this is a respect for the formalities of the medium itself – of the distinctions of size, shape and style that make writing what it is. At a higher level this becomes respect for the meaning that writing embodies. And at the highest level of all, writing can teach reading that for every reader there is a writer: another human being who has made a personal effort to communicate something, and who hopes that this communication can be received. (In the special case of reading over one's own writing this same awareness can also be approached, when 'I the reader' may develop a more objective and conscious sense of 'I the writer', and indeed of the communication itself.)

Let's look more closely at the first lesson that writing has to teach reading – the 'respect for the formalities of the medium'. It is of course possible for a person without the use of hands, and who cannot and does not learn to write in the normal way, still to learn to read. Nevertheless, reading will only emerge out of an activity that corresponds to what writing is, which could be characterised as a refined activity of shaping. If the hands cannot be part of this shaping, other parts of the body must be. It may be the left foot, as with Christie Brown. It may be the head, with a paintbrush held in the mouth. Or it may simply be the eyes. Whichever it is, *something must move* through the shape of each and every letter of the alphabet, and each movement must be felt and registered and remembered, just as with ordinary handwriting, if a person is ever to go on to read. The more physically the movements are experienced, the more powerfully and intimately they can be visualised. One of the things we can learn from the phenomenon of dyslexia is how closely the sense of movement is linked with the perception and visualisation of form. Dyslexics frequently show difficulties in both these areas, and can be helped in their imaging ability through specific movement exercises that serve to consolidate a 'whole body image' of different spatial patterns and relationships.

At its most basic level, the activity of writing prepares the activity of reading for engaging with the difference between a straight and a curved line, left and right, up and down, and differences in size. Such differences are fundamental in distinguishing between one letter and another. But writing goes further than this. Iflstartasentencelikethis, you will be relieved when I finish it like this. You will appreciate that writing – in this instance alphabetic writing – is designed not simply to represent letters, but also words. This wasn't always the case: before the eighth century the manuscripts of the Roman church were written as an unbroken string of letters – much more closely representing the reality of spoken language, which is a stream of phonemes (individual speech sounds) broken into breaths, or *phrases*, not necessarily or normally into words.

The introduction of word breaks was actually hugely significant in the development of literacy – especially when coupled with a cursive script that bound individual words together in contradistinction to their neighbours. It was followed by further refinements in breaking linguistic flow into discrete units: the use of punctuation to indicate phrasal groupings, the introduction of paragraphs to picture unities of thought, the inclusion of quotation marks to identify unities of speaker. Strictly speaking we must acknowledge that such refinements in writing were directly influenced by the way reading was developing. Historically, that is, reading urged writing to write in words, because otherwise it was very difficult to 'hear' the appropriate verbal distinctions within the pictured stream of speech sounds without an actual speaker there to articulate them.

Before this 'segregated' writing finally came about, reading and writing were both still intimately associated with speaking. Now that it *has* come about, the way we are taught to write actually predisposes us to a way of reading. Modern alphabetic writing – and as we shall see, this is especially true of printed text – encourages us to read in 'bytes'. It encourages us to make both linguistic and cognitive distinctions as we read. What this does is to make our whole relation to language and thought much more conscious. Linking this back to the point made earlier, that reading is actually seeking to dissolve the written script, to look through it to its underlying meaning, we can now say that it is precisely because writing has come to open up spaces in itself that reading has been able to achieve its objective so well. As you read these sentences now, the text before your eyes is actively helping you see the meaning I am trying to convey. The language I have used, together with its punctuation and paragraphing, has been shaped with this end in mind: in essence, it has been shaped to try and help you *think*.

The reader-writer relationship

In these last sentences something else has been happening too. Rather politely and formally, and I hope without offending your sensibilities, I have begun talking to you. Well, in reality of course I haven't said a word; nor in most cases do I know who you are, or expect to be personally known by you. And yet we have entered into a kind of conversation. I have introduced the personal pronouns 'I' and 'you' into my writing. The closest this has brought you and me together is as it were onto a literary settee, where 'we' sit imaginatively together looking at right angles to each other at the objective 'it', the subject of the book. (Does this remind you at all of the TV-watching picture outlined earlier?)

How does this become different if I now ask you actively to imagine me writing these words; and not simply writing them, but writing them to you personally, as if this were a letter coming through the post? It would be much easier to imagine this if the words were hand-written, since handwriting always carries the signature of its author. Even so, the fact that you have nothing more than printed words to go on need not wholly stand in the way of our relationship. What, you may already be asking, has a personal relation between me the writer and you the reader really got to do with a book about literacy? Very little, in one sense. As far as the meaningfulness of the book itself is concerned, perhaps the most you want and need to know about me is what my experience is of the subject I am writing about. You would like at least to be able to trust me – or rather, to trust my words. I, too, would like to be trusted.

Literacy *can* be the supreme author of lies, the great betrayer, the abuser of trust. But it can also be the embodiment of trust. Though you and I cannot see or hear one another, and may not wish ever to do so, the fact that we are both somehow present in these words with some degree of mutual willingness does at least indicate a basic openness to each other's thoughts, feelings and even intentions. We are willing to share an inner experience that hereafter will be inscribed into both our lives. If you want to stop this happening, you can do so at any time you wish simply by putting the book down. This is your freedom, and it is a freedom literacy makes much easier for you. But if you have connected at all to the fact that I am a real human being with a reason for talking to you, who has made the effort to put this in writing, you will experience the third thing that writing can teach reading: that writing invokes the gesture of a human being speaking, as reading invokes the gesture of a human being listening.

A complex of skills

This chapter began by asking 'What *is* literacy?' We identified literacy as a kind of changeling child within our consciousness, and noted that its acquisition represents a significant loss as well as a significant potential gain. We acknowledged its complexity as an evolved human faculty and its dependence upon other developmental preconditions. We noted the special challenge that modern alphabetic writing makes upon children learning it, having only a very tenuous link to the physical and sense-perceptible world. Moving from this into the realm of reading, we noted that the basic correlation between alphabetic letters and speech sounds is fraught with ambiguity, requiring experienced and contextual interpretation. We suggested that the technical aim of reading is to make writing invisible, but that our abilities in this direction may overleap themselves and lead to reading errors. We confirmed that reading needed to be apprenticed to writing at three levels: that of form, meaning, and communication.

If literacy is to be considered a basic skill, we must acknowledge that it is neither instinctive nor simply acquired. To emerge at all it must do so in the context of a complex of related and supportive activities; and to do so effectively and meaningfully it must be actively linked to effectiveness and meaning. However it is acquired, the premise upon which the whole of this book is based is that literacy changes everything. It marks the end of a certain kind of communication, the end of a certain kind of thinking, the end of a certain kind of general consciousness and the beginning of a new kind of consciousness that is focused on the inner world of the individual self. Paradoxically, and wonderfully, this same literate consciousness can also expand us far beyond our own experience to share in that of others whom we do not know!

In the next chapter we shall see what the world at large thinks of literacy, what it is doing about it and what is happening as a result of its efforts. Expect some interesting ironies around the next corner!

3. Literacy in the World Today

Back in the 1960s a theory propounded and researched by the American social psychologist Stanley Milgram captured the popular imagination and quickly became an urban myth. The theory was called 'six degrees of separation'. Its claim was that everyone in the world is connected to everyone else in the world through an average of just six personal relationships. In 2002 the young British journalist Lucy Leveugle set out to test whether the theory would still stand up as well as it had done in Milgram's experiments of 1967, given that the world's population had almost doubled since that time. She decided that she would try to establish her chain of connection to some unknown person as far away from her native London and in as remote a region as possible. She selected Outer Mongolia as her target country. In order to identify a named individual within that country she placed an advertisement in Mongolian national newspapers inviting a response from anyone interested in participating in a TV documentary. Sifting through the correspondence that followed she finally chose her target individual: a nomadic herdsman from the middle of the Mongolian steppe named Purev-Ochir Gungaa.

The idea that we all might be so closely connected with each other is an attractive one in itself, and the fact that it took Lucy

Leveugle nine rather than six steps to reach her herdsman still allows us to entertain the 'small world' notion as something more than wishful thinking. The reason I mention the story here is firstly that it says something big about human interconnection generally, but also because it offers an interesting angle on literacy in relation to communication. While Lucy Leveugle's connection to Purev-Ochir Gungaa had to be established through a chain of people each of whom knew the next link personally, Purev-Ochir Gungaa's connection to the first foreigner he had ever met came through the fact that he could – and did – read a newspaper. One of the curiosities of this story, let's say, is that Outer Mongolia, remote and primitive as it certainly is, has a literacy rate of some 94% with remarkable circulation figures for its national newspapers considering the lifestyle of its population and the terrain and distances involved in making deliveries. In the United Kingdom, by contrast, only some 80% of adults (less in many regions) are considered functionally literate, and newspaper sales are falling at an increasing and (for their publishers) alarming rate.

There are other contrasts between the United Kingdom and Mongolia. The population of Mongolia is something over 2½ million, living in 1,565,000 square kilometres of land. The population of the United Kingdom is nearly 6 million, sharing ground space of 243,305 square kilometres. Averaged out, a square kilometre in Mongolia 'houses' 1.6 people, while the same area in the UK houses 24.7 people. Geographically, Mongolians are spread thin compared with the Brits; but ethnically they are far more of a homogenous and unified community. It was their deep sense of cultural unity, coupled with their ability to relate to each other over great distances, that lay behind their extraordinary empire-building achievements under Ghengis Khan (or Chingis Khan as he might prefer to be known). Though this communality of culture and tradition has since gone through a trial by communism, amongst other things, there is still something alive out there in the fresh air of Mongolia that is positively gasping for breath over here. This is the sense of connection to one's own world, one's own people, one's own roots. Yes of course there are discords in Outer Mongolia; and the old ways are also changing. But in comparison with the kind of life that you and I know best, Purev-Ochir Gungaa and his people remain connected by fewer than six degrees of separation. They also happen to be collectively more literate than the people in whose lands this book is likely to be read.

I think it would be an interesting experiment to measure the steps between you or me and a beggar in Calcutta. Or even a beggar in London. For all the criss-crossing daily journeys of our modern city dwellers, life in the big cities seems much easier to lose track of. Isolation, anonymity, loneliness, alienation seem to increase as people press closer together. Who talks to each other on the Tube? Some people read their national newspapers; others, if they could read at all, would have little interest in national newspapers anyway. It's a different culture here. People are interested in different things.

It hasn't passed me by that what Purev-Ochir Gungaa found as he was looking through *his* newspaper was an advert by a western journalist inviting him to participate in a western experiment. An invitation that he accepted. Nor has it passed me by that Mongolia's literacy will beyond any shadow of a doubt draw it further and further out of its own culture into the global melting pot of consciousness that literacy represents. This may or may not lead to a cultural alchemy through which it will emerge the richer. It will inevitably lead to increasingly radical changes at every level of life, and many aspects of a centuries-long tradition will be consigned to history.

Economic factors

Literacy is a global force. However, the way it is growing and spreading through the world is neither uniform nor predictable. Recent studies involving global organisations like the Organisation for Economic Co-operation and Development (OECD), the United Nations Agency for Education, Science and Culture (UNESCO), the United Nations Children's Fund (UNICEF) and the World Bank reveal that the 1990 World Conference on Education for All, held in Jomtien, Thailand, was being unduly optimistic in setting the target of universal primary education by 2015. Not only is the target unlikely to be achieved, but the premise that goes with it – that primary education is effective in raising literacy and numeracy levels – has also been called into question. Surprisingly, perhaps, the most striking indications of a failure of education to achieve its own basic objectives have come from the richest, most developed countries. The follow-up Education for All conference (Feb 2000) organised by UNESCO and other UN agencies reported that nearly a quarter of 16 to 65-year-olds in the world's richest countries are functionally illiterate. This means they cannot understand brochures, train timetables, road maps, and simple instructions for household appliances. A national survey conducted by the US Department of Education showed that only about half of the American population was more than semi-literate, with the number of illiterate adults increasing by 2.5 million each year.

Relevant statistics and objectives for less developed countries at the turn of the 21st century can be seen in the following summary:

- 130 million of the world's children aged 6-11 are not in school. Of these, 90 million are girls. One in four of the girls who start primary school drops out within four years.
- More than half of these 130 million children are in India, Pakistan, Bangladesh, Ethiopia and Nigeria.

- A further 150 million children drop out without basic literacy or numeracy skills.
- World Bank research shows that investment in girls is the single most valuable development intervention any country can make.
- The World Education Forum's targets are universal primary education by 2015 and the elimination of gender disparity by 2005.
- One in four adults in the developing world is illiterate.
- More than half of women in sub-Saharan Africa are illiterate. Over 80% of women are illiterate in Burkina Faso, Sierra Leone, Nepal, Somalia and Afghanistan.
- The child of a Zambian mother with primary school education has a 25% higher chance of survival than the child of a mother with no education. In the Philippines, a mother's primary education reduces by half the risk of child mortality.
- The illiteracy rate in Sierra Leone and Liberia is 80%. They rank with Angola at the very bottom of the UN's human development index.[2]

The surveys from which these facts and figures have been drawn represent a profound, worldwide concern with the condition of illiteracy in which the majority of the world's population lives. There are different levels to this concern. The most basic level – the one that drives an organisation like the World Bank to invest so much in literacy research and literacy programmes – is that of economics. In a world whose economic processes are becoming ever more globalised, literacy is both a ticket for jumping on the international bandwagon, and also a key element in the fuel that keeps the wagon rolling. There is more than simple altruism in the goal of primary education for all: it makes collective, universal economic sense to have the world's workforce made as functional as possible; and basic literacy and numeracy are more essential to this condition than they have ever been. No doubt there is still an argument for saying that some elements within the literate world are happy to keep an illiterate element within the workforce, since illiterate people are easier to manipulate. However, the mechanisms involved in such manipulation are often cumbersome and, in a world where ethical consciousness is growing alongside economic growth, liable to backfire. In the main, it is seen to make economic sense to have a workforce that can read instructions and fill in forms – whose literacy makes it less labour-intensive to organise and supervise – and which feels itself valued, included and ultimately co-responsible within the economic process.

Social factors

Economic considerations lead to social ones. A quick glance at literacy levels in prisons confirms that the majority of those who fall out with society to the point of criminality are either illiterate or semi-literate. The lack of literacy, in most such cases, is clearly linked with a failure to achieve gainful and satisfactory employment 'above ground'. It would however be simplistic to say that lack of literacy can turn people to crime simply because it deprives them of the same level of material benefits as their literate fellows. There is another kind of poverty that attaches to illiteracy in an environment where literacy prevails, whether or not it is directly linked to employment prospects, and this is social poverty. By social poverty I mean the feeling of not being valued by society – of being socially worthless. When this feeling prevails, crime may be as much a way of striking back at society as of simply surviving. Some manifestations of illiteracy may even represent a deliberate refusal to be associated with literate society even at grass-roots level. There is certainly plenty of evidence to suggest that the so-called literacy crisis in the developed world, especially in urban areas, is indeed intimately associated with an attitude of 'who gives an expletive anyway?' If this still leaves a question as to whether illiteracy is chicken or egg in the equation, the fact that it is part of a vicious circle seems undeniable. This closed loop creates its own kind of culture: one actively iconoclastic towards educated society's 'precious things' – its standards of pronunciation, grammar and spelling, for example. As a social phenomenon the existence of an alienated and unquiet underclass isn't new; I believe, however, that the form it is taking today is radically different from anything that history has seen before. One of the reasons for this difference is the availability of a new kind of 'bonding medium' that can unite the community of illiterate or semi-literate people in a sense of shared identity, just as literature has been able to do for literates. This new medium is delivered through various orifices: television, videos, films, computer games and mobile phones in particular. What *kind* of bonding this really is remains a pivotal question within the overall concerns of this book – as indeed does the social cohesiveness associated with literacy. We shall return to the question from various perspectives as we go on.

Self and world

In rounding off this general overview of the significance of literacy and illiteracy in the world today, we must take a further step from social concern into the personal realm. We must ask how literacy or illiteracy affects an individual's deep-seated feeling of self. Although intimately connected with it, this goes further than the question of how the ability or inability to be able to read and write impacts on an individual's self-esteem,. At the deepest level of all we come to the question, *Who am I?* It is impossible to be human and not have some sort of relation to this question. Exactly *what* sort of relation we have to it is affected by influences that flow both from inside and outside our own personal consciousness. The development of a sense of self, indeed, requires us to distinguish between these two currents of experience. What ultimately enables us to make this distinction is a certain evolution in the ability to think. The essential nature of thinking is that it allows mental 'reflection' to take place in freedom from the direct influence of sense impressions. The experience of the world 'out there' can be thought about – both reviewed and developed – 'in here'. And as the thinker becomes aware of this process, he may also become aware of the fact that just as thinking is different from sense experience, so the thinker is different from the world experienced by the senses. The thinker is indeed the 'self' that is active in a thinking process that is not proceeding automatically. 'I think, therefore I can know that I am', might be the best way of putting this.

The basic connection between thinking and literacy was outlined in Chapter 2. Literacy makes thinking easier precisely because it so effectively severs the source of experience from the world of the senses – including the dimensions of time and space. In doing this, literacy also strongly reinforces the impression that the thinking writer-reader is in possession of his thoughts – is their sole present incumbent, so to speak. And in doing *this*, literacy strongly reinforces the writer-reader's inner, self-contained, self-directed (because neither the pen nor the book is mightier than the ability to put them down at will) sense of personal identity. The reader may be accepting someone else's words, but they are being accepted into the reader's world – the world of the reader's self.

Self versus tradition

And what has this to do with the state of the world out there? Put simply, literate societies and literate economies are more focused on the experience of self than those still largely embedded in an oral culture. They develop value systems that put individual rights – including freedom of thought and freedom of speech – and individual opportunities based on the principles of 'free enterprise' at the summit of their collective aspirations. This is not to deny that literate populations have and express altruistic sentiments, nor that they have collective sentiments with regard to their own local culture. Nor is this to claim that non-literate people are incapable of any real experience of self, or of differentiation from their own community. It is simply to point to a generic difference of emphasis between literate and oral cultures, the one focusing more on individuality and freedom of expression and the other more on a local-scale social conformity and tradition.

The contrast and conflict between these two kinds of culture can be very poignant. A recent Chinese documentary filmed by Wang Qinze called *Ou Dede and his Daughters* brings this poignancy home very powerfully. The documentary is set among the Nu tribe of the Yunnan Province of south-western China. The Nu people speak a language belonging to the Tibetan-Myanmese group of the Chinese-Tibetan language family. It has no written form, and, like many of their ethnic minority neighbours, the Nus used to keep records by carving notches on sticks. Nowadays, the growing number of educated Nus use the Han language (Chinese) for administrative purposes. The traditional Nus are animists, whose objects of worship include the sun, moon, stars, mountains, rivers, trees and rocks. The shamans are often clan or commune chiefs and practise divination to ensure good harvests. Apart from that, their duties also include primitive medicine and handing down of the tribe's folklore. Any small mishap becomes the occasion for an elaborate appeasement rite, involving huge waste and hardship to the Nu people. The Nus practise an extempore type of singing accompanied on the dabia (a lute-like instrument), flute, mouth organ or reed pipe. Their dances are bold and energetic – mainly imitations of animal movements. They are masters of the crossbow.

In Wang Qinze's documentary, Ou Dede was the village musician who played the dabia, sang about the life and history of his people and performed the ancient rites. Traditionally the tribal songs and dances were passed from father to son, but Ou Dede had only daughters, three of them. This was a problem. The village headman had just returned from the local government meeting, where it had been decided that the preservation of traditional Chinese cultures should be a priority, and so Ou Dede would have to pass on his knowledge to one of his daughters, or to another boy from the village. This demand to break with tradition in order to preserve tradition threw Ou Dede into an almighty existential crisis.

The ensuing crying, shouting, singing and drinking meant that this anthropological documentary began to resemble reality TV. When Ou Dede finally decided to teach one of his daughters, he inexplicably chose Third Daughter, who wanted to stay at school, instead of Second Daughter, who had her heart set on the job. (They really didn't seem to have names.) Second Daughter went ballistic, and Third Daughter went to the itinerant teacher in the hut that doubled up as the village school to ask what she should do. The teacher finally came up with his answer: 'Learn to read, but also play the dabia. Books can teach you about the world,' he said, 'but only the dabia can teach the history of the Nu.'

Sadly, Third Daughter was never to have the opportunity to take up her teacher's challenging counsel. The film ended with her father Ou Dede going alone to the grave of *his* father, who had first taught him the dabia and finally handed on both the instrument itself and the shamanic traditions associated with it. In a state of increasing distress, he invoked his father's spirit through a mixture of prayer, song and rant to intervene in this crime by culture against culture. 'What *is* culture?' he demanded, completely mystified, tears running down his face as he begged for some confirmation of a meaning to the calling from which his own people had now begun to turn away. Whether once in the past he had been able to hear his father's spirit voice we could only surmise; this time, however, there came only silence. In a shocking moment of despair, Ou Dede smashed his dabia against the earth;

and the window into this distant, contemporaneous world filled up with credits.

What is culture? What relation does it have to the experience of community? What relation to the experience of self? What relation to the world of nature and the world of the spirit? What relation does culture have to language, and to ways of thinking? What relation does one culture have to another? What destroys a culture? What sustains it? What enables it to develop?

Linguistic monoculture

All these are questions that bear on the phenomenon of literacy. In today's world they are particularly pressing questions, because thousands of individual local cultures are being overwhelmed by larger cultures, which in turn are amalgamating into something increasingly all-encompassing. A symptom of this demise is the death of languages. As John Sutherland put it in *The Independent* (March 2002):

Languages are possibly the most complicated structures the human mind has ever invented but, tragically, our species' most impressive creations are dying. According to the British linguist David Crystal, an indigenous language currently disappears every two weeks. By the end of the century, it is projected, 5,500 of the current 6,000 languages now spoken will join Latin and Greek as 'dead languages'. Those, of course, were once two of the world's top languages. Sic transit, as they used to say. What we are witnessing is linguicide. A language massacre.

What is rushing in to fill the vacuum these dead languages leave behind them?

There's no mystery about the root cause of the linguistic holocaust that we're living through. Take a holiday anywhere in the world. Your airline pilot will, as you listen to the safety instructions (in English), be communicating with ground control in English. Signs in the airport, whatever country you're in, will be duplicated in one of the world's top 20 languages – most likely English. You'll see Coca-Cola logos. MTV will be playing on the screens. Muzak will be crooning out Anglo-American lyrics as you walk through the concourse to baggage reclaim. At the hotel, the desk clerk will speak your language, as will, probably, the bellhop. (His tip depends on being polyglot.) Go into any internet café and the keyboard code that will get you best results is what you are reading now: English – the lingua franca of our times.

The spread of English is the product of naked linguistic superpower. If anyone anywhere wants to get ahead nowadays, an ability to speak English is obligatory. We take it for granted. When the premier designate of Afghanistan visited Britain a few weeks ago, the newspapers were entranced by his exotic dress – that colourful tablecloth-like shawl draped on his shoulders. No one commented on the fact that the dapper Mr Kharzai spoke better English than most of the journalists who interviewed him.

Whose English are we talking about?

Is 'English' a misnomer? Would it not be more accurate to rename what we speak 'American'?... American is, currently, the dominant English dialect. Even Tony Blair says, 'I'm a straightforward kind of guy,' – just like Tony S (Soprano, that is).

How come American?

A favourite axiom among linguists is 'a language is a dialect with an army behind it'. Follow the big armies (Roman, Norman, American, Chinese, Russian) and you'll find the 'world languages'. The most potent army, in 2002, flies the stars and stripes. If Tony had the Seventh Fleet and 500 B-52s, Dubya would be talking just like the man in Downing Street. Dream on, President Blair.

Anything else?

Another factor speeding the worldwide spread of American-English is the 'dialect levelling' induced by modern mass media. Some 40 per cent of British prime-time TV is American originated; cinema screens and MTV-style music channels are even more tilted towards the transatlantic product. The resultant levelling can be measured in the younger population's preferred 'discourse fillers': 'ya know', 'kinda', 'sorta', 'check it out'. You'll hear them as frequently in London as in New York.

And what may be bound up with the death of a language?

Be it a weapon of war or a cultural signifier, language is to Homo sapiens what water is to fish. Take it away and we're neither human nor sapient.

If this is meant to apply to the loss of language altogether, does it also have some relevance to the usurping of a local mother tongue by some larger interloper?

Save the whale, yes. But save, say, Manx (the last native speaker on the Isle of Man died in 1974) – forget it.

Forget it? Because it is inevitable, or because it is of no significance? Welsh came close to dying, but is now in the process of being saved. The same people who held out against the Anglo-Saxons and their tongue are still fighting for their own linguistic and cultural identity. Welsh is the first language in large numbers of their schools, English the second; and Welsh is taught as a second language where it is not the first. The people who produced Taliesin still produce their bards; but the best of their bards, although they may speak Welsh, largely write in English. Most reading in Wales is done in English (though not most television watching). In this small, mountainous country we find a people who have come to believe passionately that linguicide is a form of cultural murder and who are fighting to keep their language alive, not so much in the literary realm (although the Welsh road signs don't let you overlook them) as in the spoken realm – the realm of orality. Though the Welsh speakers tend also to be literate in Welsh nowadays, few if any of the native population refuse to read or write English on cultural grounds. As a people the Welsh seem to have managed to take up the essence of Third Daughter's teacher's advice: Learn to read, but also play the dabia. The reading is the English bit, the dabia the Welsh bit. Maybe the 'dabia' playing has had to go through a trial by self-consciousness that has strained its naturalness. Maybe it is not, and can never be, what it was in the heyday of the old Welsh bards. Maybe, for all its struggle, it will still go under. Or may, just maybe, it will continue to flourish as a living culture with a living language that can incorporate the global language of its neighbour as means of written and electronic exchange with the wider world without being sterilised by it. Time alone will tell. (I've just read – *The Independent*, 19 April 2003 – that the Welsh language is making a remarkable revival in Patagonia, where it was implanted by colonists in 1865. Thanks to a scheme in the 1990s by the Welsh Council to send more Welsh teachers to support this resurgence of interest, which Juan Peron tried to suppress, the younger generation is now relearning the language of their parents and grandparents 'in their hundreds'. Hardly world-shattering, but interesting nonetheless.)

Having ranged between Mongolia, China and hilly Wales it is now time to take leave for a while from the contemporary world and travel back in time to see how this thing called literacy first developed.

4. The Emergence of the Alphabet

Proto-writing

How did the Mongol hordes under Chingis Khan communicate with each other? When they were within listening range, being human rather than demonic (despite the rumours), they spoke to each other in the normal manner. When they were out of listening range they typically chose one of three options: they sent a messenger on horseback to carry a spoken message; they waved flags at each other when horses would have proved too slow, typically in the process of fighting a battle; or they made smoke signals, like native American peoples, that could be 'read' from maybe forty miles. These three steps outwards from direct speech are also three steps in the direction of an alphabet.

Listening to a messenger is just like listening to anyone else, except that the listener is being asked to believe that the messenger's words are the same as the words originally spoken by the sender of the message. In cultures that used or use messengers as a basic means of distance communication – pre-literate or oral cultures – the identification of the messenger with the message sender, and indeed with burden of the message itself, is made very readily, as the saying about shooting the messenger of bad news may remind us. We might expect this to make messengers more economical with the truth in the case of life-threatening messages; and perhaps sometimes it did, although it is typical of oral cultures that their respect for the word is fundamental, and lying is something they are bad at.

Interpreting semaphore is different from listening to someone speaking, relying as it does upon a different sense. It is also different from the interpretation a deaf person would make of someone talking, since neither lip movements nor the other natural movements of ordinary speech are involved. The beginnings of semaphore undoubtedly arose as extensions of simple arm movements such as pointing and beckoning. Gradually the process became more sophisticated, with the signals coming to represent pre-understood 'directions' rather than simply referring to perceptible realities within the physical directions of space. At all times, however, the givers and receivers of the messages remain present in the same physical, visible environment. To this extent they remain 'in touch'.

With smoke signals this latter factor disappears. The meaning carried by puffs of smoke is discarnate: it no longer requires human beings to be perceived as part of it. Originally the perception of smoke was of course experientially connected with the presence of human beings; however, the smoke can only say more than 'I am here' when an understanding of the signals has been pre-formulated. Both the constraints of the medium and limitations in the ability to deal in abstractions kept such aerial messages fairly simple; nevertheless, smoke signals represent more than just a step away from direct speech – they represent a quantum leap.

A similar leap can be observed when we trace the development of a more obvious form of writing. Some thirteen thousand years ago, in the region between the rivers Tigris and Euphrates sometimes called the cradle of civilisation, the lifestyle of the native people changed from being nomadic to being pastoral. Animals were raised and kept in one place, and crops were grown. The more people put down roots in one place, the more important it became for them to keep track of assets that might retain a tendency to wander away from them – either physically (like their cattle) or mentally (like their produce stores). 'Keeping track' meant initially just that: keeping a fix on animal tracks. Later it came to include keeping an account of all sorts of legless things as well.

One way to interpret animal tracks is to follow them in the right direction until they lead to a real animal. Another is to learn from experience what kind of animal they would lead to if followed. A really experienced tracker may even be able to distinguish an individual animal by its tracks, just as we may distinguish an individual human being by his or her fingerprints. In each of these instances, the animal leaves behind in the mud some impression of itself – an impression that points to the reality that created it.

In hot countries the impressions made in wet mud tend to get hardened in the sun. It is theoretically possible in this situation to assure oneself of the existence of an animal literally by keeping one of its hardened tracks. It would be easier, and not requiring a huge leap of imagination, for a cowherd to model something like an animal track himself and relate this to one of his animals, numerically if not specifically. Such counters, circular, ovoid and diamond shaped, have indeed been unearthed from ancient Mesopotamia.

If the archaeologists have got it right, then around eight thousand years ago a significant change took place in the basic method of keeping track of the 'tracking' counters. They began to be stored in sealed clay pots, into whose outer shells – and this is the big new step – were inscribed representations of the counters kept hidden within the pots. The pots could be shaken, and their counters *heard*, but the only visible sign of them was a kind of picture. The relation between this picture and the invisible counters had to be taken on trust; although if any significant doubt arose it was always possible to break open the pot and verify the contents. Later, as these sealed pots became more widely used as records of an exchange of goods, the participants in a transaction would impress their personal seal (being illiterate, they wore this prefabricated signature round their necks) into a special clay token that would be included in the pot with the other 'bullae' representing the objects sold. The individuals' seals could also be impressed on the pot's outer shell.

Yet another step away from the concrete representational system of the counters came at around 3,500 BC. Again, this may seem a small step to us, but for mankind it was another giant leap. Having first experimented with hiding the counters, now the counters are done away with altogether. In their place are kept simply the impressions made previously on the shell of the pot. The pot itself now being redundant, its memory is nevertheless retained for a while in the curved shell-like 'tablet' (reminiscent of the concave lid of the original pot) on which the signs are written.

It may be argued that such 'writing' is more to do with numbers than words. It *does* have to do with numbers, but it also refers to numbers of specific things that have names. Literacy and numeracy are indeed closely related, historically and inherently. They both involve the magical act of translating something concrete into something abstract. One of the most extraordinary developments in numeracy – all the more extraordinary because for us it has become so ordinary – was the incorporation of the 'number' zero. The story of zero is a mysterious one, but it seems that it also has to do with impressions in clay, or maybe in sand. The kind of concrete counting still done on an abacus has been done over the millennia in various related ways, notably with pebbles and 'counting boards'. Pebbles were pressed into either a clay tablet or board covered with sand to build up a number total, and removed from it in order to reduce that total. Without getting side-tracked into the intricacies of place value that precede the arrival of zero into mathematical thinking, both the form and the significance of the cipher were probably first derived from the impression left by a pebble that had been removed from its counting board. The point about zero as a mathematical tool (for that is really what it is) is that it is both substantial and insubstantial at the same time. It represents something that is not actually there, but whose absence asserts itself as an active and meaningful presence. The same *kind* of credibility has to be accorded to the various signs of writing.

Time and the world have produced a very large number of signs that are fit to be called writing. Most, but not all, of these signs have now been deciphered – which means, literally, that they have had their zeros removed. The meaning of some signs has remained completely elusive, and some have had to be best guessed. We cannot be sure, for example, what intention lay behind the remarkable Palaeolithic cave paintings, or sketches on bones and stones, found in southern France and Spain. Were they simply pictures of things seen, or did they carry magical or some other kind of conceptual overtone? Nor can we be sure of the significance of the numerous river pebbles of the Azilian culture (Middle Stone Age), painted in iron peroxide with dots and lines; or of the 'petroglyphs', which are geometric signs or conventionalised figures of men, painted or engraved on rocks, or on the stones of megalithic tombs and other Neolithic Period monuments scattered in particular around the Mediterranean region. We can simply be fairly sure that they all had *some* kind of meaning for those who created them.

From its misty beginnings, the art of representation that develops ultimately into writing as we know it has no clear thread either of geography or of chronology that leads from then to now. It is nevertheless possible to speak of stages of development in the writing process that have an inherent sense and natural order, and whose appearance can be correlated with stages of cultural development in the societies associated with them. This same correlation can also be recognised in terms of the stages of individual human development, as we shall explore later.

The smoke signals and semaphore of the Mongols both belong to the category of *proto-writing*, or *embryo writing*. This is the most rudimentary type of writing system. Examples of this type usually have a small inventory of signs and leave large room for interpretation. They don't denote full running texts but instead serve more like mnemonic devices for the recipient of their message. However, they are properly called writing systems because in some small way they do represent the underlying language, no matter how poorly. Some types of proto-writing are more pictorial, others more related to gesture, and yet others express themselves through symbolic tokens. An example of this latter kind can be found in the communications of the Nu tribe we visited earlier, where a piece of chicken liver, three pieces of chicken fat and a chilli, wrapped in red paper, indicate 'prepare to fight at once'. The kind of imagination that produces proto-writing is one that lives deeply in the experience of metaphor, where one thing is 'literally' identified with another. The chicken *is* the enemy; the chilli *is* the fire of wrath. The smoke of the fire *is* the spirit of the people. The dance of the flags *is* the gesture of the people. Such signs and tokens have meaning because, and only insofar as, they are directly a part of the experience of the people. Their symbology is never abstracted from this experience.

Pictography

The development of the drawing element in proto-writing leads into *pictography*, or picture writing proper. Here the painted or drawn images individually speak for themselves. What they might mean when put together in a sequence is another matter; and here again the appropriate interpretation depends greatly upon a pre-existent shared understanding and experience amongst communicators. Herodotus was kind enough to translate a letter sent by the Scythians to the Persian King Darius, which consisted of a bird, a mouse, a frog, and five arrows. Its meaning was as follows: 'Persians, can you fly like a bird, hide yourselves in the ground like a mouse, leap through swamps like a frog? If you cannot, then do not try to go to war with us. We shall overwhelm you with arrows'.

Pictography can be subdivided into two classes. The first is called *iconography*, which gives a static impression: the pictures relate to things in themselves, or things as archetypes. To a culture like ours, which has become used to comic strips and cartoon shows, iconography looks very stilted as a form of communication. However, just as a young child invests her first spoken nouns – the things she has learnt to name – with the full force of the adjectives, verbs and adverbs that she has come to associate with them in her living experience, so those early pictograms will have *lived* in the imagination that gave birth to them, interacting in the flow of consciousness rather than on the bark or parchment. The development of sequential 'action pictures' represents a significant new step in the discrimination of noun qualities from verb qualities, and thus a birthing process for what we call grammar.

A movement in this same direction appears in the second type of pictographic writing, which is commonly called *ideographic* writing, and sometimes *synthetic* writing. Here, the signs and images shift from being *metaphors* to being *similes*. While metaphors conjure magical identity, similes point to the affinity between distinct things. They begin to detach the ideas associated with a thing from the thing itself. An example of this transition has been immortalised, albeit in a sophisticated and unquestionably literary fashion, in Longfellow's *Hiawatha*:

From his pouch he took his colours,
Took his paints of different colours,
On the smooth bark of a birch-tree
Painted many shapes and figures,
Wonderful and mystic figures,
And each figure had a meaning,
Each some word or thought suggested...
Life and Death he drew as circles,
Life was white, but Death was darkened;
Sun and moon and stars he painted,
Man and beast, and fish and reptile,
Forests, mountains, lakes, and rivers.
For the earth he drew a straight line,
For the sky a bow above it;
White the space between for daytime,
Filled with little stars for night-time;
On the left a point for sunrise,
On the right a point for sunset,
On the top a point for noontide,
And for rain and cloudy weather
Waving lines descending from it.
Footprints pointing towards a wigwam
Were a sign of invitation,
Were a sign of guests assembling;
Bloody hands with palms uplifted
Were a symbol of destruction,
Were a hostile sign and symbol.
All these things did Hiawatha
Show unto his wondering people,
And interpreted their meaning...

Logographic writing

As the ability to interpret meaning from pictures develops, it runs parallel with a refinement in the ability also to perceive common denominators in different things, and to express these linguistically. The words you are reading now are mostly composite words, made up of smaller individual words and sometimes even smaller 'roots' of verbal meaning, including prefixes and suffixes. We call the smallest unit of verbal meaning a *morpheme*. The word 'understanding' contains three morphemes: under-stand-ing. When a society's language develops to the point of being able to 'spell out' relationships of ideas in the composition of its words and the ways of stringing its words together, its method of writing naturally turns from picturing things to picturing words. As with the shift from picturing things to picturing ideas associated with things, the shift to picturing words themselves is hugely significant. The generic form of writing that pictures words is called *logographic*.

The first stage of word picturing still refers essentially to the 'thingness' of words: to their objective correlatives in the phenomenal world. A word like 'understand', which seems rather far-removed from visible phenomena, would still need at this level to attach to some kind of picture. The image of Atlas holding the sky, or the world (as he appears in some depictions), up at the level of his head is such a picture. To picture 'understanding' we would need to include some image of an ongoing process to represent '–ing': perhaps a wavy line like a stream. Whatever symbols do get chosen in a logographic system of writing, they only become authorised 'logograms' through collective endorsement. The whole society, in other words, must agree to use the same symbol to represent the same meaning each time it is used: something that simpler picture writing is not obliged to do. Interesting that in German and English we 'stand' in a certain relationship to something when we understand it, while in French we 'contain' it.

Every language gives a slightly different, untranslatable perspective on shared realities. One consequence of this is that a logographic script may develop a staggering number of individual logograms: in Chinese, for example, there are some 10,000 logograms, most of which only rarely appear in everyday usage.

Phonetic writing

No doubt the sheer cumbersomeness of such writing largely explains why only eight or nine examples of it are known to us (cuneiform, hieroglyphic and hieratic, demotic, the scripts of the Indus valley people, of the Cretans, Hittites, Chinese, Mayas, and Aztecs, and probably also the mysterious Easter Island writing), and why the next radical metamorphosis in word-picturing comes about. The new and portentous development is that of *phonetic writing*. This is the graphic counterpart, not of words and their meanings, but of speech and its sounds. It is the visible representation of something quite invisible, and it both diminishes the necessary range of symbols required for writing, and hugely opens up the possibilities of literary expression. Even the main logographic scripts just mentioned could not resist its attractions, and came to incorporate a phonetic element into their writing systems. The first offspring of this marriage was a feature called a *rebus*. A rebus represents a word by using pictograms to represent its individual morphemes or syllables. To give an example using English: the name Woodbury could be depicted by three trees in a row and a berry. In one of the curiosities of linguistic history, the rebus has recently made a cultural comeback connected with the use of the mobile phone. T 4 2 & 2 4 T, ME 4 U & U 4 ME… is an example of 'textese' using the rebus principle.

   Pure phonetic writing falls into two classes: *syllabic* and *alphabetic* writing. Syllabic writing does what it says: it represents syllables – including vowels when these take up a syllable. When we listen to speech, syllables are the smallest sound units that we listen for in a word that is unfamiliar to us. (With familiar words our conscious analysis stops at the level of distinguishing the word itself from its contextual phrase.) What unifies a syllable is its rhythmic value: it is like a single note in a melody. The word 'syllable' itself has three syllables: syl-la-ble. In syllabic writing it would be a three letter word.

Alphabetic writing analyses speech sounds even further, right down to the smallest units of sound incorporated into a particular language. (These, incidentally, are never more than a respectable fraction of all the vocal sounds that human beings make.) Such a unit of sound – an atom of speech, we might say – is called a *phoneme*. The basic principle of an alphabet is that its individual letters represent individual phonemes. As in atomic theory, phonemes combine to make 'molecules' of sound, such as diphthongs (vowel blends) and consonantal digraphs like 'th'.

The world's first fully alphabetic writing system was born in Egypt around 2000 BC, as the Egyptologist John Coleman Darnell established only a couple of years ago. This proto-alphabet, distilled from existing phonetic symbols scattered amongst the body of Egyptian hieroglyphs, developed via two divergent branches: the Canaanite branch, which led eventually to our Roman alphabet; and the Arabian branch, which flowered into the modern Arabic scrip and also the alphabet of Ethiopia. (The fascinating story of this development is clearly described in *The Alphabet* by David Sacks.[3])

A significant feature of this original alphabet was that it was purely consonantal: it had no letter forms for the vowels. Both Arabic and Hebrew writing still retain this characteristic. It was the Greeks who first gave vowels a 'literal' status in their adaptation of the Phoenician alphabet The different significance of vowels and consonants is fascinating and fundamental to an understanding of how language weaves together the world 'out there' with the world 'in here'. Rudolf Steiner had much to say about this; in particular, he drew attention to the relation of consonants to the world of things and vowels to the world of feelings. A consonantal alphabet, if this is accepted, is still biased towards the world that can be pictured – and the Hebrew letters are indeed actually named and also somewhat shaped after real things. The first Hebrew letter *aleph* means 'ox', and could be related to ox qualities, if not an actual ox picture, by an erudite Hebrew scholar. By not writing vowels the assumption is – since they exist in the spoken language – that they will be supplied by the reader. Actually, the original assumption was they would be spoken aloud by the reader – for silent reading was unknown in Hebrew and all other literate cultures to begin with, and was initially treated with great suspicion when it first began to be practised. Another assumption went with the consonantal writer's omission of vowels: that the reader-speaker would already know the text he (sic) was reading. If he didn't, there was every chance that he would misread the intended meaning, since many words could have more than one interpretation – such as b-g (bag/beg/big/bog/bug) Consonantal writing, in essence, was part and parcel of a culture still strongly based in its oral traditions, which writing and reading served initially to reinforce rather than to develop. (When Aramaic supplanted Hebrew as the spoken language of the Semitic peoples it became necessary for the Hebrew texts to have their vowels indicated by punctuation marks called niqqûd, which are still retained in today's modern Hebrew.) Interestingly, the use of consonantal writing, like the rebus just mentioned, has made a comeback in the shorthand lingo of 'textese': whr u cn brve8 in whtvr wa u cn gt wa wth.

An alphabet that includes both consonants and vowels (C and V alphabet for short) is a fully sharpened tool for scribing every possible nuance of spoken language into its graphical 'objective correlative'. Well… it has the potential, certainly, to be used as such a precision instrument, leaving no blurred edges of meaning to be resolved by contextual or other means of interpretation; but the reality is that something in the development of language itself has significantly thwarted this high ambition. You read this. How? As read (present) or read (past)? There are countless examples, in English especially, where spellings are ambivalent, not to mention outlandish. The child who has to learn English spelling may grieve at this recalcitrant refusal of words to play by the phonetic rules; but the lover of language must also fall in love with all the idiosyncrasies that both history and geography endlessly write into it, and rejoice at the inability of standardisation to overcome these entirely. Even so, the C and V alphabet is a truly remarkable box of tricks – all the more so for being so simple. It can represent any word in the language that belongs to it, most other words in other languages, and even words that have never been spoken – like this word I have just invented, 'flentish' – all in a way that can be learnt by children.

Let us remember, however, that the C and V alphabet was the last of all alphabets to develop historically, and remains the most analytical and abstract representational system in common use outside mathematics. To understand it requires a specific form of synaesthesia: the ability to 'cross-wire' the senses of sight and sound in a way that really isn't natural. To assume that because its principles are so very simple means it can therefore be simply taught is both misguided and, when applied to the education of young children, dangerous thinking.

A brief overview of writing

Before we go on to look at how the English alphabet might best be taught to children, this chapter on the emergence of the alphabet needs rounding off with a summary of how the different alphabets have actually been written down. Prehistoric writers drew pictures and symbols on stones and walls of caves. About 4000 BC, the Sumerians pressed marks into soft clay, which they then baked. About 3000 BC the Egyptians invented papyrus to use for writing. In the 2nd century BC, parchment, a specially treated animal skin, began to replace papyrus as the chief writing material. The Romans constructed a new kind of book: instead of long rolls of papyrus or parchment, they made books from wooden boards and tied them together with thongs. After the invention of a brush and a suitable ink, the use of cloth as writing material became popular.

The Chinese experimented with making paper. According to Chinese tradition, Ts'ai Lun, a Chinese court official, invented paper in AD 105. He used the inner bark of the mulberry tree. Within 500 years, the Japanese also knew the craft of papermaking. The use of paper spread westward from the Far East by way of Baghdad, Damascus, Egypt, and Morocco. The art of papermaking reached Europe more than 1,000 years after its invention in China.

The Chinese were also ahead of Europe in the development of printing. Printing from moveable type was practised there in the 13th century – although the existence of so many characters in the Chinese language led to a return to block books. It took a further two centuries for the first printing press to be set up in Europe. There is some dispute as to who actually reinvented the printing process, but most books remember Gutenberg of Mainz as the man. What is beyond all dispute is the tremendous effect that printing has had upon the western world. Its ability to duplicate texts has led to both a vertical and horizontal spread of literacy. By vertical, I mean that the literate oligarchy associated with the medieval church lost sole possession of the thing that gave them their ultimate power, namely the Word of God. The reproduction of the Bible enabled the laity to gain their own access to the scriptures, and a huge shift in moral and social authority followed in its wake. The horizontal spread of literacy through printing

involved different classes of people being
more widely and quickly amongst themse.
merchants, scholars with scholars, gentry v.
eventually most classes of people with most othe.
on a newly equalised footing made possible by the
pamphlet or a book.

Printing changed religion, science, politics,
economic relations, patterns of trade and methods of pro
and above all, it changed people's relation to language. L
became ever more a meeting of minds rather than the join.
'hands' represented by handwritten communications. The flo
cursive script became the blockwork of text, an architecture
frozen ideas, feelings and intentions that could be woken to life b,
anyone who had the power. Increasingly, the printed way of
writing became the educated way of speaking: clipped, structured,
measured, standardised and self-conscious. However, the ready
appetite of the printing press was not averse to ingesting and
perpetuating the uneducated vernacular as well; and the genius of
a writer like Shakespeare was to write in the 'low' as well as 'high'
style, and so help preserve the character of orality within the very
medium that was beginning to emasculate it. (Shakespeare, of
course, didn't write initially to be read – apart from his poetry –
but rather to be spoken. Nevertheless, he was a figurehead in the
impulse to preserve the life of language through the possibilities of
printed literature, and for that we must be truly grateful.)

While printing revolutionised the spreading of the written
word, it also, as its technology developed, allowed the spreading of
images. Embellishment and illustration had long been a part of
hand-written manuscripts, but the possibilities of linking text with
illustrations and, later, photographs in printed books, ushered in a
new experience in reading. In a way, something finally
extinguished from visibility by the phonetic alphabet could now
make a reappearance. At the same time, the increasing

isucation of printed illustrations took something away from
reader's own imagination, or at any rate served to reshape the
er pictures evoked initially in the reader's mind by the words
emselves.

Fifty years ago it would have been hard to envisage a further
revolution in the realm of the written word that would take it
beyond the parameters of print and fundamentally redefine the
meaning of a 'paper' or a book. But that is exactly what has
happened. The revolution in information and communications
technology that marked the latter part of the 20th century has
proved as radical and extraordinary as anything affecting the issue
of literacy to date. It marks a further – dare we yet say final? – step
of the written word away from sensory and tangible human reality.
Now even written words themselves need have no substance: no
paper, no ink is required to embody them; they can live in a
suspension of electrical light, visible yet untouchable, instantly and
endlessly reproducible and equally instantly reducible to nothing.
They can appear in all manner of fonts, sizes and colours, and
change their shapes and colours in a blink; they can leap into the
company of other images and wander amongst them; they can
spill into their ethereal manifestation through the fingers or even
directly through the voice; they can appear fully formed and
instantaneously as answers to questions posed minimally and
ungrammatically to mysterious entities called search engines; they
can appear identically and simultaneously to people scattered all
over the globe who can respond to them in a network of virtual
conversation without necessarily knowing one iota about those
they are conversing with. Are we already so used to this wizardry
that its illusions have become simply a part of our way of life?

At the time of writing, only about 2% of the world's
population has access to the internet, and fewer than this own
their own computer. In America, by contrast, almost 50% have
regular internet access, though many use cyber cafés or work

computers rather than their own PCs. The question about the computer's wizardry will undoubtedly have different answers in different settings. Anyone who thinks about it, however, must acknowledge that the theoretical possibility of linking everyone in the world with everyone else in a live communication network is mind-blowing. The difference between a computer network and a telephone network is that even when everyone 'talks' at once, the different snippets of conversation are put on ice and can be retrieved when convenient, minutes, days or years later.

The freedom to pick one's own way through the communications of a chat-room is similarly available when reading 'hypertexts', where words or phrases that appear in blue provide instantaneous links to other bodies of text related specifically to the highlight, and which can be followed or not according to personal interest. This gives new meaning to the notion of hidden meaning in a piece of writing. A blue word no longer means just what it says. At the same time, it is ever so willing to spell out its meaning if you ask it. Its enigma is only skin deep, unlike the meaning of, say, the four Hebrew letters *yod he vau he* – the so-called Tetragrammaton or Holy Name of God – whose nature is to be ultimately inexpressible.

Many searching questions are set before us by the 'technologising' of the word. Later we shall return to them, but for now there remains a fundamental connection to be explored between the way humanity has evolved as a whole through the course of history and the way individual human beings develop biographically. The parallels are striking and have a direct relevance to choices we make when intervening in children's development through upbringing and education.

5. Lessons of Development

Both biological and psychological aspects of human development will be considered together in this chapter. The very idea, derived from Descartes, that they could be considered otherwise, that there is an unbridgeable mind-body divide, has already caused enough trouble in recent history, though this is fortunately passing out of fashion again. Body and soul may not be two words for the same thing, but they are two sides of the same coin. In childhood especially it is crucial to recognise and treat the human being as a single organism, where what is focused in one area affects all areas together. The further step of treating the whole of humanity as a single, mighty being that behaves as an individual – as William Blake did with his giant Albion – is not really a step in a different direction, though it may feel like a bigger one. For anyone working with children it can only help to feel part of something universal, predictable and familiar. Comparing macrocosmic with microcosmic pictures can also be a stimulus to finding out *why* human development naturally should take the shape it does, and make it easier for us to work with rather than against it.

So let's go back to where it all begins.

Embryonic development

In the mother's womb, where the embryonic human being is *in* the world but not yet *of* it, an alphabet is written into flesh and blood. It is an alphabet of form: of soft, suggestive shapes that slowly change from one into another without ever quite coming into full focus. Those who have studied this alphabet closely can teach us how to see it. We come to realise that the transformations of the human embryo through the nine months of pregnancy are in fact an evocation of the entirety of biological evolution. 'Ontogeny recapitulates phylogeny' is how the scientists put it. Initially in the realm of form, or anatomical morphology, the individual human being appears to go through the same run up the rungs of the ladder of evolution as we are told humankind has done historically, beginning at the cellular level and becoming more eloquently reflective from the 'fish' stage onwards.

Of course, the embryonic human being never *actually* becomes a little fish swimming in the amniotic fluid, or a little bird trying to fly through it. It reaches the form of a fish in embryo, then metamorphoses into an amphibian in embryo, then a reptile in embryo – and so on; recapitulating the latent potentialities of the animal kingdom but never the full-blown realities. Moreover, when the moment of human birth finally arrives there is *still* something embryonic about the little being that appears for the first time in the open air. Of all mammals the human being is the least mature at birth, and the slowest to develop full maturity after it. A new-born baby still has the vocal tract resembling that of a non-human mammal:

The larynx comes up like a periscope and engages the nasal passage, forcing the infant to breathe through the nose and making it anatomically possible to drink and breathe at the same time. By three months the larynx has descended deep into the throat, opening up the cavity behind the tongue (the pharynx) that allows the tongue to move forward and backwards and produce the variety of vowel sounds used by adults.[4]

Infant development

The sense of a lengthened infancy in comparison with the animal world is further emphasised through a secondary recapitulation of the evolutionary sequence undergone in the womb. This time the child does not so much repeat an evolution of form as an evolution of gesture. In her book *The Incarnating Child*,[5] Joan Salter describes the way in which a baby typically moves its body into the gestures, successively, of a fish, bird, reptile and quadruped from roughly the third to the ninth month of life (or often later), until it finally achieves its human uprightness.

Fish gesture

Bird gesture

Reptile gesture

Quadruped gesture

Human gesture

Whether these patterns and parallels have been laid down wholly by chance and then perpetuated as genetic prototypes, as Darwin would have it, or through the existence of an overriding developmental *archetype* that plays into the evolutionary process from a dimension not bound to linear time, is a hugely interesting and significant question. However this does not affect our basic common-sense recognition that human development is inherently consistent, holistic, rhythmic, ordered – and at the same time predisposed to remarkable metamorphoses. The potential for metamorphosis within a single human lifetime is indeed something that distinguishes us from all other life forms, and indicates that our relation to biological precedent, though clearly established, is uniquely flexible. We are the least predetermined of all earthly life forms. Potentially at least, we are the most free. This is why we have been able to teach our children to read at such an early age. It is not, however, why we *should* teach them to read so young.

Laterality, movement, balance and speech

No child learns to run before walking, or to walk before standing, but some children do learn to stand and walk before properly crawling. When this happens (and the reasons for this appear to spring from children's interaction with the world around them rather than from simple biological predetermination), such children typically seem to suffer for it later, not least in the way they develop literacy. In the developmental 'blueprint', the various kinaesthetic impulses associated with the animal gestures just mentioned have a definite purpose, central to which is the discrimination and co-ordination of the upper, lower, right and left sides of the body via a corresponding development in the different regions of the brain. Particularly significant in this process is what is called cross-crawling, where arm and leg move together in a diagonal relationship. The establishment of laterality, (dominance of either left or right eye, ear, hand and foot), is the most obvious physical outcome of these early activities. Normally laterality, once established, is consistent down the right side of the body. Occasionally it settles uniformly down the left side. Sometimes, however, it doesn't settle uniformly at all, but sets into a condition called cross-dominance, commonly associated with various learning difficulties.

The findings of neuroscience tell us that the co-ordination of bodily movements depends on the way these movements are perceived in the brain. The word for such perception is *proprioception*, which is a complex apprehension that combines an inner picture of one's own movement with an outer picture of how this relates to the three dimensions of space. Central to the working of proprioception is the sense of balance. Significantly, the organ for the sense of balance develops very early during pregnancy, identifiably from about the sixth week onwards. As it first begins to function – somewhere between the tenth and twentieth week following conception – its initially limited capability begins to stimulate the brain to make increasingly intricate neurological connections. These serve to interpret what the organ actually perceives. Everything that is registered via the different sense organs has a stimulating effect on the brain; but the organ of balance (which remarkably starts life as a peripheral organ that migrates inwards during embryonic development to its final resting place in the inner ear), along with the sense of touch, are especially significant in stimulating development of the brain itself.[6]

What neuroscience further informs us is that the perception, co-ordination and comprehension of movement is also linked to the development of speech and language. Attention was first drawn to this when it was noticed that efforts to change a child's handedness (left to right) sometimes induced an onset of stammering. A more sophisticated investigation revealed that the movement centre and speech centre of the brain are not separate entities, but intimately linked. Most of us probably think that speech develops through listening, but in fact the child both registers and responds to speech through a whole complex of sense activities, including sight and, crucially, proprioception. As the child listens to someone talking he is also taking in a detailed impression of the speaker's movements, ranging from body gestures through to the smallest lip and tongue movements, and even (this through sympathetic listening rather than looking) those of the larynx. But the child isn't simply noticing these movements; he is also, albeit more subtly, *imitating* these muscular activities of the other person in micro-movements: in the limbs and right through the vocal tract. These things can be measured.[7] They tell us that a child is quite literally moved to speak through the perception of others speaking.

Imitation and environment

The significance of imitation in the young child's development was signalled early in the 20th century by Rudolf Steiner. He gave it an absolutely central place in all aspects of the child's transition from being a creature of instinct to being a creature capable of new and ultimately self-directed learning. Imitation is, in the young child anyway, an unconscious process of learning, and it relies upon a foundation of biological predispositions to be effective. Unlike instinct, however, it is not wholly determined by the past. Into everything that is given genetically as the human image it weaves all that is taken in as present experience via the senses.

There are a number of well-documented stories of children who have been raised by animals – in particular by wolves. It is clear that such children do not develop normally, either in their body gesture and movement patterns, their language, or generally in the way they think, feel and behave. The biological processes of heredity, including the primitive reflexes referred to, take them to the point of being 'proto-human'; the next steps – those that would raise them above the animal – can only be taken in the context of a human environment. If these so-called feral children are not rescued early from their unlikely foster parents they will never fully develop human traits. Certain aspects of human development – in particular all that is involved in walking, talking and thinking – depend absolutely upon there being an appropriate human environment around the child in his early years.

What makes a human environment 'appropriate'? It is appropriate when it brings to the child an image and experience of the human archetype, the human ideal, which is what calls human development forward out of the future rather than simply driving it out of the past.[8] (Here the word archetype really does convey the process better than prototype.) The infant is everywhere looking for this image. It sees it even in two dots drawn upon a circle, which will draw its focus from the earliest age. It hears it in the human voice, which it immediately distinguishes from all other sounds. It recognises it in human gesture and movement. Not surprisingly, it finds the image of its search most intimately revealed in the place where it naturally first appears: in its mother's face, its mother's voice and its mother's movements.[9] The infant's first smile is a beautiful celebration of the fact that the human archetype has been recognised and welcomed in a personal way.

In saying that the infant is looking everywhere for the human image we touch upon the manner in which he opens himself utterly, in absolute trust, to all that approaches him from the world. He opens himself to this world and allows himself – cannot indeed prevent himself – from being completely and literally 'informed' by this world. Steiner uses the analogy of an open eye to express how defenceless the infant is against what streams into him through all the senses – and also how directly the outside world is recreated as an inner image. As the outer world is perceived it is also imitated. This is why it is so important to give our young children examples worthy of imitation. How we move, how we speak, how we act and interact – all this is crucial to a child's human development.

One of the general tragedies of contemporary life is the way in which modern lifestyle can deprive children of the necessary basic human contact and communication during their early years. Parents are often just too busy to be parents. There are also so many things available to substitute for what is good and healthy and natural in the child's environment. TVs, videos, computers and a whole avalanche of electronic / mechanical / sentimentalised / sensationalised / caricatured toys are obvious examples of human substitutes that have the power to mesmerise, captivate and obsess children so that they may appear, in the short term anyway, to be quite happy to do without real human interaction. In the longer term, starvation of their inner being will manifest outwardly in a lack of warmth and creativity in their behaviour and a general lack of vitality that may lead both to health and learning problems as time goes on.

Consider the following quote:

Research on the role of the environment in children's intellectual development has shown that a stimulating environment can dramatically increase IQ, whereas a deprived environment can lead to a decrease in IQ. A particularly interesting project on early intellectual stimulation involved twenty-five children in an orphanage. These children were seriously environmentally deprived because the orphanage was crowded and understaffed. Thirteen babies of the average age of nineteen months were transferred to the Glenwood State School for retarded adult women and each baby was put in the personal care of a woman. Skeels, who conducted the experiment, deliberately chose the most deficient of the orphans to be placed in the Glenwood School. Their average IQ was 64, while the average IQ of the twelve who stayed behind in the orphanage was 87. In the Glenwood State School the children were placed in open, active wards with the older and relatively bright women. Their substitute mothers overwhelmed them with love and cuddling. Toys were available, they were taken on outings and they were talked to a lot. The women were taught how to stimulate the babies intellectually and how to elicit language from them. After eighteen months, the dramatic findings were that the children who were placed with substitute mothers, and therefore received additional stimulation, on average showed an increase of 29 IQ points! A follow-up study was conducted two and a half years later. Eleven of the thirteen children originally transferred to the Glenwood home had been adopted and their average IQ was now 101. The two children who had not been adopted were re-institutionalized and lost their initial gain. The control group, the twelve children who had not been transferred to Glenwood, had remained in institution wards and now had an average IQ of 66 (an average decrease of 21 points). Although the value of IQ tests is grossly exaggerated today (...) this astounding difference between these two groups is hard to ignore. More telling than the increase or decrease in IQ, however, is the difference in the quality of life these two groups enjoyed. When these children reached young adulthood, another follow-up study brought the following to light: 'The experimental group had become productive, functioning adults, while the control group, for the most part, had been institutionalised as mentally retarded.'.[10]

Earlier I mentioned Rudolf Steiner's view that imitation is a process of development that provides a transition between instinctive recapitulation of the human image and an ultimately self-directed form of learning and behaving. In terms of the quality of consciousness involved, we could associate instinct with a condition of deep sleep, imitation with a condition of dreaming, and self-directed learning with a condition of wakefulness. Again following Steiner, we could further equate these three conditions with the three psychological activities of will, feeling and thinking.[11] These distinctions are characterisations rather than definitions, and are inherently blurred at the edges. In this last part of the chapter we will look at how a child, in the broad spectrum of normal circumstances, makes the transition from 'dreamy' into wakeful intelligence.

Cognitive development as reflection of human evolution

The development of thinking, or cognition, has been amply studied from various perspectives. Probably the best known researcher into the development of cognition in children is Jean Piaget (1886 – 1980). Though some of his methods and findings have been challenged, he is still referred to as the authority in his field in standard psychology textbooks, and offers insights that are directly relevant to the arguments of this book. Let me therefore attempt briefly to summarise his basic ideas on 'genetic epistemology' (the study of the origins and growth of knowledge) in children, and then to place these in an anthropological evolutionary context.

According to Piaget, knowledge is crystallised and modified as the child develops and interacts with the surrounding world. At the heart of this theory is the idea that children actively acquire knowledge through their own actions. Within the theory, Piaget describes a sequence of four stages through which all children must pass in developing knowledge:

1. Sensorimotor (birth to age 2)
2. Pre-operational (2 to 7 years)
3. Concrete operational (7 to 11 years)
4. Formal operational (11 years on)

The stages of cognitive development, says Piaget, are sequential: they must be developed in the order listed. Children may differ somewhat in the timing of transitions between stages, but never in the sequence itself.

So much for the general principles. If we stay within general terms it is further possible to see within Piaget's four developmental stages how they correspond to the 'macro' picture of the cognitive development of humankind. To begin at the beginning: Piaget's period of sensorimotor intelligence refers to the development from the primitive reflex level to a co-ordination of the senses and motor actions leading to the manipulation of objects in the immediate environment. This stage, we are told, is obviously a practical one, involving perceptual and motor adjustments to things, but not yet grasping the symbolic manipulation of things. It can be seen as a transitional stage between biological and psychological organisation.

If we are to seek for correspondences between early infancy and the early developments of the human race as a whole we must acknowledge that the ground we tread is not altogether solid. The physical evidence that exists from the dawn of human time is scanty and open to differing interpretations. However, there does seem to be a clear evolution of activities amongst the various hominids on earth, leading to those activities which are indisputably human. Key amongst these is the emergence of bipedalism in the Australopithecines in the Pliocene era. Walking upon two legs frees the hands for new activities, and Homo Habilis ('Handy Man') surely progressed the art of hunting, adding the ability to throw things, and also gathering, bringing the world towards himself rather than forever chasing it. With Homo Erectus, in the same epoch, we see evidence of the first use of tools and – of huge significance – the first use of fire. Maybe this last activity should remind us not to expect literal correspondences between the micro and macro pictures, although learning that something is hot is a universal early lesson, followed by learning how not to get burned.

The pre-operational stage represents the beginning of a process of conscious reflection still centred essentially around the child's actions. Rather than simply performing actions instinctively or through unconscious interaction with the environment, the child now begins to form mental pictures of what he or she is doing. Initially these representations are focused on a complex of specific memories: movement memories, context memories (including what led up to, what went with and what followed a particular action), and memories of feelings associated with actions. As the faculty for language develops alongside cognition, the ability to verbalise mental processes begins to loosen cognition from specific memory experiences, as well as current sense experience, and extend it into the dimension of associative imagination. This could be described as an intermediary activity of consciousness, where mental experience is still distinctly 'organic' in character and influence. One particular feature Piaget stresses in relation to pre-operational cognition is that it is 'egocentric'. By this he means, not that the child has a well-developed and exclusive sense of self, but rather the opposite: that the child has not yet clearly distinguished its own self from the totality of its experience of the world. In the very beginning the child avoids the use of the personal pronouns altogether, referring to himself by name. Then 'me' comes into currency, and finally 'I', usually after the child has turned two. Even here, however, the sense of self is still very embryonic: it needs the protective envelope of a sense of 'we'. My own term for Piaget's egocentricity would be egoperipherality, albeit at the risk of offending the Society for Plain English.

The historical parallel that can be drawn here is between pre-operational cognition and that of the first Homo Sapiens, with the beginning of reflective imagination and thinking as evidenced in cave art, the practice of religious rituals, the considerations given to the afterlife, and the 'egocentric' anthropomorphic perception of nature. The transition to the next stage is marked by the beginning of agriculture in the Holocene epoch, which as we have already noted is also when primitive forms of writing began to develop.

The concrete operational stage brings the child to a clear awakening of the type of knowledge referred to by Piaget as logical-mathematical knowledge. The root of 'logical' is 'logos', meaning 'word'. We think of logical as referring to relationships of meaning, and it does: the same kind of meaning that is inherently present in meaningful sentences. The relationships of mathematics are of the same order. As the child becomes increasingly conscious of the use of language, so a concrete operational thinking develops that is highly organised, with the ability to understand ever more clearly the interrelationships of concepts, e.g. adding, subtracting, multiplying, dividing, infra logical operations involving quantity, measurement, time, space, and (initially within concrete situations) causality and moral judgements.

In the historical picture we have the advent of complex societies utilising irrigation systems and civil administrations; the philosophies of Buddhism, Taoism, Platonism; the Mesopotamians, Egyptians and Greeks developing astronomy and mathematics; and finally Galileo concluding that the earth was not the centre of the universe. Galileo graphically demonstrates the eventual metamorphosis of the egocentric theology of the pre-operational stage to the highly organised understanding of the interrelationships of concepts of the concrete operational. Already the foundations of the formal operational stage are beginning to develop.

The fourth stage, the period of formal operational thought, is where the aspect of unrealised potential comes into its own, rather than present and tangible reality. Linguistically, the special character of the conditional sentence – the 'if' sentence – is a vehicle for such thinking. This stage displays the capacity to reason about the abstract, and the integration of concepts. The combination of identity, negation, reciprocity and correlation is the central feature of formal operational thought. Obviously such reasoning doesn't develop all at once: it is the only open-ended stage of Piaget's system. Here some of the macro parallels are: the Enlightenment, Marx and Engels, Darwin and Wallace, the Industrial Revolution, psychoanalysis, atomic physics, Braque and Picasso, space travel…

The trials of maturity

Interestingly, when the human organism reaches physical and mental maturity in a post-industrial society it 'leaves home'. I think it was Carl Jung who predicted that human consciousness would be changed forever once the earth was perceived as a whole entity, from outside itself. Initially it was cameras, now human eyes themselves have seen this sight; and every astronaut has testified to the profound, life-changing experience it has been.

Has consciousness been changed for the rest of us? Assuredly it has: not simply because we have seen the photographs, but because of all that has percolated down into society through revelations from scientific heights. We know that we are no longer bound to the earth as once we were. The cord to the mother of all mothers has been cut. The human race has come of age.

Please read the previous sentence again. It's scary. For thousands upon thousands of years human beings have felt parented by the earth beneath their feet and the world of the stars all around them. Now, really only within the last millennium, we have finally left home: physically, emotionally, intellectually and spiritually. We have an unprecedented freedom in the realm of both thought and deed. Less and less do we feel ourselves subject to nature; more and more do we feel that nature is subject to us. Significantly, our moving away from earth, as evidenced in space travel and the whole dimension of astro-physics that has accompanied it, has been paralleled by a deeper penetration *into* the nature of earth substances and material processes. We are now manipulating the very foundations of Darwinism, bringing human purpose into what was thought to be random genetic mutation. Our freedom from the earth is becoming a new freedom from our past – and a new freedom to determine our future. Moreover, this capacity for freedom is accelerating at an extraordinary rate: it has developed more over the last hundred years than over the last thousand.

All of which represents a fundamental 'atmospheric' condition in the environment of the developing child. Think of it like this: until a moment ago, historically speaking, the child was parented by those who felt themselves to be parented by the earth and the stars. Now the child is parented by those who have stepped out of this relationship and who are setting up home on their own. Today's children, we might say, are examples of 'first child syndrome' – and of very young parents to boot. Many new ideas and impulses have been and are being practised upon them. Many mistakes are being made. The proliferation of books about parenting is testimony to this: collections of advice that seem quite laughable to those salt of the earth types who still carry the talent in their bones and blood, but nevertheless books that have become essential reading for our latest generation.

Through the course of this chapter we have been examining how the principle of recapitulation plays into children's physical and cognitive development, linking their 'micro' biography to the macro biography of the human race. Within this recapitulation there appears a distinctive open-endedness: a picture of the human being as nature's great unfinished symphony. Inheritance and instinct take us up to a certain point, and then they hand over to another developmental principle. This is the principle of imitation. Through the young child's remarkable ability to register impressions and weave them into every aspect of his own development, the influence of the environment becomes paramount at this stage, beginning with the child's parents and carers and panning out from there.

Ideals and pressures

Parents have dreams and ideals for their children. These dreams are informed, we might say, by the spirit of the times, at both a conscious and unconscious level. They are dreams of the future, of something yet to be realised. And they are woven deeply into the child's development, because the child imitates *intention* as well as activity from its human environment. (All of this is expanded in considerable detail by Rudolf Steiner and his commentators.)[12] As parents are the medium through which a template of the past is genetically communicated into the physical body of the child, so they (and the whole environment of which they are a major part) are a medium through which an impression of future possibilities is communicated into the child's will, feeling and thinking. With some parents, and in some environments, the pressure for a child to develop in a particular way is stronger than in others.

Is there any more to it than this? James Hillman, the American psychologist, international lecturer and author of twenty-odd books, is one of those who are convinced that there is. In *The Soul's Code*[13] he sets out what he calls his 'acorn theory'. Briefly, the theory states that just as an acorn contains an imprint of what it is ultimately destined to grow into, so does a human being. In Hillman's analysis this appears as something more than genetic predisposition coupled with environmental influence; it is an 'innate image' of the person each of us uniquely intends to become – an archetype of each individual's total (but as yet unrealised) self. Hillman does not directly tackle the question of where this image comes from; for him the crucial recognition is that we each have a sense of it, and that it plays into our lives in significant and extraordinary ways. He cites many examples of episodes in individual biographies where 'moments of destiny' appear to occur: moments that with hindsight appear prophetic, and that are experienced in the moment with emotions ranging from excitement to terror, but always with the sense of the experience being deeply personal. One particular example that has a special place in our book about literacy is that of the French writer Colette.

Colette was one of those individuals who appeared to show no sign of her future calling during childhood. Indeed, she appeared to deny it:

No, I would not write, I did not want to write... No, I did not get up secretly in the night to scribble poems on the cover of a shoebox! No, I never flung inspired words to the West wind or to the moonlight! No, I never made good marks in composition between the ages of twelve and fifteen. For I felt, and felt it each day more intensely, that I was made exactly for not writing... I was the only one of my kind, the only creature sent into the world for the purpose of not writing.[14]

Curiously, what the young Colette did do, and do with a passion, was observe her father writing and crave for the implements of his 'mystery'. She would sit at his desk and take in every detail of his pens, pencils, blotter, sealing waxes and so forth; but choose to write she would not. She herself explained this later by saying that she needed her childhood to be a time of deep experience – of sensing, smelling, feeling – so that her writing, when its time came, would have something to draw from. Maybe she also sensed that her calling would in many respects prove a torture to her. In any event, one reading of her life is that she had the inherited potential to write, the paternal influence to focus and encourage this, and the inner sense to hold back until both she and her talent had sufficiently come of age, and could express all that she had in her to put into words.

For those of us who are in the business, professional or otherwise, of helping young people to read and write, there is intense societal pressure to achieve specific results within a specific time frame. This is no longer the time frame of nature. It is 'designer time' – a human construct that can look extremely clever and convincing on paper, and that can even have a positive effect on statistics in certain contexts and, again, time frames. Typically, today's designer time may include the arrangement of the moment of a human birth around a consultant's opinion, and perhaps sometimes a consultant's convenience. It then promotes all kinds of ways for the young hopeful to 'get ahead', from weaning to walking to talking to problem solving to reading and writing and counting. There is little time in designer time for lingering in the echoes of the past and drawing nourishment from processes that are older than the hills. Designer time has an image of its own outcomes and is driven to realise that image before other influences distract its purpose. It is future oriented; but the future that is shaping young peoples' lives through our collective societal imagination is not necessarily their own future, and may sometimes prove its antithesis.

Alienation, limiting projection and distorting expectation

I believe that the crisis of disenchantment referred to at the beginning of this book has, again, three strands to it. In the first place, many young people are being, and are feeling, cut off from their 'mother', at one or another or at all levels. 'Mater' has become mere 'matter'. Secondly, many young people are infiltrated by an image of who and what they should become in a way that confines and inhibits them. Traditionally it has been the father who has nurtured ambitions for his children and 'whipped them into shape'; today the paternalistic influence (which still seems the right way to describe it) has become increasingly subtle, working more out of the general environment than through the father figure as such. Everywhere there are images of 'ideal' human beings: on advertising hoardings, on television, in the celebrity columns of newspapers, and even in the politically correct representations of human society given to children in their schoolbooks. Let's not be under any illusions: these images are profoundly influential. Whether they are motivated by seemingly altruistic motives or by the motives of the market place, there can scarcely be a child left in the developed world who has not been shaped by them – who has not tried to measure up to them, with greater or lesser success, and who has not in the same process been either deluded or deflated by them, at least in part.

The third strand in contemporary disillusionment is twisted with irony. This is the strand that links us to our sense of individuality – the sense that we are something more than just the product of mother nature and society's ambitions. Humanity, we said, has come of age. Humanity as a whole has weaned itself from nature and borne children who have rejected its traditional gods. Humanity as a whole is beautifully and dangerously catching fire with its own sense of self. As the new-born infant gazes into its parents' eyes in search of universal human love, so the parents are searching the eyes of their child for uniqueness, for an answer to the question, Who are you? There is generally a deep sincerity in this questioning, and certainly I can think of no more important question for a parent to ask. But two things can happen to turn the well-intentioned impulse into something that works against its own purpose. Firstly there is the tendency for parents to answer the riddle of the child's individuality *for themselves*. And secondly there is the tendency to expect the child to have an answer, long before he is ready with it, and in a manner that must inwardly burden him with a responsibility that he actually does not yet want.

Much of this chapter has been concerned with general questions of child and human development. I am utterly convinced that this is essential background for approaching the question of meaningful literacy. Literacy is more than just a communication skill; it is a means of transforming consciousness, and via this, a means of accessing the self. If it is to achieve its fullest possibilities it must be a faculty that unfolds along with a person's development as a whole. Some aspects of our development are universal and predictably patterned, and others are individual and open-ended. Unless we are fully aware of *both* these factors, as the basis for raising and educating children, our budding new generation must inevitably suffer limitation. What, do we imagine, the future will make of this?

Part Two: Making the Difference

6. *Tuning to the Mother Tongue*

The origins of literacy go back to the beginnings of life. Its foundations are laid in the pre-school years, and in the ideal world these more or less establish themselves. The fact that we are not living in an ideal world is the reason for this chapter. It is especially addressed to those involved in raising and caring for young children at home, but belongs integrally with our theme as it is the area where literacy problems typically begin and also where real differences can be made.

The chapter will consider the elements that combine to provide children with an early experience of living language. It will encourage parents and carers to take their lead from children themselves and the natural response children can evoke – rather than from second-hand ideas about what child-rearing *should* be about. It will remind us that our contemporary conditions of life are not absolutes: they are subject to change at all levels, most easily and significantly at home. And above all, I hope, this chapter will establish that language has its own genius capable of working the most extraordinary wonders. What a privilege it is to work in partnership with it!

What is our first experience of language? It isn't the midwife's exhortation to 'Push!'; it comes earlier than that, and thankfully weaves a more subtle linguistic fabric into the foundations of our developing organism. Already in the 'inner ocean' of the womb there are sounds to be heard by the embryonic ear. The character of these sounds is influenced by the medium through which they are transported: they are 'water' sounds, perceived in darkness and part and parcel of the rocking, swaying, rising and falling of the amniotic waters that cradle the curled foetus in the season before the seasons of the sun begin. Ever-present amongst these mingled water sounds is the beating of the mother's heart. Never again, once the moment of birth has passed, do we experience the pulse of life coming simultaneously out of the world's periphery and equally out of our own centre. Never again can the two sides of our eardrum be quite so intimately linked.

When we place our heads underwater, or even just our fingers in our ears, something of this original experience is re-invoked. The sound we hear (assuming no outside sounds intrude) is difficult to describe without appearing rather 'Zen': I would choose, for example, to call it a 'whispered roar'. It is unmistakably different from sounds borne through the air. What we hear is something like a 'sound soup' – far less differentiated, specific, sharpened than anything we normally experience through dry ears. This remains the case when we listen through water to sounds not emanating from our own organism. Voices heard underwater at the swimming pool are certainly still human voices – that is something the water is happy to leave intact – but can we understand what they are saying? Can we distinguish word breaks, syllables, single sounds? No: what we hear is essentially a rise and fall of melodies, rhythmically punctuated and with a certain tone quality, but otherwise indistinct. Waterborne language speaks to us musically, and we hear it *feelingly*. Intellectually, it makes little or no sense.

So with our first perceptions of language before birth: they are musical experiences. With our modern ability to measure things we don't simply have to deduce the linguistic significance of this through guesswork. We can show, for example, by measuring a baby's reactions in different situations, that right from the beginning, even in the weeks before birth, an infant can recognise both its own mother's voice and also its mother's mother tongue.[15] A French baby is notably happier when people are speaking French around it than any other language. The sounds of French are integral to the sounds of her mother. This has nothing to do with the actual words being spoken, but is rather a response to the nuances of vowel sounds in particular and to the musicality of phrasing that identifies one language as distinct from another. Through the faculty of imitation, whose sophisticated capabilities we have already referred to, the unborn child attunes herself to the mother tongue so that she, too, may become an instrument for expressing that tongue. What sounds into the child becomes a formative power that shapes the physical organism and sets its seal upon that organism's utterances. The basic equipment and capability for making vocal sounds, including those of speech (in any tongue, whatever the child's nationality), is given by heredity; the tuning of this equipment is achieved through imitation. The Japanese statesman who is reputed to have followed President Clinton's 'election' with interest was physically unable to avoid a prophetic *faux pas* with that word: the 'l' sound is not a part of Japanese speech, and if not learnt through exposure to another language in early childhood will invariably come out more like an 'r'. The Japanese vocal tract cannot manage otherwise. Significantly too, when a speech sound is not incorporated in childhood and is therefore not clearly pronounceable later on, it is not fully audible to that person either. That is to say, the person cannot clearly recognise whether the sound is 'right' or 'wrong', especially when she is the one trying to pronounce it.

Parents of bilingual families may feel alarmed here. Will the formative influence of separate mother and father tongues make for confusion? In general, the answer is no. Languages themselves are not mutually exclusive, and the young child is a natural language genius. The one situation that can appear to complicate things is where the mother does most of her mothering in the father's tongue. Especially where this second language is not at all natural to her, the mother is thereby instilling a degree of unnaturalness into her child's developing speech. Language is communication, and the mother's communication with her child should be as pure and direct as it can possibly be within the context of her life circumstances. If each parent's special moments of intimacy with the child are expressed in his or her own tongue, the general outcome is likely to be positive. Indeed, the inherent gift of bilingual parentage is a mobility of speech which in turn is associated with a mobility of feeling and thinking, since language is a formative influence within the entirety of human development.

What is far more confounding to a child's development than having two languages spoken at home is having less than one language spoken at home. It happens. Languages, which should be something whole, can be broken, just as homes and spirits can be broken. A language is inseparable from the relationship between those people who speak it. Where the relationship is incomplete, the language is incomplete. Where the language is incomplete, the relationship is also incomplete. Let me say straight away that where there is deafness or dumbness in a family there can still be complete human relationships within that family. Language is not wholly and simply a matter of words spoken. Indeed, words are not language but rather vehicles for language. Language is the life of meaning and the communication of meaning (by which word I mean not simply intellectual meaning but the whole spectrum of what can make sense and matter to us.) Words are one way, but not the only way, to communicate what we mean. What matters within any community of people, and above all in a family, is not firstly how, but whether, real communication can and does take place in any form. Where there is communication breakdown, above all between parent and child, language begins to suffer. In the extreme case of abused and neglected children, language development can be very seriously impaired. If such children then grow up to have children of their own, the language impairment is passed on through imitation – and with it, something of the human loss that impairment represents is handed on as well.[16]

Love and literacy

As we noted earlier, the proliferation of books on parenting is a testimony to the fact that many or perhaps most of us do need help in this area. The world we live in draws us out and away from the oldest and simplest of its mysteries. We have become strangers to our own original condition, unclear how to recognise and relate to it even when it is there in our midst. Are the books a help? I suppose as the writer of another book I am bound to hope so; but I cannot believe that the books themselves have the answer to the conundrum. If we want to know what best to do with children we must learn how to ask the children themselves. We must learn how to listen to them, how to 'read' them in their own language. Everything else must be put aside, with the time that we have, to tune in to the being that is before us. What that being is asking us is that we make music with it – that we 'play' with it in its own key, remote and strange as this may initially appear to be. To appreciate what this key really is we must first silence our adult modalities. We must let go of intellectual thinking. We must let go of over-anxious feelings across the whole range from eager anticipation to the sense of failure and guilt. We must silence our own intentions and approach the child openly and with deep and honest interest. Even when the child is kicking and screaming and seeming totally unapproachable and unappeasable – even there is a wonderful possibility for spontaneous understanding and sympathetic communication. We too were children once, and kicked and screamed and babbled and cooed and laughed and loved being loved. Love, language and literacy are interlinked; and in an environment that is loveless, or short on love, no programme on earth can bring language and literacy to life and give it a future.

Of course, no programme on earth can bring love to life. If love is lacking, however, the best hope of restoring it is children. Maybe that's why they keep coming back to us. Maybe that's why, in the most desolate circumstances imaginable, such as those faced by the world's street children, they continue to show us the bottom line: the six-year-old in a shop doorway tucking up her little sister whose toes have been gnawed off by a rat, doing what she needs to do to keep her parent-less sibling alive, offering what comfort she can; or the four-year-old boy who ran away from his violent home in Moscow and found more kindness in the pack of wild dogs who adopted him than in humankind, begging on the streets for food that he readily shared with his new brothers and sisters, and in return being fiercely protected by them (ultimately unsuccessfully) against efforts to retrieve him.

I told this last story as part of an assembly at school to our collection of six- to fourteen-year-olds. As I did so I was aware of the special quality of listening that was growing in the room. Children's natural love of animals is of course something that speaks for itself. Here, though, was a story that placed this in stark contrast with human love. When the moment came in the narrative for the boy to be 'rescued' by his own kind, two of the younger boys sitting in front of me, oblivious of the attention they would draw to themselves, simultaneously cried out 'No!' These were not themselves abused children, although they had suffered confusion and loss in their family lives. They were two children amongst many millions who knew in their hearts that nothing is more important than love, yet whose faith in human love and consistency had been shaken; children who found it safer, somehow, to trust and embrace the bonds of sympathy represented by 'dumb beasts' than the more complex liaisons of humankind – not least when these creatures themselves had been transformed from 'man's best friends' into outcasts.

I continued the assembly by telling the children about an African boy who had been stolen away as an infant by a band of chimpanzees. This was a toddler whose parents had become too sick to mind him properly and who had strayed too far towards the trees. No full-scale hunt was made at the time to recover him, and he was fed and raised by the apes until he was 8. When he was finally recovered by a band of well-intentioned Christians he had to be given another set of surrogate parents, his own now being dead. He clearly came to feel loved by his new 'family', and despite early struggles with getting dressed and other 'non-chimp' features of his new regime, in most ways he became increasingly integrated into his human way of life. One thing, however, remained unchangeable, and that was his inability to become fluent in language. He could learn words, but he couldn't put them together properly out of his own resources. What he could do, and that in a quite extraordinary way, was sing. When I gave the assembly he had just visited our area with his choir on a world-wide tour. It was said that the quality of this boy's voice was unlike anything heard before. Was that hype – a part of the tour's promotion? Or has his vocal tract been moulded to communicate through sounds rather than words? I didn't get to hear him myself, so I can offer no answer. What I wanted to bring to the children at school was the strange pathos of a child who, though raised by beasts, could sing Gospel songs 'like an angel' and who yet was unable to speak naturally with his own kind, and never in his lifetime would.

Language as a whole

The life of every human being is a mystery. When children are born into extremity, or have extremity thrust upon them, or aspire to extremity through the drive of their own inner natures, the strangeness of life is brought closer to home. At the same time the common threads of human nature are also reconfirmed. In the stories I have mentioned here the need of every child to live in sympathy with her world is paramount. Young children seek such a relationship everywhere, and if it is denied to them in one place they will seek it in another. Through the bonds of sympathy develops the language of communication. To begin with this language is pre-verbal: it is the language of movement and gesture. The activities of feeding, washing and dressing are fundamentally linguistic activities. (With animals, the tongue – *lingua* – retains a more obvious relation to this type of communication than with humans.) The infant's vocal accompaniments to these early ministrations are expressions of pleasure and displeasure, articulated through a musical vocabulary of changing pitch, timbre, rhythm and volume. The attentive parent tunes into this language and learns to interpret it. Though musical rather than verbal, it is a language with its own inherent grammar and syntax: it is designed to express emotional meaning just as clearly as words may express intellectual meaning.

The attentive parent not only tunes in to the child's vocal expressions but responds to them vocally in the right way:

Now, thank goodness, researchers with all their instruments and neurological expertise confirm that a close, bonded mother will quite automatically use tones and rhythms and intonations which are calculated to promote early language development.[17]

This is the origin of what has come to be called 'Motherese' – or 'Parentese' in more PC circles. I'm sticking with Motherese, if that's OK, because it seems to me so completely a part of the archetypal experience of nursing. Fathers and others, however, can be very maternal too:

Are we going to get you in the bath? Come on. Are you going to wash yourself or have I got to do it again? Hey? That's a good boy. Is that nice? Wash your feet and your arms. Is that good, hey? What are you looking at, hey? What are you looking at? Smiley, smiley. Hey, smiley smiley, is that nice? Shall we wash that big belly?[18]

Motherese is a language of sing-song: of words mixed with pure sounds in a modulating rise and fall, more in the upper than the lower range of the voice but with all sounds softened. The words are generally meaningful, though liberally blended with endearments and often repetitive. Often the question form is used, not because an answer is expected but because it is a more engaging form of speech.

Let's put you out here. What can you see? What can you see? Can you? Do you want to stand up? Up a bit. There. Did you have a lovely sleep? Did you? We'll get Conny in a minute. Mmmm. Do be de do be de do be ded do. Do be de do be de do be de do. Ohh. Big hug. Big hug. I can see you. I can see you. Hello gorgeous. A diddly diddly do. A diddly diddly do. Ready? A diddly diddly do. A diddly diddly do. Do you want to sit down there? She's trying to reach for it. Pardon you. Can you see that green chair? Pardon. Mummy's fingers, that's right. Big stretch. Big stretch. Big stretch, ready? Pat a cake, pat a cake, baker's man. Bake me a cake as fast as you can. Pat it and prick it and mark it for me. And put it in the oven for baby and me.[19]

There is no linguistic requirement for Motherese to extend into such mutations of adult words as 'doggy-woggy' or 'pussy-wussy', and Rudolf Steiner for one was keen to advise that this kind of extreme baby-talk be avoided. The high purpose of Motherese is to draw the real meaning of words out of the music and movement and inherent grammatical relationships of words. These relationships do not need creating; they are pre-existent in all natural language, and, as Stephen Pinker[20] and others have demonstrated, are fully appreciated by a child's innate language genius wherever they can be felt and heard. For them to be *felt* as what they are they must be experienced as emerging directly out of the meaningful relationship existing in the 'conversation partnership' of child and adult. This means that verbal communication with infants needs to be accompanied by eye contact and a natural expressiveness in the face especially, but also the entire body. The child is all sympathy and takes everything in as whole. That is how language is meant to be taken, and that is how we need to offer it.

Mothers find that they can move the baby's body in rhythmic ways and chant and sing songs and the babies like it... So we find for example that mothers sing nursery songs which have got very clear phrases in them. The baby is vocalising on the final vowel at the end of the phrase, synchronised with their mother, and they often do it in tune. They can pitch their voice so it matches, so in fact the two of them are trying to produce something together.[21]

Song into speech

As soon as the question of actually singing with children is raised comes the worry, What if the parent isn't very musical? At this level, no parent is unmusical. What matters is not the finished product but the *process* of *tuning in together*. To share a nursery rhyme in the manner just described is worth infinitely more than putting on a recorded version, however charming. The notion of musicality is not an absolute, and the 'well tempered' music of our western civilisation is actually at some considerable remove from the more primitive rhythmic and melodic modalities that reflect a young child's natural soul condition. To be a bit out of time and out of tune need be no bad thing. The crooning of a Hebridean lullaby was never born to be hammered into the latticework of bar lines and staves. It rises and falls like the waves of the sea – fluid, unbroken, absorbing itself into itself with unselfconscious ease. Frequently with such music we search in vain for a key note, or for the distinction between 'minor' and 'major'. It's all still 'in the mix'. It's true that not everyone – in fact very few people – can actually sing authentic Gaelic music or other traditional folk music in the 'old way'. We can, however, develop a feel for the essence of unsophisticated singing from the heart, both by going out of our way to listen to it being sung, and by daring to do what Ou Dede did, which is simply to improvise little narratives incorporating the simplest of made up melodies ourselves. Intellectual self-consciousness is a terrible enemy of intimacy, and really needs banishing from the nursery world altogether.

Rudolf Steiner spoke of the 'mood of the fifth' as being appropriate to music for young children. The interval of the fifth is sounded at the beginning of 'Twinkle, twinkle little star'; violin strings are tuned to it; it is a natural harmonic interval that can be produced simply by changing the breath pressure on many wind instruments. In folk music the interval is often sounded as a drone – a kind of musical warp into which simple melodies may readily be woven. It resounds as the heart of the octave, within which all musical scales are patterned. Most modern western scales in fact bring out the mood of the octave itself, with a clear key note that defines it. A different kind of musical scale can be used to help bring out the mood of the fifth more readily. This is called a pentatonic scale, composed of five rather than eight notes. The black notes on a piano give one ready-made example of such a scale. If a violin had an extra string tuned to a fifth above its top E string, the five strings would give the notes G, D, A ,E and B. By transposing these same notes into the compass of an octave we arrive at the singable pentatonic scale of D, E, G, A, B (the D being one tone above middle C). By adding an octave D' and E' we extend the melodic possibilities to the upper vocal range for most women's and children's voices, with men of course being obliged to do their singing an octave lower. Many songs have been collected that use only these notes, including some that have been specially composed for children in recent times. One book that gives a very persuasive rationale for developing such music consciously in homes and early years settings is Dr. Julius Knierim's *Songs in the Mood of the Fifth (Quintenlieder)*.[22]

Every culture, including stiff-upper-lip English, has a storehouse of folk songs, rhymes and folk tales for the young and very young. They are full of life and a natural wit and wisdom that is educational in the fullest sense. Take one of the simplest, appropriate for youngsters at the beginning of their language development:

> Round and round the garden
> Like a teddy bear;
> One step, two steps,
> Tickle you under there.

This is of course not simply a rhyme to be spoken. During the first two lines the speaker's finger is traced round and round the little one's palm; with the third line the finger takes two steps up the child's arm; and finally, usually after a dramatic pause, the tickling and giggling follows with a delicious inevitability.

Leaving aside what the words mean, a kind of primitive drama unfolds simply through the vowel sounds of this little rhyme. The 'a-u' of 'round', twice repeated, combines the first and last of the sequence of the five pure vowels, 'ah', 'eh', 'ee', 'oh' and 'oo'. It is the vowel sound of the ancient, sacred chant of AUM – the sound of the beginning and ending of all things as they are brought together – round and round – in the cycles of life. Then follows the 'ah' of 'garden', the sound of open-mouthed wonder, voiced from the back of the mouth and uniting in its gesture of formation what is most inward with what is most outward, as a blossom opens and offers itself to the sun. The second line moves into the two broad 'eh' sounds of 'teddy bear'. These are voiced in the middle of the mouth, with an increased contraction of the tongue and palate. The breath that streams from within now has to pass through a kind of threshold before uniting with the outer world. As the 'ah' sound evokes communion, the 'eh' sound evokes duality. In the third line of the rhyme the sound comes twice again in 'step', this time further contracted into the short 'e' and pushed further towards the front of the mouth by the vowels in 'one' and 'two'. The whole drama is leading to one place, and that is the 'i' of 'tickle'. Of the five vowels this is the most pointed, the one that directs the breath so as to penetrate the outer air like a spear. It expresses both contraction and release together – like laughter.

The vowels of 'Round and round the garden', in other words, move from a relaxed openness through an increasing tension into an ultimate moment of release. As the little one participates in the experience she is urged more and more into her own body – step by step, from the periphery of the hand inwards – towards the ultimate muscular contraction of tickling that finds its necessary counterbalance through laughter. The 'pedagogy' of this nursery rhyme is that it lightly and playfully leads the child into an experience of herself as the inhabitant of her own body, without binding her too heavily into it. It does this through the actions that accompany the rhyme, but also through the progression of vowel sounds within it. Both of these constitute direct communications to the child. On top of this, gradually, the actual images represented by the words begin to add their own layer of meaning. The 'garden' is the child's world, innocent and 'unfallen'; the 'teddy bear' is the child's body; the 'steps' are a picture of child development; and the tickling is a crisis of transition such as punctuate all life processes in their unfolding. In this case, it should be added, the acute moment of physical self-awareness represented by the tickling is equally an experience of the 'other' – the tickler. For one cannot tickle oneself.

Even if you feel this is 'reading' too much into a trifle, the general recognition must surely be granted that the essence of the nursery tradition in every culture is to consolidate the child's sense of being 'at home': in the body, in the family, in the world. Through rhythm and repetition, both of sound and image, the nursery rhymes sing themselves into the child's consciousness and memory. Repetition confirms experience as an enduring reality. The more specifically things are repeated, the more real and meaningful they become for the little child. Experiments have shown that children actually learn words that are repeated by the same speaker far more quickly than the same words repeated by different speakers.[23] This, to repeat, is because language in its origins is inseparable from relationships.

A further word about rhyme:

Some time ago we set up a project which actually looked at how responsive children are to rhyme and how well they judge whether words rhyme or not... Then we followed these children over the next three to four years and looked at how they learnt to read and to write when they went to school and how they learnt other things at school too... We found that there's a strong predictive relationship between their sensitivity to rhyme at ages three and four and the progress they later made in learning to read and write. We found that this was quite specific. In other words these rhyme scores taken early on predicted how well they learned to read and write but didn't predict well how they did at other things at school, for example mathematics.[24]

Research in the US has also found that children with dyslexia and reading problems can make great advances by learning to sing in tune.[25]

Some children are innately more sensitive to rhyme than others. All children, however, become *more* sensitive to such consonance of sound through repeated early exposure to it.[26] One of the games children like to play together – and with adults who have the appropriate abandon – is making up rhymes simply on the basis of sound, regardless of whether they are creating real words or not: 'I'm going to see my mummy'. 'I'm going to see my dummy.' 'I'm going to see my plummy'. . . Another game is substituting the initial consonants of a string of words for a common consonant: 'D-I'm d-oing d-o d-ee d-y d-ummy.' 'D-o d-ou d-aren't!'

Grown-ups sometimes get rather concerned about whether children's speech is 'proper' enough. But 'correctness', like 'musicality', is frequently more to do with the vicissitudes of fashion than inherent linguistic dictates. Language is magical, playful, infinitely creative but also religiously lawful. And children are the same. The one thing that really matters is that language is experienced with reverence. This doesn't mean prim and prissy piety; it means appreciation, care, openness and wonder. Sadly, much language that children hear is spoken without reverence. Sometimes it is punctuated by expletives; sometimes it is simply empty phrases. All of which children are compelled to take into themselves and recreate. It's a bitter medicine, and it does them real harm. Then they get told off or simply ignored when they begin to talk that way themselves, and it's little wonder that they lose respect both for language and its perpetrators.

Needless to say, not all communications with young children need be in rhyming couplets or sing-song. The crucial point always is that they are natural, and that they spring from a living relationship. While musical speech especially helps develop active listening and sensitivity to the nuances of sound that will later be relevant to reading and spelling, something more is needed to consolidate a wholesome link between language and meaning. At its simplest this involves relating words to people and things – to the giving of names. One of the infant's earliest deliberate actions is pointing, and in due course the endlessly repeated word 'Dat' assures us that she has become as desirous of receiving a *word* to get the feel of as the actual object being pointed at. The child appreciates and begins to speak of things generically at first; so, for example, a flower is 'flower' regardless of whether it is a daffodil or a daisy. The way the little one perceives associations between things is often quite eye-opening for us, and we should take care not to insist on pedantic distinctions too early. It isn't for very long on this earth that we are granted such a 'universal' consciousness, and in this age of particularity we need more than ever to treasure and protect what we can of it. The child herself will let us know when she is ready to move into further differentiation. Typically the change comes all of a sudden, usually around eighteen months – though children differ in this respect. And when it does come we should have the feeling that every new word we give to the little one is a sparkling jewel, each one differently faceted and shining with its own colour and light. The delight with which a child will repeat a new word over and over again should be confirmation enough of just how significant the experience really is – and just how capable words can be of working wonders out of their own nature. Language has its own genius, just as children have a genius for learning it. In learning words they are not merely learning labels for either things or thoughts; they are engaging with living entities, hearing and visualising them as beings in their own right – beings that have something to tell them.

Language as creative principle

The more we take notice of the way language unfolds through childhood, the more we are drawn to acknowledge that language is as much creator as creation in the realm of human life. Its activity is profoundly influential in shaping the very being of the evolving child, in thought, feeling, voice, gesture and the ultimate ability to act humanly. Such a perspective is by no means new. Its most matter-of-fact expression is probably the opening of the St. John's Gospel, which sets the tone for a testimony to the divine creative power described as the 'Logos' – whose original Greek usage combined the sense of 'word', 'meaning' and 'spirit' – that incarnates into human life and thereby unites humanity with its divine origins:

In the beginning was the Word, and the Word was with God, and the Word was God. . .
. . . All things were made by him; and without him was not any thing made that was made.
In him was life; and the life was the light of men.
And the light shineth in darkness; and the darkness comprehended it not. . .
. . . And the Word was made flesh, and dwelt among us.

Which might also be interpreted and expressed as: The archetype of language expresses the creative power that underlies the world as a whole and human beings in particular. It is the bearer of both life and consciousness. Its revelation is present even before it can be fully comprehended; and the mystery of the Word becoming flesh is that of the divine creative principle flowing and resounding through the physical body of a human being and ultimately flowering in human speech.

Language originates in unconscious darkness. It announces itself as a manifestation of life before it becomes a manifestation of meaning. It spirals into the 'listening' flesh of the human embryo, resonating with what is already imprinted there so as to advance the formation of the organs that will both further receive and further express the 'spirit and meaning' that the being of language eternally seeks to bring to life. In the beginning it wells into consciousness simply as a stream of sound. The babbling of infants is like the rippling of the surface of this river, where the watery depths begin to catch the light and to move with the air. This first differentiation of the unified impulse of the Word is into phonemes, which are the basic elementary sounds of all human speech – English, Welsh, Mandarin, whatever. Then syllables emerge, gathering the phonemes into themselves according to the different linguistic roots that define each mother tongue within the family of world languages. Then come words, which further shape universal experience into the local dialect of culture, country, region and family. Then come sentences, through which each one of us can become individually co-creative with the spirit of language itself, expressing universal experience according to our own voice and inner disposition.

What makes it all work? We could call it a process of attunement. Biological nature prepares the child's physical body as a fit instrument through which language may resound, but the real tuning of this instrument is an interactive process involving the child and the totality of her environment, in particular the human environment most closely associated with the child's biography. The more attuned this environment and its inhabitants are to the child, to each other and to the spirit of language that expresses what is common to them all, the more the child will also be enabled to tune into her own voice within this general harmony, and to 'rhyme' herself with her world. Once all of this happened more or less naturally; now it is necessary for most adults to attune themselves and the environment over which they have some control quite consciously to the condition of childhood. They may have to go through a barrier of self-consciousness to achieve this. They may have to let go of certain attitudes and assumptions that have become ingrained in them through the habits of a lifetime. They will certainly have to give the undertaking time. But it is all entirely possible, wholly desirable and actually a quite wonderful and rewarding adventure that can bring as much to the adult as to the child.

7. Animating the Word

This chapter, like the last, will focus on the early years. It will follow the development of language from broader contexts through to the child's meeting with books. Parents and early years teachers alike should find plenty to relate to here, while those concerned more with older children may find their attention drawn to things that are missing in these biographies, and discover therapeutic value in returning to activities overlooked at an earlier stage.

Orality and community

The early years of childhood, like early stages of humanity, are characterised by an experience of life in general that is fundamentally animistic. Everything is experienced as alive. Even the mineral realm appears ensouled, and all things and all creatures in this condition have a listening ear and an answering voice: they are all potential conversation partners. The spoken word becomes the medium for a magical communion with nature, with the spirits and with other human beings. Just listen to a young child talking away to 'himself': the last thing he is experiencing is being alone. The spoken word brings everything into touching distance.

In all oral communities of the past, and those that still exist today, the most traumatic experience possible is to be exiled from the community. Some readers may remember being 'sent to Coventry' by schoolmates when they were young, and the pain such 'excommunication' caused. Exclusion of this kind has always occurred, sometimes as a punishment equivalent to eternal damnation, but sometimes as part of a process of initiation that will end with reintegration into the tribe. In either case they represent profound, life-changing experiences which are only bearable to individuals who have achieved a certain evolution in their own development. 'Go to your bedroom!' is an evocation of this ancient exile in the soul of a young child. So, in the wrong context, is 'Get out your book and read it.'

Orality is fundamentally holistic, and for literacy to emerge from it in a healthy way the experience of wholeness must be kept intact. We have spoken of the importance of constant human relationships in this regard. We have spoken of tuning in to the mothering ministrations of language that give voice firstly to universal human utterance (infant babble), then to the soul of one's 'folk' in a specific angle on the world offered by the mother tongue, then to one's immediate human community and finally, when the time is right, to one's own individual voice and self. We speak of 'personal voice' or 'finding a voice', for instance in reference to poets, as the most individual form of utterance in which a common language is individualised to the greatest possible extent. We have touched on some of the environmental influences that can work to undermine a child's holistic relation to life, including non-human parodies of human beings, voices and activities – such as appear in the vast catalogue of today's mechanical and technological toys and animation. These typically distort the human or natural world, and render it grotesquely, but pretend to have life and soul, and effectively (strong stuff here) sap children's life forces and sense of living engagement with the world in order to keep that pretence alive. All inanimate toys and images are indeed 'animated' by the children who engage with them, but when the character of this animation is dictated down to the last detail by the toy or image in question, allowing the child no freedom to imbue it with his own character; and when the toy or image is essentially non-childlike – then unhealthy obsessions are spawned, and the child's living relationship to his own natural and human environment, and to himself, begins to be severed.

Living toys

The availability and integration of appropriate toys and puppets is a vital and irreplaceable element within a healthy childhood. The Steiner Waldorf nurseries and kindergartens (and books about them) contain many wonderful examples of playthings that reflect and develop a simple, healthy love of life. They are made of natural materials, and are objects and images drawn from the natural world of early childhood, including not only its visible and obvious manifestations – conkers, shells, logs, toy animals, toy people, toy implements that people use – but also anthropomorphic (humanised) forms drawn from imaginative realities: for example gnomes, fairies and all sorts of other fairytale characters as archetypes that embody diverse and vital energies at work just below the surface of life.

The place of puppets deserves a special mention here. More than any other kind of toy, puppets are designed to 'come alive'. They can do this in a number of different ways, each of which invokes a different quality of relationship between the three players involved, namely the puppeteer, the puppet and the audience (if there is one). Some of these relationships are more appropriate for younger children than others. Used inappropriately, puppetry can be very scary and disturbing; used appropriately it can be healing, energising and inspiring.

With younger children it is particularly important that the

puppets should remain visibly related to the puppeteer, whether as finger puppets, self-standing fleece-filled dolls that can be picked up, moved around and placed on a decorated table top, or simple, soft-featured marionettes. Children have no difficulty whatsoever in suspending their disbelief in the puppets' reality; and the fact that this reality is also fundamentally part of a human reality is absolutely appropriate and welcomed by the child. The puppets with their human operator are indeed a picture of the human being's higher and lower (or, if you like, non-physical and physical) nature working together – visibly connected, even if only by thin threads. Equally they are a picture of the essential relationship that exists between childhood and adulthood, without which connection a child will feel wholly cut adrift and lost. Certainly there comes a time to cut the apron strings, and for children no longer in their milk-teeth stage (see next chapter) puppets that appear animated without a visible animator can come into their own as dramatisers of the life of soul. But even here there is a world of difference between a puppet with an invisible human operator and one having no human operator at all, in other words a mechanical puppet or doll that moves and 'speaks' by itself. Such robots, in my view, are appropriate playthings only for those who can make them themselves and who can retain the creative power to live in a mechanistic environment without becoming subtly mechanised in their inner life.

Central to all good puppetry is the relation between the puppets' movement and gesture, and human speech. The one should express the other, but it should always be speech that leads. Often, in our culture, it is the other way around, and human speech becomes secondary and subject to physical impulses. All expletives are of this order – and there are a hell of a lot of expletives about today. Children who are exposed to this kind of impulsive language (which goes way beyond swearing) will inevitably fall strongly under its influence and their entire development may be shaped by it. Puppetry is a wonderful medium for creating and restoring the right relations between the higher and lower impulses of human nature. At the heart of its potential is the controlled and creative power of speech made visibly eloquent through bodily movement.

For many adults puppetry may also prove one of the easiest ways to get back into the spirit of childhood and find release from the cramping inhibitions with which adulthood tends to fetter us. It isn't even necessary to have ready-made puppets to do this: thumbs and fingers make a good beginning, and there are scores of little finger games like 'Two little dicky birds sitting on a wall' that can be found or invented. Hands dressed in socks are also good. All kinds of things are a way in to this special realm of make-believe; and so long as care is taken not to go too far there can be some very healthy magic in every house, home and playspace.

Living pictures

A variant of puppetry's holistic animation can be achieved in two dimensions through moving pictures. Pop-up books offer a ready-made example of pictures that move in response to human movement, and it is quite possible to supplement off-the-shelf versions with one's own creations, and to encourage children who are capable of it to make and manipulate their versions too. A picture need not pop up to be animated; the animation can be as simple as a cut out figure (human or animal) attached to a cardboard strip which is slotted through an extended slit in a drawing or painting and moved along it. Very basic, very simple, but very effective in drawing the child into the imaginative scene and unlocking the spirit of a story from that scene: a spirit, once again, which springs from the animator rather than some anonymous, invisible creator behind the screen, as is the case with mechanically or electronically produced animations.

Animating images is integrally part of the process of drawing and painting as such, regardless of whether the finished product moves outwardly or not. Children love and need to draw and paint, and it is important to encourage this in the right way. In the beginning what matters is the activity itself. The youngster simply needs the materials to get going and the rest takes care of itself. It begins as scribbling, which could well be described as all animation and no image. Even when the first suggestions of imagery begin to appear it is a mistake to draw the child's conscious attention to this by asking or guessing what the picture is – or even to compliment it as 'good', as if it might be anything else. The process remains the all-important thing until the child himself begins to talk about the content of his pictures. Early drawings spring not from the impulse to represent outer visual perceptions at all but rather to experience archetypes of movement: the oscillation between polarities that defines the straight line; the swirling round and round that defines the spiral and circle; the transpositions of movement through the different dimensions of space that define the cross, the rectangle, the triangle etc.. Insofar as this connects with anything physically perceptible to the child, the character of this perception is defined by the child's senses of touch, life, movement and balance.[27] If Rudolf Steiner is right in his interpretation here, then the actual object of such perception is the child's own body. In this view the child is actually drawing – quite unconsciously, of course – his own physical 'incarnation' as this proceeds from the head downwards through roughly the first seven years of life. Michaela Strauss, in her book *Understanding Children's Drawings*[28], offers a detailed analysis of this correlation, with many examples of children's (and also historically 'primitive') drawings to give body to the argument. One of the practical implications of such a perspective is that a child's development may be 'read' quite directly, once one has developed an eye for it, through the details of his drawings. Audrey MacAllen elaborates this diagnostic approach in *The Extra Lesson.*[29]

As the little child grows older there is an increasing overlap between his 'organic' inner perceptions and those shaped by the world around him. Figures and objects in his drawings are given names, notably those belonging to home and family. However, the child is clearly not involved in a process of conscious copying here, such as an adult does when sketching; he is drawing what are still essentially 'egocentric' inner pictures of his world. This remains strongly the case well into school age. Having said this, the process of drawing is one through which the child begins to make his experience of self and world distinct and articulate, and there is a natural accompaniment to this development in the realm of language. Taking the lead from the child himself in the way he talks about his drawings, an adult can engage with what the child has produced in many wonderful little conversations. If we appreciate that a child is really baring his soul in his drawings, we can develop appropriate sensitivity in finding the right words to affirm his experience. This, in turn, can blossom into resonant, living concepts in the realm of thought – or more accurately, to begin with, in the realm of feeling. Such conversational reflections can be ever so simple. 'Don't those flowers look pretty in the sunshine? Daddy must have remembered to give them a drink, otherwise they wouldn't look so fresh.' Or, 'The princess looks happy today. I expect with a smile like that she's going to make other people happy too!' Or, 'Is that Grandpa? Do you remember when he fell over on the lawn? Everyone laughed, didn't they – even Grandpa? Which is funny, because some people cry when they fall over, even if it's on the grass.' But not, 'Why have you put the chimney on our house at a funny angle when you know it points straight up in the air?' Reflect on what the picture evokes in the realm of 'shared experience', but not on the way the picture is drawn.

Conversation to story

Immediate experience, especially shared experience, is the inexhaustible source of meaningful topics of conversation. By talking over events that a child has recently witnessed or participated in, in a quite simple and matter-of-fact way, those events are confirmed as realities and woven into the fabric of memories that become the basis of his feeling of continuity and identity. The child's own past is, for him, the truest of true stories. It is the one essential narrative that he must hear. The members of an oral community spend their entire lifetimes telling each other stories of their communal past, including their spiritual past as recollected in the form of myth and legend. The storyteller – the one with the gift of translating memories into words, and remembering those words – is a figure of crucial significance in such cultures: he, or also she, is effectively the bearer of the ego of the tribe. So we, parents or those in loco parentis, are the ones who can articulate the sense of identity spun from the daily experience of each child in our care. Our responsibility here is all the more pressing given that we are all more or less caught up in the white water rush of twenty-first century time: we need to be quite deliberate in slowing this tumult down, creating backwaters and eddies where we, and our children, may catch breath and come more fully to ourselves. Given young children's love of, and need for repetition we should not be averse to repeating ourselves; indeed, we *have* to repeat ourselves when conversing with children. Experience recollected once is only a beginning; we are called upon to tell the special stories again and again, the biographical ones as well as the fictions. The process bears fruit when the child can repeat these stories himself, word for word.

One of the more hopeful signs of our times is the re-emergence of storytelling in primary schools. This is part of a growing recognition of the vital role that orality plays in a child's early life. Sadly, much of the storytelling is being done exclusively by professional storytellers brought in for the occasion. Really, the lifeblood of orality is what lives in a particular human community. It should be the teachers, like the parents before them, who take on the burden of this role – although burden is altogether the wrong word, since it quickly proves the greatest of delights. And to begin with at least, it should be story*telling* rather than story reading that the parents and teachers devote their best efforts to establishing within the daily routine. Those who have done both know for an absolute fact that there is a world of difference between the two activities. Storytelling is a conversation; reading a story is ultimately a monologue, no matter how sensitive and animated the reading. A narrative drawn from memory, or spun directly out of the imagination, requires real inner activity; and this communicates itself as a gift, not merely of the story but of one's personality with it. It also enables the communication to adapt itself moment by moment to the fluctuations of attention and comprehension within the listener. In the special instance where one has made up a story oneself with a child or children in mind, something truly magical can occur in the telling of it: a sense, not merely of communion, but of the story telling itself, with the narrator becoming a co-listener alongside his audience.

Reading: inclusion or exclusion?

If the several thousand words of this book so far have done little to promote the cause of books themselves, now is the time to correct such a misapprehension. There is certainly a place for books in the world, and equally in a child's life from the moment the outer world comes into clear focus within the child's consciousness. Books are part of the furniture of an adult environment – at any rate a literate adult environment. Bearing no obvious signs of life themselves they are initially quite uninteresting. They begin to become interesting only when they move. The most interesting they can get for ages is when they spread open like a Chinese fan in the child's hands. Many books are innocently brutalised by youngsters simply for this special effect. Most adults are wisely against this sort of thing in practice if not principle, and keep their books out of baby's reach on shelves where they merge into the wallpaper and disappear into the realm of background 'harmonics' – still a part of home, but a part yet to be grown into.

The issue becomes more complicated when the youngster sees books in other peoples' hands. Hands, like mouths, are very interesting to infants and toddlers because they have everything to do with movement and life. Things that other people hold in their hands become interesting by association. Children are also drawn to the quality of interest itself: they know when someone's interest – especially a parent's – is focused on something, and they naturally want to be part of that something. This is a problem when that something is a newspaper or an adult book. The child's attempt to get involved physically is doomed to meet with rejection; and even from a distance the child is aware of being closed off from the person in question. The more this experience is repeated, the more a child will begin to associate books with rejection – a very particular kind of rejection, too, since books don't actually *do* anything themselves and people don't *do* anything with them either, as far as the child can see. They actually make people seem to be asleep – or dead.

It is therefore a kindness to children, where possible, to do one's reading out of their sight if there is going to be competition for attention, certainly until books have begun to reveal their interest for the child too. This is where the pop-up books and other picture books come in. Once the child is actually able to distinguish one picture image from another a great festival of naming can begin. As with Adam in the Garden of Eden, the realm of the animals has a special place in this early human activity. Pictures of animals are of course different from living animals, and when the child learns the name of a living animal from real experience he is learning a name that incorporates the size, sounds and movements of that creature, plus the feeling of its living presence, and not simply its colours and shape. His animal nouns are also active verbs and expressive adjectives. Animal pictures in books are drawn with differing degrees of artistry, some catching the essence of their animals better than others.[30] It is good to choose books that have warmth in their illustrations – not undue sentimentality, but a feeling of the essential being and archetypal gesture of each creature. The way in which the parent or other adult animates these pictures through speaking about them – or through giving voice to the character of the animal in question – will be different from the way a living animal would 'speak' for itself, and different too from the way Walt Disney would animate the creature; it may or may not be particularly 'realistic', but it will allow the animal to become an immediate part of the child's human family in the same way that puppets can be seen as a living extension of their human puppeteer.

The way that we actually share a book – any book – with a child is as much a part of the child's experience of that book as whatever is drawn or written in it. How we sit down with the child, how we pick up and hold the book, how we turn its pages, how quickly or slowly we move through it, how we talk about it, how we invite the child into appreciating its content: these are the keys to unlocking the life within it. Think of the book as an extension of the arms and hands, not the head – a kind of cuddle, if you like. Watch how the child 'reads' to his toys, if indeed he is inspired to do this at all: is it a real gesture of sharing, as we would hope it to be? Is it comfortable and natural? Does the book 'belong' to the child in the same way as his toys do?

A word about our tone of voice when sharing stories with young children. We are often tempted to over-dramatise stories, using a range of strongly different voices for different characters, making the scary bits scarier and the exciting bits real edge-of-the-seat stuff, without necessarily noticing the effect this is having on the little child. Perhaps there is an element of our own amusement mixed up in the proceedings. In fact the *way* we tell a story can prove much more disturbing than the story's content. Getting eaten by a wolf, narrated in the matter-of-fact way proper to fairytales, is not typically a bad or troubling experience for a four-year-old – but it certainly becomes deeply disturbing when the narrator *becomes* the wolf, leaping out of the dreamtime of the story into the real time and real place of bedtime and the bedroom. 'Long ago and far away' is the essence of the timeless, dreamy 'soul histories' that the classic fairytales tell of, and even when telling stories of other kinds this crucial sense of the 'otherness' of the story world should be maintained, not because it makes that world more distant but because it doesn't create confusion before the child is ready to reconcile it.

If we take on board the importance of *telling* stories to our children, and begin to practise this, at least at the level of recalling shared experience, the more our reading resembles telling, the better our children will appreciate it. It is obviously easier to do this when the content of a book is familiar; and with first books especially it really is a pity to have to read them 'blind', regardless of whether they turn out to be good books after all. When the reader's attention is glued to the book rather than the child, the latter is inevitably somewhat excluded. The experience becomes a more intellectual, head-focused activity, and it is easy to lose the warmth of connection.

Everything that we have been considering in relation to the inherent musicality of spoken language, and the young child's intimate relation to this element, applies directly to the choice of appropriate first books for children to have read to them, and in due course to read themselves. Books of illustrated nursery rhymes are an obvious first choice, not just because their language is musical but also because much of their content is (or should be) already familiar as a part of home life. Stories written in rhyme can take their place alongside these, albeit with choices to be made when it comes to storyline, illustrations and the actual vocabulary and use of language. Literature based in the well-worn folk tradition generally has most to recommend it at the early stage, whereas many modern rhymes and stories exchange warmth and depth for cleverness and humour, and perhaps satisfy adults more than they do children. It is not, however, my wish to be dogmatic here: a few inappropriate books are likely to do little harm if the general soil is healthy. Certainly we should think carefully about our choices of first books, but equally we should avoid exuding anxiety, which our youngsters themselves may pick up on, about whether some books might be 'bad' for them – just as we should in the case of people who might not always be the best influence. Of course we should do our best to protect children, but not by encouraging them to lose trust in their world. If a book comes to have the same status as a stranger – the sort we don't talk to – then its magic will become darker, but no less potent than its acceptable associates. There's nothing at all wrong with saying that a book is for later, when you are older. Children *know* that they are children; they are excited by growing up; the sense of becoming ready for new things is a soul force that generates focus and strength of purpose. Saying that a thing will be right for you later is different from saying that it is wrong for you now. It's also different from saying that it's right for you now when it isn't, and different again from asking whether the child thinks it's right or not.

Now, dear Reader, it is time to move on from the early years to the middle years of childhood, and firmly to grasp the nettle of literacy proper – as a child must grasp it in formal education, with conscious and specific focus.

8. First Writing and Reading

With this chapter we come to the transition between what children normally learn from their parents and what they mainly learn from their teachers at school. Some remaining aspects of preparation will be considered first, related to building bridges from the spoken to the written word. Then we must face up to the whole question of how and when children should start school, and the influence that different kinds of schooling may have on them. We shall here consider 'literacy readiness' as the main focus for general school readiness, while giving pointers towards other broader considerations around this theme. And to bring our theoretical arguments down to earth we shall compare approaches to literacy adopted by the Steiner Waldorf schools with other contemporary mainstream practices.

The sense of sound

The assumption we are proceeding on in this chapter is that, prior to being introduced to the mysteries of literacy, a child will already have developed a rich sense of the spoken word. She will have an ear for the spoken soundscapes of words, borne on the air. She will have her favourite words – words she likes to 'toy' with, words that conjure up sensations, feelings, memories, other words. Some words she will associate clearly with the people she first learnt them from, or who say them most characteristically. The words she knows and uses will be a part of her life: they will link her powerfully and directly to her own sense of meaning and identity. They will also have a life of their own, because that is what spoken, air-borne words do have.

For the child who is approaching literacy without this fertilised sensibility, everything possible must be done to make good what is missing. Obviously experiences appropriate for younger children will need adapting to fit the needs of older ones, and some suggestions to this effect will be offered as we proceed. It will be seen that much of what is done anyway in the Steiner Waldorf schools continually underpins literacy with orality. In any event it cannot be sufficiently stressed that, without a living experience of spoken language as its basis, literacy teaching is likely to prove worse than a waste of time.

The bridge between spoken and written language is a bridge between hearing and seeing. The child who has learnt to speak properly has learnt to hear not merely sounds but meaning in words. So now the child approaching literacy must learn to see not merely forms but meaning in text. With alphabetic writing, the very fact that meaning can be seen in a written word at all is a major challenge to a child's credulity. Without believing there will be no seeing, so the first preparatory steps of literacy lie here.

Long before the child even thinks to ask about it we can begin to forge some basic links. With no trouble at all we can encourage the child to experience writing and reading as an extension of speaking. When we are writing something down in the child's presence – say, a shopping list – we can say out loud what we are writing. We might also ask the child if we have forgotten anything, and let her see that the thing she remembers gets written down on the list as well. Such an exercise connects the word list with more than just speaking. It relates it also to the activities of daily life, and more specifically links the written words to a process of naming real and familiar things.

Demystifying script

Another obvious area where literacy links into ordinary life is in the writing of letters and cards. Here again, if composition is done aloud when the child is present then the process is demystified, and in most cases the child can also be invited to contribute to the composition herself. The young child naturally has a very matter-of-fact relation to the way things hang together in life, and shouldn't initially need to have writing explained to her in order for it to have a meaningful place in her universe. If she does ask, we might explain simply that writing is a special way of drawing talking – something that you learn when you've done lots of other drawing. If the child then wants to do 'pretend' writing and reading, that's fine, so long as it doesn't become obsessive and is done in the context of ordinary drawing. Together with the wholly made-up kind of 'emergent' writing – or 'mark-making,' as it often gets called these days – that many children love to do, a limited amount of copying of actual words can come into the equation too: perhaps the child's own name and the names of those closest to her. If at all possible, though, it would be better to avoid speaking about the individual letters and their sounds altogether, since the child's experience of words is (or should be) of living beings, living entities, whose wholeness is essential to their being alive. In this respect it is certainly best to have nothing to do with ready-made letters as playthings in the pre-school years. Magnetic plastic letters on fridges may indeed familiarise the alphabet and give it a brief novelty attraction – but living literacy isn't a matter of solving intellectual puzzles; it's a revelation of life and soul. Fridges freeze food on the inside and these days frequently freeze language on the outside. I really wish they wouldn't!

The foundations of living literacy are laid via the operative principle of imitation. What this powerful learning impetus does *not* do is raise its achievements into full consciousness. Imitation is essentially an activity of the will; the cognitive process that accompanies it is dreamlike: an activity of spontaneous associative imagination and fantasy rather than directed rational thinking. Imitation and imagination forge connections; consciousness, whether applied to doing, feeling or thinking, sunders the totality of experience into separate distinctions. The compulsion to make everything conscious is really the bane of our age – at least where it is applied to the realm of early childhood. Intellectual consciousness *actively inhibits* the spontaneous genius of imitation and associative imagination. In neurological terms it actually limits the learning process to a much smaller and less creative area of the brain. It also weakens the memory, which is at its strongest when it involves the full range of the senses, not just the 'higher' ones. The question isn't whether consciousness is worth having, since it is integral and essential to our humanity. The question is how and when it should be awakened.

Slow awakening

In Chapter 4 we compared the developmental timetable of children according to Piaget with the historical development of human culture and civilisation. We suggested that the historical emergence of literacy, with its significant accompanying shift of consciousness, corresponded with the transition from the child's 'pre-operational' to 'concrete operational' stages. In Piaget's picture, this occurs when the child is around seven years old. This is also the age recommended by Rudolf Steiner for the beginning of a child's formal education. In a book that I co-wrote with Martyn Rawson called *Ready to Learn*[31] we discuss the question of school readiness at length, bringing forward both argument and evidence to support Steiner's approach, which has been practised by Steiner Waldorf schools throughout the world since 1919. There is not space to recap all the arguments here, but the following points are central:

- A child's first developmental need is to develop a physical body that will serve as the best possible instrument for expressing the child's inherent capabilities and creative impulses through the rest of her life.
- It really does take the best part of seven years for a child to grow into and possess her body, right into the fingers and toes and the fine motor skills that their movements are part of.
- Social, emotional, linguistic and cognitive development are inextricably interwoven with early physical development and also take around six to seven years to reach their first stage of organic maturity. Thereafter they naturally become more free of physical and physiological constraints.
- Abstract and 'head-based' learning before a child has completed this first developmental chapter will either bemuse, confuse or confound the child; it may also precipitate a precocious leap into the next developmental stage, leaving significant 'unfinished business' in what is properly called the foundation stage.[32]

In *Neuropsychological Fundamentals in Learning Disabilities*[33] we find confirmation of the fact that a child's ability to orient herself properly in space and inwardly perceive her own body structure and movements 'is the basis of a fundamental psychological process, i.e. the ability to differentiate between external space and the body schema which is actually the core of consciousness and the pivot of interaction between 'ego' and 'non-ego', subject and object.' Things don't get much more significant than being 'the core of consciousness'. In the same work we find what we might call the basic 'incarnation' skills summarised and their relation to subsequent academic skills indicated as follows:

- Purposeful equilibrium, body image and the integration of the postural system which are basic for the use of instruments or objects

- Independence of both halves of the body
- Learning of non-conditioned language
- The possibility of developing creativity
- The capacity for higher-level learning[34]

The argument in *Ready to Learn* is that English and American education systems in particular have got it badly wrong in terms of their prescriptions for school starting age and the beginnings of formal learning. Comparison with countries where formal education begins at 6 or 7, for example Finland and Norway, immediately challenge the 'hothouse' approach with clear evidence that, both educationally and socially, starting later produces better results. The absence of a constant regime of testing is also part of the 'Scandinavian' model, and may well be related to its successes. So too, of course, may be the more generalised aspects of Scandinavian culture that influence children's upbringing before and alongside the process of education as such.

The world has moved on since *Ready to Learn* was written, with some educational developments appearing to moderate the hothouse approach while others, sadly including Norway's, seem to be turning up the heat. There is certainly still a need to keep the education debate alive; and above all there is a need to get hold of and hang on to the core issues that underlie it. Of these, the one that matters above all is the nature and development of the human being.

In recent modifications to the Foundation Stage of the National Curriculum in my own country there are some very promising new emphases. I would like to celebrate these in the hope that they may continue to flower in their country of origin, which rather desperately needs such a flowering, and perhaps be part of a larger humanising of education generally. First and foremost amongst the positives in this latest reform is the clear recognition that early years education should be promoted and pursued as an extension of the life of the home. Parents are not to be left feeling bereft and redundant exiles from the province of educational professionals. Their perceptions and involvement are to be welcomed and given a formal status within the 'partnership' of adults working together for the best interests of the children in their care. There is a place for their observations in the Foundation Stage Profile that has replaced the earlier form of child assessment at the end of this period. The practitioners of early education are also counselled not simply to be 'aware' of each child's background, but to form a living relationship with the child's home circumstances so that the child can really *feel* the connection. Continuity and consistency are seen as desirable in terms of both personnel and daily routine. The basic necessity for the child to feel included, secure and valued is paramount, involving an appropriate awareness of ethnicity, culture, religion, home language, family background, special educational needs, disability, gender, and ability.

In the realm of 'Communication, Language and Literacy', the very formulation of the heading puts literacy in its rightful place as the last stage in our efforts to make sense of things. Communication is put first and established as at least a two-way process. Attention is drawn to the pre-eminent significance of body language, eye contact and facial expression in the development of communication, and practitioners are advised to include and encourage the use of gesture in tandem with talking, in some cases actually 'signing' as they communicate. The relation of language to movement and 'whole body' learning is also hinted at, albeit only in generalised terms, suggesting that language may be used to reflect the way children are being 'articulate' in their limbs. The value of song and rhyme, rhythm and repetition, in developing the musical appreciation of language is clearly established, as is the central place of stories in nurturing both language and imagination. Practitioners are encouraged to tell as well as read stories, and also to make them up – or at least, to make them up with the children. In a general sense practitioners in early years settings are rightly seen to be more effective as role models than as instructors, and in the realm of language much importance is attached to how they make an example of their own speech, in the way it is formed and the way it adapts to different contexts.

So far this chimes quite harmoniously with the arguments here regarding communication and language development in the early years. Two things, however, need to be distinguished. One is the age at which the English National Curriculum introduces the formalities of literacy and numeracy. The other is the particular emphasis that is highlighted as prescriptions for teaching these 'basic skills'. In respect of the literacy curriculum, you get the feel of it when you start counting words like *think, reflect, compare, predict, explain, categorise, identify*. It quickly becomes apparent when reading the Curriculum Guidance document that while most of what really does belong to the foundation stage of human learning is far more clearly acknowledged than in previous directives, the whole thrust of the approach to working with these prime realities is still effectively to anticipate, encourage and precipitate their metamorphosis into conscious knowledge and faculty.

The italicised words in the previous paragraph invoke the mental processes belonging to Piaget's concrete operational and even formal operational stages – processes which in his (and to a large extent Rudolf Steiner's) scheme emerge naturally at ages 7 and 11 respectively. The Curriculum document gives special emphasis to fostering language as a tool for the development of thinking.[35] In the same vein, creative play is highlighted as an opportunity for problem-solving, to be undertaken by the children with either more or less guidance and then reflected upon by and with the practitioner with the aim of learning some general principles from it. Everything gets talked about in the scenarios presented as examples of good practice; everything quickly gets analysed and brought into clear focus. It's a wake-up call, all of it; and as it jollies the children out into the light it brings to an inevitable end the magic of their dreamtime; and, since it is premature, the effect is comparable to being woken too early from actual sleep. Perhaps this effect may not be clearly apparent in the shorter term, though in many cases it certainly is. But then it is often the afternoon or evening when actual sleep deprivation really begins to show, and in similar fashion the effects of early education may wait till adolescence or adulthood to reveal their consequences.[36]

First steps to literacy in Steiner Waldorf schools

In order to appreciate more fully the range of options available to educators at this crucial transitional stage, let's look at how things are done in the Steiner Waldorf schools. The background to first reading and writing in a Steiner Waldorf school is all that happens in the school's kindergarten and the child's home. All that you have read in this book about the living culture of orality is understood to be an essential aspect of this early experience. Songs, rhymes, stories, puppetry, finger games and play acting are basic ingredients in the weekly round of activities. The encouragement for the children to play freely in a harmonious environment with creative and natural materials, and with each other at their own level without the constant intervention of adults, is equally significant. The assumption at this stage is really that education will take care of itself if the right conditions are provided – including the presence of 'exemplary' adults whose activities and attitudes can be imitated by the children without needing to spell out or analyse the details.

Formal education begins with a change of setting, though in most cases not with a change of school, as Steiner Waldorf schools aspire to take children from nursery right through to school-leaving age. One of the most crucial features of the new arrangement is that the child leaving kindergarten will come into the care of a class teacher who is committed to teaching that child for the next eight years. Early in this book it was noted that today's children often suffer from the lack of continuity in their lives. The class teacher in a Steiner Waldorf school is there, above all, to keep alive the fundamental relation between learning and human life during this period that could be called the heart of childhood. The Steiner school class-teacher is responsible for teaching most of the 'core curriculum' over the eight years, and will do most of the teaching orally. Her voice will be, in a sense, the central oracle through which the world speaks to a particular group of children whose parents have chosen this special learning community. It is a daunting task, and not without its dangers; but where it works – which it has continued to do in the vast majority of cases since 1919 – it goes way beyond anything set out in terms of curriculum content or teaching method to create an education founded on what William Blake called the Human Image. The class teacher stands there as a representative of humanity. The teacher's knowledge, morality, talents *and* failings are all part of what the children experience as bound up with education's purpose. The fact that the teacher is also learning through this shared process is perhaps the most significant gift of all to the children, no less than it is for the teacher.

The classes in a Steiner Waldorf school are essentially oral communities within which the written word becomes a growing presence. Lessons are taught orally and are then consolidated and extended through writing. The class teacher is first and foremost a storyteller and 'characteriser': not a lecturer, not a preacher, but a weaver of images, feelings and events through the living power of words. Any teacher needs to command attention; the Waldorf teacher tries to deserve such attention by creating living imaginations that captivate the children because they speak directly to their souls. It's nothing like as easy as it used to be to achieve this: children who come from a world more and more filled with voices not actually talking to them and pre-animated images which require no inner visualisation on their part– these children are losing their ability to listen and respond creatively to the human voice. Nevertheless, the magic of story is too deep and powerful to be wholly overcome, and the same is true of every child's yearning for direct human communication. After a few days, or weeks, or perhaps months, almost every new Waldorf class becomes attuned to a new habit of active listening through which – and only through which – the children really come to live in their teacher's words and the powerful experiences these words may evoke.

The stories told to the first class (ages 6–7) are mostly traditional fairy tales. Why search for anything more modern when children in their souls are still living in that land of long ago and far away from which these stories spring? So much has been spoken and written now about the wisdom of fairy tales that we hardly need to justify them further[37] – except to confirm through experience that children naturally delight and find the utmost reassurance in them. They tell children what they want to hear – that life is a wonderful adventure in which good always ultimately triumphs over evil – in a language within which the children feel fully at home. They are simple, pictorial and also musical. They are punctuated with the 'formulaic phrases' so characteristic of orality, from 'Once upon a time' to 'They all lived happily ever after.' Their narrative structures and motifs are repetitive and predictable, with events following one another as summer follows spring. Their characters are archetypes of the human soul, and the resolution of their relationships is a study in both social and individual harmony.

Form drawing

As fairy tales form the bulk of the stories that are told in this first school year, so they support the transition from orality to literacy. Before the real business of writing and reading begins, however, the class teacher normally prepares the children for the complexities of recognising and reproducing the forms of the alphabet by introducing a period called 'form drawing.' The time devoted to this activity varies, and some teachers like to lead quite quickly into writing proper, although still with the essential principles of form drawing remaining operative. In the bibliography you will find references to published expositions and developments of this art form that Steiner initially adopted and adapted for pedagogical educational purposes from the motifs of Greek and Teutonic decoration in particular.[38] In essence, the activity begins with the practice of straight and curved lines which are put together in a variety of rhythmic and sequential patterns, both contiguous and continuous, that gradually increase in complexity and inner dynamic. The patterns are drawn quite large, and before being drawn at all are rehearsed through a sequence of body movements that often begin with walking the forms on the floor, then tracing them in the air with the whole arm, carefully following the movement of the hand with the eyes and perhaps also repeating the arm movements with eyes closed and the eyes still following the patterning as an inner visualisation.[39] Hand-eye co-ordination is one obvious focus of such a discipline, as is the inner perception and control of body movement generally: a raising of proprioception into consciousness, to refer back to an earlier chapter.

In fact the value of form drawing extends a long way beyond simply helping to develop spatial awareness and motor control. It leads, slowly over the course of the first four or five school years, into perception and understanding of symmetry: firstly mirror symmetries on a vertical axis, whose archetype is the human face and limb structure; then mirror symmetries on a horizontal axis, whose human embodiment is in the arrangement of the teeth; then the fourfold 'mandala' symmetries based on the cross, whose archetype is focused human consciousness. In addition to such formal symmetries the art of form drawing incorporates and develops a dynamic feeling for complementarity, where one aspect of a form dynamically balances another, as for example where a convex feature is reflected in a concave feature. A further and deeply significant theme within the form drawing lessons is that of metamorphosis, where one form is developed into another through a sequence of transformations according to its own inherent formative principles. The following is an example, appropriate perhaps for 10 or 11 year olds:[40]

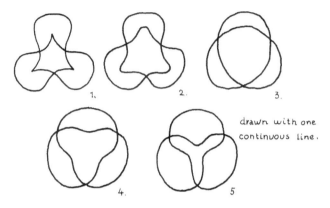

1,   2.   3.

drawn with one
continuous line.

4.   5

The poet-scientist Goethe beautifully elaborated the nature of metamorphosis in his studies on the 'archetypal plant', and also the human skeleton.[41]

As children work with such exercises they are developing movement skills that are, simultaneously, artistic skills; and in their growing consciousness of the processes involved they are also developing their ability to think. This works at a much deeper level than what we might call head thinking; it is thinking infused through and through with life processes. The Greek philosopher and scientist Heraclitus described the universe as an egg that is constantly turning itself inside out. Contemporary philosophers and scientists are starting to talk the same way again. Try drawing a two-dimensional egg that turns itself inside out in stages and you'll start to appreciate what Plato was talking about when he said that 'God geometrises.' In the Waldorf movement we often say that form drawing leads on the one hand into handwriting and on the other into geometry. This is true; but its greater significance is that it helps develop dynamic, living and reflective thinking. Such thinking is equally the basis of living literacy, living science and living mathematics. Form drawing is an activity that could very easily be incorporated into any educational curriculum with far-reaching results.

From movement into letters

Once the activity of moving and drawing spatial patterns is underway, the teacher can approach the specific forms of the letters of the alphabet. Because letters *are* forms, and need to be learnt as forms as well as symbols, the same preparatory activities apply to writing as to form drawing. The shapes of the letters need to be fully *perceived* by the children before they can be memorised. Perception of a shape is the end result of a perception of movement – so the first step in learning a letter is to move through it. Walking it on the floor, tracing it large with the whole arm while following the movement carefully with the eye and then retracing the movement with the eyes closed serves, as stated above, to raise proprioception to consciousness, helping embed it in the memory.

Because the letter forms are not in themselves easy for children to memorise, the more *physically* they can experience them the more help they will get from their 'muscle memory'. It was partly with this in mind that Rudolf Steiner suggested it would be appropriate to begin with capitals rather than lower case letters. The capitals are for the most part composed very clearly of straight lines and semi-circles, which invite a deliberate, almost sculptural approach to their formation. It is important that the children learn to form the strokes in the right sequence and direction. Vertical strokes need to be drawn from above to below, not simply because the movement is more fluent but because this is the direction of 'incarnation', of bringing an impulse down to earth and embodying it. Children draw their first human figures in this way, just as they grow into their own bodies, from the head down. Later they may also build a figure up in the reverse direction, just as in cursive script they will begin many letters with an ascending stroke; but this is a very different process when it is part of a return journey, so to speak. Such details are more significant than commonly acknowledged. Some children have a strong resistance to forming their letters and numbers from the top down; these same children frequently show a spectrum of other signs that they are not fully ready for the earthing of consciousness that literacy and numeracy represent. Once the decision has been made to place the children in a context where writing is being formally taught there is nothing to be gained from turning a blind eye to wrong writing, which will actually make it harder for a child to catch up – developmentally as well as technically – as the writing activity proceeds. Properly formed writing (with a proper pencil grip to go with it) is a developmental catalyst; it can actively *help* a child get right into her own body and out of it again through the words on the page. Only when a child is really too young (as they often are), or specifically and abnormally retarded in development, may the formal teaching of writing prove significantly damaging.

The horizontal direction of movement in writing needs awareness also. Teaching children to make their horizontal strokes from left to right is obviously practical in a culture where writing proceeds in this direction. There is also an inherent human significance in the difference between left and right, as the separate functions of the two sides of the brain indicate. Moving one's hand across the midline from left to right actually carries an impulse across from the right brain to the left brain – from the region belonging to artistic consciousness to that belonging to intellectual consciousness, as it is often put. We might also say that the movement from left to right (from right brain to left brain) is the direction from orality into literacy. In an earlier chapter we observed that Hebrew and Arabic developed their scripts within a context where writing was written to be spoken. The right to left direction of their writing can be seen to confirm this 'harking back' to the oral traditions from which they sprang.

From picture to symbol

So much for the spatial dynamics involved in the choice of capitals for first writing. There is another reason why Steiner recommended them. In addition to being more sculptural they are also more graphic – closer to the character of a pictogram than their lower case offspring. One of the things that anyone familiar with Steiner Waldorf schools knows is that 'they teach writing out of pictures'. We do – though not arbitrarily, and always in association with teaching writing out of movement. In fact Steiner suggested that even before we begin to focus on the individual letters we should begin our first real writing lesson by writing a short sentence on the board, reading it to the children and then having them copy it.[42] The rationale for doing this is one that underpins the approach to teaching everything in a Steiner Waldorf school; it is that children learn best, and learn most meaningfully, when they proceed 'from the whole to the parts'. The basic unit of meaning in language is the sentence. The archetypal sentence is like the archetypal human being. It has a head, heart and limbs: the nominal subject, the mediating activity of the verb, and the extension of the subject into the objective world. By giving the children the wholeness of a sentence, in that ceremonial moment (for such it surely must be) when one of the greatest mysteries of life is about to be unveiled, we are confirming that language is coherent, complete in itself, comprehensive and comprehensible. Steiner suggested that the chosen sentence should have some significant moral content (e.g. 'The person is good.') because morality is also part of living meaning.

So the context is set. Now the teacher can make a quick review of some highly salient points. She can confirm that writing is something that is meant to make sense, just as we try to do when we talk. Unlike talking, writing has to make sense even when we are no longer there ourselves to explain it. We tell the writing what to say, but then the writing must be able to carry our message by itself. The teacher can confirm that she has written something called a sentence, which is a collection of words that make sense together. She can say that within the sentence there are the different words themselves, and within the words the things we call letters that stand for the sounds that live in each word. She can make it clear that letters are shaped in a special way, and that sentences are written from left to right. And now, finally, she can say that once upon a time letters were drawn as real pictures, and that if we look carefully we can still find the pictures that are hidden within them like a special secret. Discovering these pictures will help us remember and understand the letters for the rest of our lives.

'Once upon a time. . .' The teacher tells a story. It may be a traditional fairytale, or a story she has made up herself. It will be a story rich in images. Amongst these images will be one – just one, to begin with – that will be specially highlighted in a picture drawn on the blackboard on the following day. The children will have 'slept' on the story, and the drawing will reawaken them to it in the manner of a remembered dream. The central image within the picture will carry the whole life of the story in it. It will also carry its own life: the life of what it is in itself. And because the teacher is being canny here, the image will also carry the life of a particular *sound*. Cannier still, the teacher will further be able to draw from the image the shape of the letter that represents this sound. 'Canny' is actually the wrong word here, because these are not just clever correspondences. The sounds of speech are embodiments of archetypal living qualities. The hissing *S* evokes a universal feeling of alertness, even in Ireland where there are no snakes. The liquid *L* has the reassurance of a lullaby, and with it the living quality of water. Steiner chose the golden fish in *The Fisherman and his Wife* to illustrate the principle of an appropriate letter-picture. *Fish, fin, flash, flicker* – the fish is a figure of living movement, and this same quality is embodied in the sound *f.* In the italicised lower case letter *f* printed here it is very easy to see a fish – easier in fact than in the capital form. This needn't challenge the principle of beginning writing with the capitals: what the teacher must anyway do with his letter-image is metamorphose it from image as such into a letter as such. A piece of chalk can bring out the *f* from the fish rising out of the sea; this *f* can then be written separately, and another quick sculpting with the chalk will translate it into F. The children will copy both the original picture and its metamorphoses; the capital F will then be carefully practised over the following days and weeks like a form drawing – but it will carry within it a living image and a living sound.

Living literacy has everything to do with metamorphosis. The historical evolution of pictograms into alphabetic letter forms is itself an example of metamorphosis. Steiner was clear, however, that the class teacher need not feel bound to try and reproduce specific transformations of pictures into letters based on historical models; the principles of inner resonance and inner coherence are the important ones. The requirement that the children make some kind of imaginative leap during the translation process is actually part of what distinguishes true metamorphosis from simple variation on a theme. The plant makes such a leap between bud and blossom; the chrysalis is a real alchemical crucible in which caterpillar becomes butterfly. Alphabetic letters are *not* pictures; they are symbols. One of the dangers of the Waldorf approach is that children may actually get hung up on their specific pictorial image of a letter and not so easily take the next step, liberating it from a prototype into an archetype capable of diversifying into innumerable other word images. Another of Steiner's own examples illustrates this 'non-literal' correspondence of image and letter very clearly. He was speaking of introducing the letter D.[43] He suggested drawing it out of the picture of a dome or roof. (In German the word for roof is *Dach*. From the picture emerges this:

Which is fine as a dome or roof, but not obviously a D. So we rotate the image 90° clockwise, and hey presto! The ability to see the same image in its various reflections and translations is not confined to dyslexics; we all have it as a hand-me-down from our pre-differentiated brain-function days. One of the requirements of developed consciousness is that we take hold of our primitive capabilities and make them subject to our own intentions. The spectrum of dyslexia represents a failure to complete this process in one or another area of faculty. Rotating a dome into a D is in fact a consciousness-raising exercise through which picture *has* to become symbol, and symbol has to be *actively* related back to its picture. Having said this, what anchors this particular transformation is that a dome is always the way up it is. The picture is referenced in reality. Drawing a left-facing fish in order to represent an F would leave things too much swimming in the mix and therefore an unwise prototype letter-image. However, if unconscious mirror-writing is persisting beyond the seventh year it may help a child to draw a right- and left-facing F back to back simultaneously with right and left hands, many times over, until the crucial differentiation is established both visually and kinaesthetically. A variation of this exercise that focuses attention (kinaesthetic, not visual) right on the midline axis of symmetry is where the child draws the same form simultaneously with both hands onto a two-sided blackboard extending forwards between her hands.

Consonants and vowels

In looking at the historical development of writing we have already noticed that some alphabets give a clearly different status to consonants and vowels – some even omitting vowels altogether. Steiner reinforced this distinction in his own suggestions for teaching writing. His recommendations for teaching the letters through pictures apply specifically to the consonants, which he characterised as being sound-pictures of the outer world. Vowels, by contrast, are sound expressions of the inner world – the soul world. Where consonants are inherently pictorial, vowels are inherently musical. Waldorf teachers often describe them to the young children as 'singing sounds', and often actually sing them. One of the distinguishing features of vowels is that they have a range of sounds associated with a single letter. How, for example, does the 'a' sound in the following words: *father, angel, hand, image, what, agree, integral*? Partly to distinguish vowels from consonants, and partly to make them easier to work with, Steiner recommended that we teach the children to call vowels by their name and consonants by their sound. The children should clearly understand that each vowel has a broad range of sounds that it can 'sing' (not least as it appears in different regions and lands); and also that the pure sound of a consonant doesn't have the '*shwa*' – a short, nondescript vowel sound – that we normally add when we say, for example, muh for 'm' or kuh for '*k*'.

This chapter has focused on the introduction of writing. Learning the letters is not learning to write, though it is of course a crucial part of it. Just as Steiner urged us to preface our teaching of the letters with a real act of writing, so our aim must be to get back to real writing before the children have forgotten what letter-learning is really about. My own recommendation, shared by many others in the Waldorf world, is that the whole of the alphabet should be introduced by the end of the first term of the first class at the latest. Given all the other things there are to do as well, this requires a speeding up of the process as it continues. The crucial thing is that children develop the feeling that the letters themselves are full of individual life. Once the first ones have been introduced individually the rest may be pictured in groups within a story illustration, or even, towards the end, introduced simply as pictures. Such introductions really are only the beginning. What matters hereafter is that the children preserve their initial recognition and respect for these new companions. There should be the feeling of a handshake each time a letter is practised, and a sense of disappointment when it is misrepresented. And there should be real joy when the letters are ready to take hands themselves and stand together as words.

From writing into reading

In concluding this chapter we must look at how reading can come to birth within the same imaginative and holistic process that should apply to writing. Steiner's recommendation was very simple on this point – and so very effective. He said that we should introduce reading directly out of the children's own writing. Regarding *what* the children write, he said, they should write down what is most alive in them: little sentences from the stories they have heard, little messages to real people about real things. To begin with it is the teacher's task to formulate appropriate sentences with the children and write them down for the children to copy. In writing down what they already know the children then metamorphose their writing activity into the activity of reading what they already know. Reading is thus, at this first stage, a personal act of recognition. This is a vastly different experience from that of decoding text with little or no prior familiarisation. The latter is rather like a form of post-mortem; the former is like recognising one's own living baby. There will be a lot more to it than this as time goes on, but in the beginning the sense that the child is really reading, even when mainly remembering, should be fostered with the greatest care, because the child's living connection to literacy is utterly bound up with her sense that it is intimately part of her.

The sensible teacher will try to keep these first sentences generally simple, but should avoid being stilted or simplistic. It matters more at this stage that the words should feel familiar and 'right' to the children than that they should fit nicely into a spelling scheme. The ground for a phonic approach to reading has been laid in the introduction of the letters, but the full-on phonics approach to reading words is the opposite of holistic and needs bringing in gently and carefully on the back of a 'whole language' or, better, 'whole experience' approach. We shall be looking at the details of this as we proceed. According to Steiner, it should be the teacher's aim to have most of the children in the class writing and reading little sentences of their own by the end of the first school year. For some children this will simply happen, but for the majority it will require more than just stories, drawings, practising letters and copying and reading back sentences. Keeping alive the spirit of language through speaking and listening is something the Steiner Waldorf schools do very well. Stitching this into literacy is both an art and a science, and while by far the majority of Waldorf pupils go out into the world both articulate and literate, often exceptionally so, for some the crossing into fluent literacy is delayed in a way that becomes uncomfortable for them. This is not how it needs to be. Steiner *did* say that the most developmentally appropriate time for children to be reading was from their twelfth year (around the beginning of Piaget's 'formal operational' stage) – but he was quite clear that this was an inappropriate curriculum marker in the world of his own day, and would surely say the same today. Many of those who struggle with literacy do in fact make a sudden quantum leap around their twelfth year, but by then they may consider themselves 'slow' or 'stupid', not least because the reading material available for their reading level is designed almost exclusively for younger children. This is bound to leave some kind of scar tissue in their souls, however wonderful and fulfilling the rest of their school experience may have been and may still be. Living literacy can and should also be effective literacy. There is nothing in Rudolf Steiner's own recommendations that does other than promote this being the case, and the fact that they haven't been systematised into a detailed and prescriptive curriculum, together with the fact that a number of Steiner Waldorf teachers haven't met the rigours of state school expectations in their own training, may account for a significant incidence of inappropriately late reading and poor spelling in some of the schools. As a class teacher I have myself been guilty of allowing some of my pupils to dream on for longer than I now feel was in their best interests.

9. Developing Literacy as Faculty

Watching someone struggle to decode a piece of text, word by intractable word, can be painful enough for the observer. How much more so for the struggling reader! If literacy is not to establish itself as one of the most unappetising of all human experiences it needs to become second nature. Its techniques must become embedded as instinctual faculty. We shall explore in this chapter the different elements required for such a transformation and point towards different literacy strategies that may be employed to promote it. Since the differences we shall be discussing typically appear in exaggerated and unbalanced forms in children with so-called learning differences, the special needs teacher should find much relevant material here too. The next chapter will offer some further suggestions for practice, and the chapter after that will expand the more technical discussion of faculty development into personal, social and cultural considerations that play a complementary and equally significant part in how literacy 'works' for different people.

Elements in the development of faculty

The following points are relevant to the development of all human faculties:

- Developmental readiness
- Impulse and motivation
- Communication
- Perception
- Concentration
- Memory
- Conceptualisation
- Selection and application

Let's consider these elements one by one.

Developmental readiness

We have already explored different aspects of this theme during the course of this book; and the reader is reminded that *Ready to Learn* (see Bibliography) is a book all about it. In focusing specifically on the development of skills, the key point to register is that every skill depends on other skills. A child who cannot count cannot calculate. A child who cannot distinguish between a 'b' and a 'd' has a reading and writing difficulty. A child who cannot hear the difference between 'v' and 'th' has a language and literacy difficulty. And so on. Learning is a stratified process: it builds upon itself. The teacher of skills needs to know what a child must be able to do in order to do something new. The School Readiness checklist in the appendix is also very much a literacy readiness checklist.

Impulse and motivation

People are motivated differently at different levels of their being. In this chapter we will concern ourselves more with what might be called 'lower' impulses to learn, in the sense that these are especially related to physical, sensory experience.[44] The chapter on the 'culture' of literacy will further explore the 'soul and spirit' influences that may work with or against the body's predispositions.

The urge to do and achieve things is generally affected by what we might call the 'feel-good factor'. Even our most noble deeds, though we may not like all that goes with them, are impelled by an underlying good feeling that is associated with them. Whatever makes it feel good to learn something should be considered relevant to the learning process – even if it is not necessarily judged good in itself or automatically adopted into one's practice. Children will feel motivated to learn when they connect learning with a reward. The giving of sweets has been used often enough in this regard; lately the giving of money to encourage young people simply to turn up at school has become part of some local authorities' provision in the UK. The flip side of reward is punishment. Often enough children get punished when they do badly at school on the assumption that it will make them feel better about learning than not learning.

It would be nice, wouldn't it, if children were happy to accept learning as bringing its own reward? For this to be the case, though, learning must be able to compensate for any discomfort it causes along the way, including at a physical level. Prolonged intellectual activity does bring discomfort, above all when it is unmitigated and challenging intellectual activity. One of the keys to promoting willing literacy is to balance its purely intellectual component with other forms of activity that feel invigorating. The younger the child the more these should include physical activity, and the shorter the bursts of head work should be in themselves.

(The notion of a compulsory daily 'literacy hour' for young children seems to me wholly misguided.) Through all schooling there should also be a constant association of intellectual with imaginative activity of the right kinds, such as we have indicated in the suggestions for introducing the alphabet. And though sweets as such may not be such a healthy offering, other forms of physical sustenance, including snacks and meals and shorter and longer breaks from any compulsive activity, are vital.

A further, very obvious requirement if learning is to bring its own reward is that it should be experienced as successful. Failure weakens the will and success strengthens it. The recognition of success is most complete when it comes from both without and within. The teacher's ✔ is an invaluable little educational tool, and the good teacher will ensure that enough of these ticks can be given to keep a child's sense of progress alive. This means balancing more challenging activities with easier ones, and also encouraging the child to acknowledge that the successes really mean something. It can be very daunting when a child is aware that some children are achieving a lot more than he is. The teacher must do everything possible to prevent a culture of failure developing in this situation. Part of this means working with the class as a whole; part of it means setting and continually resetting appropriate targets for individual pupils and making each step count.

Communication

What has been said about impulse and motivation has everything to do with communication. A child who is doing well needs to be told he is doing well. A child who has learnt something needs to be able to communicate to others what he has learnt, and that he has learnt it. In the case of literacy skills the ready-made vehicle for communication of success is reading and writing itself, where the reading is done out loud and the writing is written to be read. It is important to keep this feature alive as much as possible in the common arena of class work, so that all the children are reading and writing as a form of shared communication. Reading text out together is one way of doing this, especially where the content of the text relates to a shared experience. Reading aloud from each other's individual work is another way.

Choral speaking is practised rather seldom these days in western mainstream education though it is still part of the tradition in Asia and Africa and absolutely part of the tradition in Waldorf education. What choral speaking does first and foremost is register speech as a communal act. In uniting the individual voice with the communal voice it empowers the individual voice, lifts it and gives it wings. This is more than just a matter of volume. Modulation and dynamics – all the features of melodic expressiveness – are communicated through a powerful osmosis between the members of the group, and can be consciously influenced and improved by the teacher's example. Without the teacher's conscious input, in fact, choral recitation has a natural tendency to become chant or drone and sound more like a religious service than is necessarily appropriate. Poems learned as choral recitations may then be spoken individually from memory, and also written down and read out by individual children. This is a very different experience from being asked to read a poem blind – a process that might better be termed reading 'deaf'.

A lovely complement to choral speaking is practised in the Waldorf schools. This involves the class teacher giving every child in the class a special verse for each school year which that child will recite in front of the class on the same day each week as part of the two-hour morning lesson. Often the teacher will have composed the verse especially for the child. It will certainly be given as a special act of communication between teacher and child. Its purpose is to help the child, from the level of strengthening his own self-image to developing particular features of language, thought and temperament. For over twenty-five years of teaching I have observed children saying their verses and listening to each other's verses, and I have often felt it to be the most profound moment of the school day.

Another characteristic 'Waldorf' feature that helps strengthen oral communication skills and prepare for more expressive written work is the way children are asked as a matter of course to recall aspects of the previous day's lesson. This process links spoken language to memory and imagination and furthers both linguistic and cognitive development simultaneously. It also links all of this into the writing process that will normally follow it. The teacher may often notice, especially when the previous day's lesson content was given in story form, that the children's recall – at least in the early years when imitation is still a strong factor – will include many of the same words and phrases, even the same modulations, used in the original telling. This is a clear incidence of 'receptive' language becoming 'expressive' language, which is the way language develops anyway in early childhood but which needs continued stimulus. Summoning something back to consciousness after a night's sleep is part of the development of conscious faculty. Where the pupil is learning linguistic faculties from a teacher it matters greatly how consciously the teacher is aware of and careful with his own language.

If the teacher has a special role to play in the communication process within a classroom, so do the individual pupils. I have often found that one pupil in my class can explain something to another pupil better than I can. Teacher-centred learning needs to give way at times to pupil-centred learning. We could coin the phrase of being 'childhood literate' – and acknowledge that by definition children are likely to better at this than their teachers. Children, simply by being children, are on the same wavelength. However well an adult may tune in to this wavelength, the communication process is inevitably different when different ages are involved. Peer learning can still be generally stage-managed by the teacher in a classroom setting, since few children can be a step ahead of the current lesson in the way a teacher should be. But the teacher must be closely attentive to what each child has to offer the other, and how they are able to offer it, and actively facilitate this.

The activity of paired reading is an obvious setting for communication to be linked into literacy, both in the child-adult and the peer group context. Paired reading can be organised in different ways, but it should always be an experience of sharing – the work as well as the pleasure. Care should be taken that the more able partner doesn't do too much of the work for the less able one. Nor the other way around. In some cases it will be appropriate for the two partners to read together; in others to alternate the reading while the silent partner carefully follows what is being read; in others for the less able partner to do most of the reading, with the other stepping in to help when the first gets stuck (which doesn't mean instantly correcting every word read wrongly).

The question of correction bears closely on that of communication. When we correct a child we are communicating something about that child's learning. When we correct something in the realm of language and literacy we are also passing comment on a child's communication skills. We need to be very careful here. Many poor readers and writers are excellent communicators. If we give the impression that misspelling or misreading a word is inherently a communication breakdown we may seriously dishearten the struggling reader and writer. We may also be telling a lie. Spelling, after all, is only a convention, and usually a practised teacher can make out what even a severely dyslexic child means. At the same time we can't avoid the fact that misspelling and misreading *may* involve a significant communication breakdown. We need to establish some priorities.

What are the most important words to be clear about? In a general sense they are the words most frequently used in communication. Sometimes it may be vital to learn a technical term, like 'danger', but the words that will be written and read time and time again are those that all children most need to learn. Every effort should be made to teach these words to the child early in the process – and these are the words on which correction should be focused. While the teacher should have a list of the most commonly used words,[45] these words should be brought into focus as much as possible through the child's own use of them, not learned separately as spelling lists that fall from the sky. In fact the word-frequency lists that one normally comes across are not age-discriminated; a children's list would surely feature words like Mummy and Daddy, cat and dog – and possibly gerbil (or is it jerbil?).

We shall consider other aspects of correction under the headings below.

Perception

'The fool sees not the same tree as the wise man sees,' says William Blake. The child sees differently from the adult, and children from each other. Perception involves all sorts of different senses together. Rudolf Steiner speaks of twelve senses and has fascinating things to say about their interrelationships which will be elaborated further in the next chapter. It is more usual, and still very useful, to focus on the visual, auditory and haptic capacities, the latter including tactile perception and kinaesthetic perception. We have dealt in some detail with the haptic side of life, and may here remind ourselves of the basic principle that a child should move through the individual letter forms using large movements before transferring the activity to the fine motor system. This experience can be made more tactile by writing the letters large with a glue stick and sprinkling sand over them; the child can then trace over the letter forms with eyes closed or covered and strengthen inner visualising of the movements in this way. Writing onto one another's backs can extend the individual experience of touch into a social one.

Also in the realm of touch and movement it makes a significant difference whether a child writes in print or cursive script. In the Waldorf schools cursive writing is introduced normally at the beginning of the second school year, and the children are expected to use this rather than lower case print. The advantage of this method is that words are kinaesthetically perceived as a whole. The flow of ink (or probably graphite) is a thread that stitches each word together. Most dyslexia specialists recommend this approach for their students. The difficulty with it that needs to be recognised (and I'm not sure that every Waldorf teacher has recognised this clearly enough) is that kinaesthetic wholeness can prove a difficult entity to discriminate visually. The word mummy, for example, easily resolves visually into a single wavy line in cursive script, especially where it is written carelessly. Are the ascenders and descenders part of a letter, or aren't they?

Visual discrimination has its own complexities. Its primary ability is to distinguish one colour from another, including black from white and all the shades of grey between. Secondarily, as a product of experience and connected very much with the sense of balance, it distinguishes foreground from background, not merely in terms of near and far but in relation to focus. As you read these words you are constantly promoting and demoting individual parts of the text between the foreground and background of your visual attention. Visual discrimination further involves the ability to distinguish one shape from another, which it does by moving through the shapes and kinaesthetically sensing the difference between them. What we see is also connected directly with what we know: When recognition is involved this is a different process from looking at something for the first time. The more seeing is linked with recognising, the less actual looking takes place. The fully literate person, as we noted in Chapter 2, needs only the briefest of glances to take in large chunks of text. The same FLP will be able to cope with missing bits of the picture: the Gestalt principle of closure comes into play, and the p-ct-r- g-ts c-mpl-t-d as a cognitive rather than strictly visual process. This is all much more difficult when a person cannot distinguish left from right.

Mirroring is part of the visual function: an image does not merely fall on the retina the wrong way round but the retinal image is communicated from the right eye to the left brain and the left eye to the right brain, each of which then has to compile and co-ordinate a single mental image that corresponds with a unified reality. Helping a child to see this process through is of the utmost importance when it doesn't happen by itself. It is common practice to give a child mnemonics to refer to when in difficulty: the picture of a bed, for example, to help distinguish 'b' from 'd', or to refer to the left hand as the watch-wearing hand, the right as the writing hand where this applies. These things may certainly help, but the trouble with them is that they involve a process of *consciousness* where the aim is to achieve something automatic. Far more effective, in my view, is to work intensively, in short bursts, with the kinds of exercises described in Audrey McAllen's *The Extra Lesson*.[46] Particularly relevant here are 'body geography exercises' (touch your left ear with your right forefinger, etc.) and form drawing exercises involving mirroring procedures.[47] Really, until 'automatisation' is achieved in proprioception it cannot be expected in visualisation either. Automatisation requires things being done in the right sequence and repeatedly so. The significance of repetition will come up again below.

We mentioned focusing as an aspect of visual discrimination. Some children find it particularly difficult to select the relevant textual focus when they are reading. It may be helpful for such children to use something like a postcard to place under the line they are reading, or even to make a 'reading window' from a

5x10cm rectangle of paper with its centre cut out that can be moved along the text revealing a word at a time. The size of print is obviously relevant too. If children are copying from the board it can be particularly frustrating to have to struggle to find their place again each time they look down to write: changing the colour of each sentence on the board is one way of helping here; another is not to ask such children to write from the board in the first place, but rather give them a paper version of the text to copy where this is what is wanted. (And one should always ask what a given child is actually learning from the copying experience anyway, rather than making general assumptions about 'receptive learning'.) In some cases it has been found that a child can focus on text far more easily when looking at it through a coloured filter. Obviously this is something to investigate further when the difficulty is pronounced and persistent.

Another perceptual difficulty children may face is that of auditory discrimination. They may find it difficult to distinguish aurally between certain speech sounds as such, for example v / f / th – a perceptual confusion which is typically reflected in their own speech. Or they may have problems 'segmenting' the phonemes within whole words, which becomes a reading difficulty. Or they may be poor at 'blending' phonemes together to build up words, which becomes a spelling problem. Assuming that hearing as such is not impaired, the problems of auditory discrimination all concern the relation between listening and speaking. This connection needs to be made more conscious. It will always help such a child to learn to listen better to his own speech. One way of doing this is to ask a child to say a poem known by heart while stepping on every word. Poor discrimination occurs when one thing flows directly into the next; stepping at every word makes each single word become much more intentional. Tongue twisters and speech exercises also help. Saying things backwards can help (as sounded rather than as spelt, either reversing the order of syllables but not the syllables themselves

– cup-ter-but – or reversing both – puc-ret-tub). Working with music is especially to be recommended. In the Waldorf schools we do a lot of singing and also teach all the children a musical instrument from Class 1 (age 6–7) – usually a recorder or pipe. This is done by listening and looking, initially, with no reference to notation. We can work individually with the children using little aural exercises in music, focusing variously on melody, rhythm and timbre or tone quality. All this helps all aspects of listening.[48] If a teacher shouts all the time this generally *doesn't* help listening. When the teacher suddenly whispers, this generally does.

Concentration

Is there anyone who hasn't heard of ADHD yet? Attention Deficit Hyperactivity Disorder has made Ritalin patent-holders an awful lot of money. Dealing with the symptoms by drugging them has also allowed society to go on its way without really having to face up to the causes or change the 'Normal' template of its lifestyle. Let's assume, for this chapter, that we are stuck with the fact that children are coming to school with an increasing inability to concentrate. Is there anything we can do about it educationally?

There is – especially if we can offer a school setting that isn't itself hyperactive, changing from one focus to another, unconnected one (sometimes in a different room with a different teacher) before the pupils have really been able to sink into anything. Having a two-hour lesson each morning with a class teacher who will be teaching the same class over eight years is unquestionably an aid to concentration. Staying with the same subject during this 'main lesson' over three or four weeks at a time is equally unquestionably an aid to concentration. Dealing with new 'head' learning early in the morning, rhythmically practising what has been learned during the mid-morning period, and doing practical, limb-related work in the afternoons is an aid to concentration. Methodically recalling what has been learned on one day during the main lesson of the following day before trying to work with it further is an aid to concentration. Having a curriculum and methodology that continually cross-references itself and builds on what has gone before . . . you've guessed, it's an aid to concentration. And finally, repeating things over and over again *can* be an aid to concentration.

But before it gets boring the activity must change. The secret of concentration is the secret of breathing. Breathing in is concentrating, breathing out is relaxing. Some aspects of learning are more like breathing in, others are more like breathing out. Listening is breathing in, speaking is breathing out. Writing is breathing in then breathing out, reading is breathing out then breathing in – because writing is first inwardly hearing the words, then spelling them out, and reading is first spelling the words out, then inwardly – or outwardly, if the reading is done aloud – appreciating them. The more regular the rhythm between in- and out-breathing, the more it is an aid to concentration. So with the rhythm of activities in the school day, week, term and year: the more they resemble a process of breathing, the more they will aid concentration.

Where a child sits in the classroom can make a difference to concentration. The presence of the teacher can make a big difference to a child's concentration – not only where the child is somewhat fearfully impressed by the teacher but also where the child is lovingly impressed by the teacher. A teacher is in a position to lend an unfocused child his presence of mind. With practice this can be done at a distance. It can only ever really be a short-term loan, and the child must be expected to pay back the interest with interest – but it remains a worthy investment, and sometimes the only thing that will make the difference. What I mean by lending a child one's presence of mind is that during the whole of the 'lending' period one remains actively mindful of that child. This is much easier, of course, in a one-to-one or small group situation, and sometimes this is what we must do with some children. But our aim should be to try to do it effectively also in the whole class situation. Sometimes a particularly impressive 'whole class' teacher will fail to notice that, despite his excellent presentation, there are some children who are off with the fairies. This is absence of mindfulness on the teacher's part, and may ultimately represent a failed lesson.

Memory

The development of memory is linked with all the other aspects discussed in this section. Rudolf Steiner describes four different kinds of memory, which, he says, are developed sequentially between childhood and full maturity. In the beginning comes geographical memory. The little child revisiting the place where he bumped his head yesterday may start crying, because the place recalls the whole of what has been experienced in it. Steiner suggested that megalithic monuments were erected partly as places to focus geographical memories: the ceremonies that were enacted there could be recalled by revisiting the sites. The so-called medieval 'memory theatres' use the principle of geographical memory, albeit now as an imagined place. The theatre is an inwardly visualised, self-created setting through which one can imaginatively walk around – and it must actually be big enough to do this in. When one wants to remember something one carries it into the memory theatre and places it somewhere very specific – at the foot of a column, perhaps – not too close to any other memories left there earlier. To remember it later one simply walks in and gets it. One way to establish a useful memory theatre in the classroom is to have a 'matchbox dictionary', where different matchboxes are placed in specific places within the classroom containing little bits of paper with phonetically related spelling words in them. To recall those spellings a child must literally walk to the reference point and get them. Later, one hopes, this collecting process can simply be a mental recollection.

The second kind of memory is rhythmic memory. Experience that is repeated, especially when the repetitions are regular, is embodied into rhythmic memory. Using the rhythmic memory also strengthens it. Learning the times tables by chanting them over and over again, especially when involving the whole body in the process by stepping and clapping routines, is both easier and more effective than learning them just in the head. Learning a spelling by revisiting it regularly is better than trying to cram it in on one day and forgetting about it for the next three weeks or whatever. The limitation that goes with rhythmic memory is that, like geographical memory, it is contextual: it is embodied into a temporal sequence just as geographical memory is embodied into a spatial framework. A child may know all the normal times tables perfectly as rhythmic chants but be unable to say what six threes are without starting at the beginning of the table and 'rowing' his way up to the required point. Rhythmic memory, therefore, must be metamorphosed into 'abstract' memory.

Abstract memories are effectively generalisations. They are detached from the specific experience that gave them birth and can be recalled at will (if the memory is strong enough) to suit one's purposes. Knowing all the possible sounds that a letter or group of letters can represent and being able to fit these into words, like keys into a lock, involves an exercise in abstract memory. Teaching children the skills of 'phonics' involves them using their abstract memories. For this to be effective it needs to be grounded in a form of rhythmic memory. This involves the repeated revisiting of whole words in the context of whole sentences. These words need to be fully learned in their own right, both visually and aurally. Then they can be 'segmented' into their different sound-letter components – and only then, when this *analytic* activity has become an actual skill, should attention be transferred to the *synthetic* activity of 'blending' letter-sound units into words. It is normal mainstream practice to go very quickly into phonics; and while this is a vital skill that children must accomplish, and that some 'whole language' enthusiasts may downplay, it is like building a house on sand if this is not based on solid linguistic foundations. Put in another way, premature phonics is literacy with the life taken out of it.

Abstract memory involves being able to call things to mind at will. It involves bringing consciousness into the memory process. This can be done in the realm of the different senses, each of which informs the memory in one way or another. In the visual realm, for example, we can play games such as the one where children are shown a tray full of objects for a limited period of time from which one object is then removed while the children have their eyes closed. Which object is missing? After all the objects have been removed the children may then be asked to put back the objects, in reverse order if possible, either physically or simply verbally without the original objects actually reappearing. A variation of this game can be played using pieces of writing on a blackboard. The children may be asked to read a sentence or short paragraph which is then covered or otherwise hidden from view. Who can remember how many capital letters there were? What was the first word of the third line? And so on and so forth. Another way to help develop visualisation and spatial orientation together is to give 'drawing dictations'. As with writing dictations, begin by giving the children an impression of the 'whole thing' first – in this instance by showing them the picture. Hide the picture and ask what was in it. Show the picture and check the results. Hide the picture and ask about the spatial relationships between the different details of the picture. Show and check. Now hide the picture and 'dictate' it to the children, detail by detail, giving the spatial co-ordinates that relate the details to each other and also to the framework of the page. Finally – perhaps the following day – have the children dictate the picture back to you – and draw on the board what you are told! Vary this and other such exercises a hundred times as your imagination and educational sense encourage you.

The fourth form of memory described by Steiner is 'moral' memory. Where geographical, rhythmic and abstract memories relate especially to the processes of will, feeling and thinking respectively, moral memory has to do with the core of who one is. Here the word 'moral' has nothing to do with right and wrong as abstractions or dogmatic generalisations; it involves, instead, what an individual actually regards as good and bad, beautiful and ugly, true and false at his particular stage of development. The healthy development of moral memory requires a cultural environment that can distinguish between social values and individual values, and allow the latter an appropriate freedom to develop. In the classroom setting the teacher must be constantly attentive to what really matters to each child and encourage each child to articulate these things. The keeping of a diary can, at the right time, become a significant means of preserving moral memories.

Conceptualisation

Conceptualisation raises perception into the realm of conscious thought. Some children find this more of a struggle than others. Difficulties can arise in a child's ability to form concepts when the perceptual process is too strong and also when it is too weak. Just as a child who eats too much or too little – or too much of the wrong kind of food and too little of the right kind – will have a poor assimilation of nourishment, so with the balance of sense impressions. Equally, a child whose digestion is weak will suffer loss of nourishment even with a healthy diet, and a child with impaired thinking will be unable to make good sense of even the most moderated sense impressions.

Working artistically is the key to bringing life to thinking and thinking to life. Artistic work both strengthens and balances the senses as such; it also involves reflecting on one's sense impressions. This reflective process can be intensified by the teacher talking about what is being or has been created artistically by the child – or by getting the child to talk about it. Maybe, in a drawing or painting context, the discussion will focus on what is actually there in the picture. Or maybe it will focus on what is not actually to be seen in the picture, but what could be imagined as being hidden in it: inside a cupboard, for example, or behind the house, or under the ground, or beyond the hill. Using form-drawing to help develop conscious thinking has a special relevance, since the language of pure form is really the language of pure thought. Asking a child to visualise, say, what a triangle would look like if its apex were moved up, down, right or left will exercise that child's powers of conceptualisation. Getting the child to talk about relationships of form will further bring the visualisation process into consciousness. So will getting the child to talk about the processes of mathematics. In this area literacy and numeracy are closely related.

Just as conceptualisation emerges from and is dependent upon developmental readiness, impulse and motivation, communication, perception, concentration and memory, so it leads into and is completed by:

Selection and application

The more specific a skill, the more limited its usefulness. Literacy involves an exceptionally large range of sub-skills, each of which requires a degree of 'focus'. Such focus, however, may work against the thing it serves when it becomes myopic. The wood must not get lost in the trees, nor the rule in the example, nor the meaning in the text. Children who have successfully learned many individual literacy skills may not be fully and fluently literate because they cannot automatically select between them and apply them appropriately. Perhaps they have learnt a spelling rule, but faced with reading a word that breaks the rule are stalled by the 'wrongness' of the word rather than immediately referring to context to make sense of it. Or it might be the other way around, that a child guesses a word from contextual reading without looking properly and applying phonic principles to see that its meaning is otherwise.

Approaches to teaching reading

There are a number of different literacy strategies being practised in the world today, each with its own justification and emphasis. Some of the more popular approaches are briefly described below.[49]

Phonics approach

The phonics approach teaches word recognition through learning grapheme-phoneme (letter-sound) associations. The student learns vowels, consonants, and blends, and learns to sound out words by combining sounds and blending them into words. By associating speech sounds with letters the student learns to recognise new and unfamiliar words.

Linguistic method

This method uses a 'whole word' approach. Words are taught in word families, or similar spelling patterns, and only as whole words. The student is not directly taught the relationship between letters and sounds, but learns them through minimal word differences. As the child progresses, words that have irregular spellings are introduced as sight words.

Multi-sensory approach

This method assumes that some children learn best when content is presented in several modalities. Multisensory approaches that employ tracing, hearing, writing, and seeing are often referred to as VAKT (visual, auditory, kinaesthetic, tactile) methods. Multisensory techniques can be used with both phonics and linguistic approaches.

Neurological Impress technique

This is a rapid-reading technique. The instructor reads a passage at a fairly rapid rate, with the instructor's voice directed into the student's ear. The teacher begins as the dominant reading voice, but gradually the student spends more time leading these sessions. Students who have learned mechanics without adequately learning reading fluency frequently benefit from this, as do students who read slowly or who hesitate over a number of words but are able to identify most of the words in a sentence. A student is directed to read a passage without errors. This method functions most effectively when it is practised for short periods every day.

Language experience approach

The language experience approach uses children's spoken language to develop material for reading. This approach utilises each student's oral language level and personal experiences. Material is written by the child and teacher for reading using each child's experience. This can be done in small groups and individually. Familiarity with the content and the vocabulary facilitates reading these stories. Each child can develop a book to be read and re-read. This approach helps children know what reading is and that ideas and experiences can be conveyed in print.

Reading comprehension support

People with learning disabilities who need work on reading comprehension often respond to explicitly taught strategies which aid comprehension such as skimming, scanning and studying techniques. These techniques aid in acquiring the gist, and then focus is turned to the details of the text through use of the cloze procedures. The cloze procedure builds upon a student's impulse to fill in missing elements and is based upon the Gestalt principle of closure. With this method, every fifth to eighth word in a passage is randomly eliminated. The student is then required to fill in the missing words. This technique develops reading skills and an understanding not only of word meaning but also of the structure of the language itself.

It seems to me that every one of these approaches has something to offer. Some children might benefit from more of one than another, but I do not see any child being best served by following one approach exclusively. The argument of this book is that the whole should precede the parts. Therefore a 'whole language', 'language experience' and 'multisensory' approach seem the right methods to begin with. But once the whole has been analysed into its individual components it then needs putting back together again. This is where phonics and reading comprehension support come into their own. While some of the skills of literacy need to become automatic, the literate child should never be an automaton. Literacy should be organic, not mechanical, in the way it is developed. If it is cultivated in relation to life and life's processes it will remain adaptable, both in itself and in its service of humanity.

10. *Further Suggestions for Practice*

As a practising teacher over the last 25 years I have collected and developed all sorts of ideas for things to do in lessons. The following chapter includes a selection of these. The problem with publishing them is that I am no longer sure exactly where some of them have come from. Leaving aside the philosophical question of whether any ideas are ever truly original anyway, I would certainly not want to offer the contents of this chapter as anything other than a collective effort of creative practitioners working both within and without the Steiner Waldorf movement. I will of course give due acknowledgement of authorship where possible.

Following on from the themes of the last chapter I will group the different exercises according to the particular capacities they may help develop and strengthen.

Auditory discrimination/articulation

Hearing clearly and speaking clearly are closely connected. Rudolf Steiner was very keen that teachers should develop their own listening and speaking as a fine art, and he gave collections of speech exercises to this end which secondary literature has developed further.[50] Steiner was very specific about the character of different speech sounds and the effects they may have on both speaker and listener, and anyone wishing to work seriously in this realm should certainly study these suggestions in depth. At the very least teachers should be aware of the basic groupings of speech sounds and find or devise specific speech exercises or other recitations that are child-friendly and that between them will involve the full range of articulation. The consonantal sound groups, defined according to their vocal formation, are as follows:

Labials:	B, P, M, W
Dentals:	F, V, S, Sh, C, Z
Linguals:	N, D, T, L
Palatals:	G, K, Ch (as in loch), Ng

Speech exercises, in my view, needn't be meaningful in the ordinary sense of the word, since the sounds of speech and the activity of forming them are realities that can carry conviction in their own right, in the way that music does. This is not to say that a pictorial or thematic element might not also be part of a speech exercise; for younger children, indeed, this may often be of benefit. But once formal work with phonics has begun, it would be well worth including in one's repertoire exercises that work simply with the individual phonemes. For example one can take the lingual consonants and form them into a cycle where each successive consonant is emphasised in turn:

<u>N</u> D T L
N <u>D</u> T L
N D <u>T</u> L
N D T <u>L</u>
<u>N</u> etc.

What matters in any such exercise is that the speech is kept lively and conscious – no mechanical droning! It is also vital that speech isn't debased by being made to feel an embarrassment. Children normally have a fine sense of humour, and many healthy speech exercises may be given and accepted in the form of humoresques. A very portable example from this genre – one that children do out of themselves anyway, as we noted in 'Tuning to the Mother Tongue' – is when a single consonant is substituted in place of the initial sound of each word in a sentence or series of sentences. This could be sentences from a nursery rhyme:

Doh dear, dot dan de datter dee . . .

All manner of traditional tongue twisters are readily available and can be woven into lessons until at least the 9th year.

Children commonly confuse particular speech sounds – notably f/v/th; k(c)/g; b/p – and in many cases it will become appropriate to focus on this quite consciously. One might, for example, compose sentences with many instances of one of the 'tricky' sounds in them, then substitute this for one of the confusingly similar sounds, having the child both listen to the difference and then speak each version clearly. Making articulation problems conscious can be painful, and great tact is needed. Where attention does have to be drawn to the physical details of vocal articulation this should as far as possible be linked with imaginations, such as the visualisation of a jet of flame for f, the velvet hum of bumblebees for v, the bulldozing forward of the tongue in 'earth'.

Vowels as well as consonants need to be worked on. We noted earlier that the pure forms of the vowels – ah (a), eh (e), ee (i), oh (o), oo (u) – represent a forward-moving sequence in terms of their vocal formation. In comparison with the consonants, vowels need to be carried clearly upon the flow of the breath. Exercises with the pure vowel sequence can help speech penetrate and carry meaning. In addition to working with the vowels alone it helps to cloak them in consonants:

* hahm, hehm, heem, hohm, hoom…
* Rah, raise, race,
  Rush, ruse, ruth, review, roof!

The projection of such exercises can be assisted by a slow-motion javelin throwing gesture accompanying either each word or some or all of the sequence.

Children are often too busy looking to do careful listening, and it is very good to include 'eyes shut' exercises in auditory discrimination. Variations of 'Squeak, Piggy, Squeak', where a speaker's identity has to be guessed, are appropriate for younger children – and the sounds that the chosen 'Piggy' makes can vary from animal cries to lines of poetry. For older children simply listening to and then recalling whatever sounds happen to be in the air around them over a given period of time can be very fruitful: it could lead into a discussion of acoustics or the composing of a poem.

Listening to speech can be improved by consciously listening to music. Musical 'communications' are especially relevant here: the teacher may for example develop specific musical commands that are used in place of verbal exhortations. Children very easily switch off to routine verbal commands, and when a teacher is driven to raise her voice to be heard then sensitive listening and basic respect is not being encouraged. Simple melodies played on a musical instrument, or hummed, can be remarkably effective and positively educational additions to normal classroom management strategies.

Dictations are an obvious way of raising listening to greater awareness. Right at the beginning of literacy work very simple dictations can be given, including the dictation simply of single consonants. And it needn't always be the teacher who gives the dictation: the class could be invited to compose their own strings of letters and dictate them in turn to each other. When children are being dictated sentences, which should be part of life by the time they are 8 or 9, it is important that the sentences are first spoken as a whole before being delivered again in smaller chunks. The teacher should establish a standard formula for how dictations are given, including the number of repetitions given to each phrase, and try very hard to stick to this so the children know clearly the kind of attention required of them. Steiner, by the way, felt that it shouldn't be necessary to dictate punctuation, since this should be apparent in the way the dictation is delivered. Some teachers may feel they need to dictate some of the punctuation some of the time.

Speech sounds can be fascinating and fun. Different regional accents and the sounds of foreign languages are a rich listening and speaking resource. Try listening with the right and left ear independently to people speaking: each ear is associated with the opposite hemisphere of brain and is attuned to different qualities of cognition. Have the children make up lots of mumbo-jumbo spells and incantations, including rhymed ones. Create families of made-up words that create a similar 'shape' in the imagination, for example rounded words like 'malooma' and spiky words like 'taketi'. Discriminate words that could and couldn't be English:

ptak	thale	hlad	plaft	sram	mgla
vlas	flutch	dnom	rtut	toasp	myip

A variation and continuation of this is to make up '4 element' words: water, air, fire and earth 'language'. How would a river or tree speak if it could?

Discriminate subtle nuances like the changed sound 'i' makes before an unvoiced consonant (cf. write and ride – rite and raieed; prize and price – praieeze and price) and –ed after a voiced consonant (cf walked and crawled – waukt and crauld). Draw attention to the 'shwa' that is normally added to the pure consonant sounds when they are vocalised, giving 'p-uh' for 'p' and 'd-uh' for 'd' etc. Phonetic spellers can get very confused by these distinctions.

Remember that the synthetic 'brick by brick' approach of phonics should follow exercises in whole word recognition. The first steps in phonic discrimination should be to recognise the onsets (initial sounds) and rimes (final sounds) of words. What is the first sound in 'man'? – 'm'. What is its ending sound? – 'an'. What is the end of its ending sound? – 'n'. Once children have some facility in this a game can be played that further incorporates a basic recognition of syllables. One child thinks of a single-syllable word, for example 'sit'. The next child must think of a two-syllable word that begins with the last sound of the first word. So we might get: 'sit – ta/ble'. Then back to one syllable: 'sit – ta/ble – lap'. Then another two-syllable word: 'sit – ta/ble – lap – pe-tal' etc. This is still a listening rather than a spelling exercise so it is about first and last sounds rather than first and last letters.

I would suggest that before proceeding to tear words any further into shreds it would be appropriate to treat the principles of phonics like a jig-saw, dealing with sound combinations as sound combinations rather than specifically as elements of words. One might set out a collection of letters like this:

Using the short 'a' sound, ask the children to couple each of the outside sounds in turn with this 'a', giving 'ca', 'ra', 'fa' etc. Repeat the exercise putting the 'a' first. Then experiment with consonant-vowel-consonant blends. Some of these will produce real words, which the children will be delighted to recognise.

Further work with phonics will go on to include the recognition of word families which may be united either by sound or spelling. It is important to begin with recognition of sound consonance, and then to establish that there are in fact different ways in which particular sounds can be pictured through different combinations of letters. It will be very useful for children to learn all possible letter combinations for each sound as a collection of 'phono-graphic' sets. (The 'matchbox dictionary' could be used to help here, where the full range of vowel sounds, at least, are given their possible letter combinations placed together in matchboxes stationed in different parts of the room.) In due course children should also learn to use a standard spelling dictionary.

Which brings us on to the development of:

Auditory memory

Being able to discriminate and articulate speech sounds isn't the same as being able to remember them. The following exercises aim to strengthen the ability to retain and manipulate mental sound-pictures for shorter and longer periods of time.

- A word is given for the children to say the sounds of backwards, e.g. tale-late; peel-leap etc. This can be done with increasing numbers of syllables, as in the earlier example given of 'but-ter-cup' becoming either 'cup-ter-but' or 'puc-ret-tub', depending on the rules.
- Sounds or words can be linked to specific physical movements and remembered kinaesthetically as well as aurally. (Rudolf

Steiner developed such a linking through the art form of eurythmy which is incorporated into the curriculum of Steiner Waldorf schools.)

- Sounds can be linked with other senses (what colours, elements, classmates fit these sounds?)
- Give mumbo-jumbo words/phrases for recall over increasing intervals. Do the same for coherent phrases/sentences, noting the difference in the quality of remembering when something has meaning.
- Read out a piece of text rich in adjectives and adverbs. Repeat with one of these missing. Which one? Again. Which two? etc.

Visual discrimination / hand-eye co-ordination

We have already referred to the significance of learning to perceive form through movement. The reader is directed to Audrey MacAllen's book *Teaching Children Handwriting* for some excellent detailed suggestions in this department.[51] Here are some more ideas:

- Write a word or series of words for the children to look at for a given period of time. Cover the writing and ask questions about it. How many letters / capitals / commas / letters with ascenders or descenders / words including –er etc.?
- How many letter shapes can you make with your hands?
- How many letter shapes can you see in this room / this picture?
- Copy a form / word without looking at your hand. Do the same with your non-writing hand.
- Write a letter / word in different sizes; make it lean backwards, forwards; make it more rounded etc. – then establish the most desirable form.
- Draw a letter form and its vertical mirror symmetry

simultaneously with both hands. Try the same exercise with hands crossed. Vary which hand does letter the right way round.

- Draw conscious attention to the letter forms that mirror each other (in lower case) : b-d; b-p; p-q; d-q; u-n; w-m; (s-z).

- Draw conscious attention to potential confusion between letter forms and their linking strokes in cursive script. Practise strings of ms, ws etc. with much heavier downstrokes.

- How many words can be made from EVERYBODY? etc. There is also a nice game with this (and other) word(s), losing one letter each time:

  EVERYBODY
  VERYBODY
  ERYBODY
  RYBODY
  YBODY
  BODY
  ODY
  DY
  Y (with rhythm)

- Metamorphosis: change 'cat' to 'pet' with, let's say, three intermediary steps changing only one letter each time and always making a new word: (cat), can, pan, pen, (pet).

Visual memory

Rudolf Steiner emphasised that visual memory will always be improved through strengthening auditory memory. We live in a very visual culture, so this connection is one to consider especially carefully. It is equally important to transform the passive reception of images into an active process of visualisation and image retention. These exercises should help:

- Arrange some items on a tray. Give the children a period of looking, then one item gets secretly removed. Which one? Continue to the last item, then have children say which items should be restored in reverse order of disappearance.
- Same idea – removing words from text on board
- Same idea – removing letters from words.
- Remember colour sequences. Enhance perception by speaking of relationships between neighbouring colours.
- Link to geographical memory. What has moved in the classroom? Which bit of the board was the word 'place' written on yesterday?
- Use coloured pages in word books as means of classifying words. What categories? (Same sound feature? Same spelling feature? Words connected with particular experience, e.g. main lesson story?)
- Write sentences, single words or other sequences backwards from memory. (What difference if this is done orally?)

Kinaesthetic memory

Sometimes called muscle memory, this underpins visual memory. We have discussed this in detail through the course of the book, and the following are really just general reminders as to what is involved.

- Enhance the inner perception of movement through various blindfold activities, ranging from stringing beads to walking an obstacle course to word writing.
- Ensure movements to be remembered are sufficiently big, bold and often enough repeated.
- Remember that cursive writing strengthens kinaesthetic learning of whole words. Sand tray writing is helpful, also 'painting-writing' on board with brush (or finger) and water.

Feeling for sentence structure
(and other elements of grammar)

Steiner insisted (as have others since) that our sense for grammar is innate. He said that raising this sense to consciousness 'in the right way and at the right time' is of central importance to the development of the ego.[52] He suggested that a living sense of grammar is most directly experienced in uneducated or 'dialect' speech. Educated and uneducated speech are distinguished in their vocabulary and phraseology, their syntax and their musicality. Since most of the children we teach have been raised on an educated (or worse, a TV) version of their mother tongue, we have a particular responsibility as teachers to re-enliven language in all sorts of ways as the essential basis for then drawing attention to the 'stubborn structure' that binds all human language together.

Here are some thoughts and suggestions relevant to this special need:

- The language of fairy tales is full of primitive life. It is perhaps worth learning one little story verbatim, and thereafter to learn at least a number of key phrases in each tale to be told. The children can be encouraged to repeat and savour such phrases during recall.
- Nursery rhymes and everything belonging to traditional playground culture obviously have a bearing here.
- The appropriate use of a 'sing-song' voice with younger children should be encouraged, though this mustn't become stilted.
- Conscious variation of the voice through each lesson is important – cf. volume, rhythm, pitch, timbre.
- Work either directly or indirectly with the different sentence moods of the Command, the Exclamation, the Statement and the Question. (There is a wonderful exploration of this in Paul

Matthews's *Sing Me the Creation*,[53] from which many of the following exercises are borrowed or adapted.)

- Draw gestures for the four sentence types. Relate them to the four elements.

- Describe a picture/setting with
  a) statements, emphasising nouns and noun phrases;
  b) exclamations, emphasising adjectives and adverbs (or equivalent phrases); and
  c) commands, emphasising verbs. A complementary exercise takes text replete with all these parts of speech and omits each in turn. ('You don't know what you've got till it's gone.')

- Explore the different qualities a statement can have when describing a scene from the world 'out there', a painting, a memory, a dream, a fantasy, a lie. How are simple statements changed through the use of figures of speech such as similes and metaphors? What is the effect of putting 'I am' before each of a series of noun phrases describing perceptions of the world around us (e.g. 'I am the sunlight warming a wall...')? What is evoked through the process of personification (e.g. 'He clasps the crag with crooked hands...')? How may a collection of attributes and activities be associated together in the naming of a thing/being? (the 'wall-warmer', the 'crag-clasper' etc. Cf. the 'kennings' of Norse mythology, or the names of Allah in Islam...)

- Explore the exclamation in relation to wish, wonder and surprise, three archetypal moods of soul. Focus on the musical qualities of exclamatory expressions, e.g. in onomatopoeia (ding-dong, bow-wow), alliteration, expletives (careful!) in slang, made-up name-slinging, made-up tongues for the 4 elements, the play of echoes... Extend from simple interjections to expressions of prayer, praise, gratitude, sorrow and joy, love and loathing, excitement and terror.

- Explore the command ranging from everyday experience in

school and at home to commands within the realm of story and imagination: humans commanding animals, God / gods (including animal gods) commanding humans. Commands may be gentle, as in lullabies; and may include wishes, charms, invocations – 'May the...' , 'Let the...', 'Give us this day...'

- Explore questions in relation to the primary question, Who/what are you? (And who, in this relation, am I?) The realm of the riddle, the guessing game. (Lots of riddles in *The Oxford Book of Nursery Rhymes*; in Norse and Germanic literature; in Jaffke's *Guides for English Teachers*[54]...) Versions of the game of consequences (these can be very creative and varied) are examples of an extended question. The question lends itself to working in pairs – e.g. one partner writes a question, the other writes an answer (maybe with a further question); and with opposites (antonyms), and correspondences (synonyms and homonyms). A nice exercise is to think of pairs of antonyms and try and find a word that unites them, e.g. light – sunset – dark. Questions may be explored in relation to nouns (Who are you? What is it?), adjectives (What are you / is it like?), verbs (What's happening?), adverbs (How / when is it happening?) and prepositions (In what direction or position is it oriented?). There are the 'What if. . . ?' and 'How could it be different? questions. And the ultimate questions, like 'What happens when I die?', 'How did the world begin?', 'How will it end?', 'How may I know God?'

Communication exercises

- Write sentence in hieroglyphs. Partner translates.
- Write story between two or more people, taking sentence (or paragraph) each. Try to make joints seamless.
- With older pupils, give extracts from literature and ask them to continue writing the piece in the style of the author.

- Create a scene or a character with a partner, writing sentences in turn.
- Write many different kinds of conversations. Examples could include conversations between colours, elements, plants, animals.
- Write a story (with appropriate theme) as a series of written correspondences.
- Write a letter to one's guardian angel. The next day, write a reply!
- Write many different real letters, cards and notes to real people – including those in the class and the school, and those at home. Try to have such correspondence feel like a proper conversation. Later, teach and practise formal letter writing – again, keeping it all as real and relevant as possible, for example through pen-pal relationships.
- Give instructions to one's class through writing. Maybe even a whole lesson could be directed in this way – with the teacher sitting watching!
- Encourage children to write down some of their questions as these arise during a lesson. Point out that this may make both the question and response more considered.
- Find kind and creative ways of characterising each other – e.g. with the guessing game (also known as 'the Furniture Game'): If this person were a colour/flower/house/musical instrument etc., which would he be? Perhaps do such exercises orally first, then translate into written (poetic) form.
- Find imaginative (and non-morbid!) ways of writing epitaphs for each other (e.g. with emphasis on achievements, using verbs and adverbs; on qualities, using simile and metaphor; on personal relationships. . .)
- Ask older pupils to explain the mysteries of text messaging! Play with this in the classroom context, and discuss the differences between a live conversation and this shorthand textual alternative.

- Try and write in another person's handwriting.
- Have a little improvised conversation with a partner, then write down the memory of what was said by the other person. Put the written conversation together at the end.
- Play a game of written compliments/complements with a partner – e.g. You have such deep and fiery eyes. (2nd person) Oh, but your eyes are like the surface of a sparkling stream. (Allowing this to be done in a somewhat tongue-in-cheek .and not necessarily wholly accurately observed way can free the children from self-consciousness and still allow them to enjoy a real relationship through language.)
- Practise accurate and truthful accounts / descriptions.
- With older pupils work more consciously with the devices of rhetoric, where one is addressing a group of people and trying to persuade them of something. (Such devices include addressing the audience as if they were a single person, giving them the impression that they are a valued, knowledgeable, 'good' audience, using musically patterned speech, repeating things rhythmically, especially in groups of three, deflating any counter arguments before they arise, concluding with a memorable QED.) Bring examples of great persuasive speeches, and discuss the part played by oratory in history, and, of course, in advertising.

We have moved here from exercises relating to literacy as a technique to literacy as an act of communication. We have also approached the essential connection between literacy and culture. The following, concluding chapters will explore these latter dimensions more fully.

11. Literacy and Learning Differences

One of the greatest inherent challenges in education is the concept of what is normal. There is no question of doing without such a concept: education cannot be expected to reinvent itself on a daily and individual basis any more than you or I can. Certain basic assumptions and expectations are necessary, of which the most basic of all is how human beings 'normally' learn things. Two risks are apparent here. One is that an accepted 'normal template' may not in fact accurately or sufficiently represent an existing truth. The other is that it may be applied, whether 'true' or not, in a way that is exclusive rather than inclusive. The present chapter will pick up the threads of 'Developing Literacy as Faculty' and expand further on what could be called our common human differences, relating these to the kind of educational curriculum and teaching style that might help such differences express themselves through a common language, so to speak. The relation of this common language to literacy will be implicit throughout.

Picture to yourself a class of children. Imagine them as mixed gender, mixed background, mixed ability and mixed motivation. Your task as a teacher is to help them learn about the world and to develop their fullest potential as citizens of the world, including the ability to be articulate within it. This means finding a meaning for 'world' that all your pupils can share and feel related to, in their thinking, their feeling and their will. The challenge facing you is that your class includes children who have been actively predisposed, through their cultural, social and economic backgrounds, to feel different from one another – sometimes, indeed, to feel 'worlds apart'. You will also be faced with children who look at the world in a different way regardless of their family background. Some of these differences will group themselves into families of temperaments (see below); others will remain purely and simply individual. So what do you do?

You start with the individual child. You use every faculty you possess to clearly observe, appreciate and form a living and sympathetic relationship with that child. Because it is so very easy to project our own preconceptions onto other people it helps to begin our observations with what is most physically perceptible. How does a child actually 'look'? How does he express himself through his physical body? How 'at home' does he seem to be in it? How well does it seem to serve his inner purposes? The child's body is the instrument of his life's music and needs to be in working order and in tune before the music itself can sound. As a teacher you may sense problems at this basic level and be drawn to make further investigations, possibly involving professional assistance from other quarters.

If a child's body can be likened to a musical instrument, it can also be placed within a particular section of the human 'orchestra'. Children have different constitutions, and these affect the ways they learn and express themselves. The relation between who the child really wants to be and the limitations imposed upon him by the physical body he inherits at birth determine his characteristic temperament. Forming a picture of children's generic temperaments is as much an art as a science, and can be developed in the first place through a process of imaginative picture forming. We can ask ourselves questions like: If this child were a musical instrument, would he belong in the brass, wind, reed, string or percussion section? If he were a tree, what kind of tree would he be? What kind of house would suit him best? What colour, season, time of day, quarter of the compass or 'element' (earth, water, air or fire) might be the fitting backdrop to his nature? Is there a period in history where I can imagine him living? Or another place on earth? One's answers to such questions can be collated, and common themes noted. These can then be compared with the general insights into constitutional and psychological 'types' that have been gained through one's own and other practitioners' experience.

The four temperaments

Rudolf Steiner had many things to say to teachers about children's temperaments. He hearkened back to the traditional schema depicting four basic temperaments and revitalised it as a modern, practical approach to teaching. The background to his propositions belongs in the large body of insights that he called anthroposophy, and Waldorf teachers are expected to be aware of this background in working with any of Steiner's specific methodological or curriculum suggestions. The following summary of Steiner's exposition of the temperaments is offered really only as a taster, with the assurance that it is only part of a much more complete educational banquet in which the individual reader is freely invited to partake further.

Summary of the four temperaments in the period 7-14 years

	Choleric	Sanguine	Phlegmatic	Melancholic
Temperament	Choleric	Sanguine	Phlegmatic	Melancholic
Element	Fire	Air	Water	Earth
Body focus	Circulatory system	Nervous system	Glandular system	Skeleton
Build	Short, angular	Graceful, harmonious	Soft, rounded	Thin, bony, drooping
Taste	Likes spicy; needs more bland	Likes sweet; needs more salt	Likes bland; needs more spice	Likes salt; needs sweetening
Nature	Wilful, assertive, loves challenges, concerned with main task not details	Impressionable, caught up in sensations and thoughts of the moment	Absorbed in own life processes, placid, equable, hates hurry, likes routine, harmony, comfort	Weighed down by physical nature, self-pitying, envious of others' talents, a perfectionist
Educational access	Responds to authority based on competency	Responds through personal love	Responds symbiotically to others' interests	Responds to others who have suffered
Educational tasks	Set tasks just beyond ability and help when asked	Set succession of small tasks – longer when asked	Set regular boring tasks – more varied when asked	Set tasks arousing sympathy and compassion for others
Orchestra	Brass/Percussion	Wind	Reed	String

Please do not peel things from the summary and use them as sticky labels!

In working with the temperaments, the aim is ultimately to make the temperament into a good servant rather than a bad master: to focus and channel its positive aspects into consciously chosen directions and to balance its extremes with aspects of the other temperaments. As effective educators, Steiner counselled, we should begin with what is already there. Rather than plunge straightway into 'moderation' exercises we should initially attempt to engage the child directly through his existing temperament, through approaching him in the right 'key' and offering him temperamentally suited activities and learning strategies. By first intensifying the temperament we then invoke nature's tendency to moderate itself; and we may assist this process by guiding the child into a natural metamorphosis that transforms his original activity into its complement. For example, a choleric child might be given a form-drawing that initially radiates out powerfully from a centre point in straight lines and angles. Then, when the choleric impulsiveness feels somewhat satisfied, we can suggest that the child now circumscribe the form with containing curves.

On the same 'homeopathic' basis of treating like with like, Steiner recommended seating groups of the same temperament together in the classroom. This allows the teacher to address each temperament economically during whole class teaching. It also encourages each temperament group to 'self-modify'. Where a certain set of characteristics become the norm, a social group seeks to polarise itself from within rather than being thrust into opposition status from without and feeling 'reactive'. The ability to feel 'normal' is the starting point for freedom.

Extremes of temperament do certainly arise and can be a significant factor in learning differences. However, a single temperament does not normally predominate powerfully and exclusively in a child. More commonly it combines with a neighbouring temperament as viewed in a circular scheme :

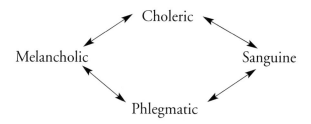

Often it may prove easier to sense a child's dominant temperament by considering the temperament that fits him *least*.

Temperament is one of a cluster of general headings under which we may begin to organise our perception of the differences between children and the ways they learn. I and many of my colleagues have found it useful to refer in this respect to the '5 + 1' formula of Else Göttgens, a Dutch educational adviser who has roamed three continents dispensing practical Waldorf wisdom. She offers the following summary:

The main causes of learning differences

1. Organic physical causes
2. Different 'intelligence quotient' / ability to conceptualise
3. Emotional disturbances
4. Imbalance of temperament
5. Dysfunction (ADHD, Asperger's Syndrome etc.)
6. '+1': Real 'late developer'

Children may be physically impaired in many ways that affect their learning, the most common (which affects the development of literacy) being impairments of hearing and sight. Teachers obviously need to look and listen out for such problems and seek advice and help when appropriate.

Differences in IQ are realities, though it is equally the case that intelligence tests tend to measure more what a child has *learnt* than a child's underlying capacity for understanding, and in any case refer only to a very distinct and limited part of any child's being. The one useful purpose that an IQ test may sometimes serve is to indicate that a child's low performance is not obviously connected with low intelligence: the dyslexic child is frequently an example of this sort, and certainly should not be labelled slow or stupid.

Emotional disturbance can have a profound effect on learning, and may sometimes take the guise of a so-called dysfunction. This is an area where the teacher must move from the foreground to the background of the picture that a child presents. The Waldorf schools normally ask for written biographies of the children they admit, including specific questions about trauma in early life. Sensitive as such questions may be, they are vital to a proper understanding of a child's needs. Working with emotional disturbance may sometimes go beyond an ordinary teacher's capability, and this should be recognised. But much can be done in the classroom context, and the realm of language and literacy can be especially therapeutic. Curative stories, for example (see Appendix 5, p. 244), can be composed especially for such children, who may also find great relief in composing their own.

The basic aspects of temperament imbalance have already been indicated, and also some general approaches to dealing with them. A general awareness of temperamental differences should colour all teaching during the class teacher period, from age 6 to age 14. In English, for example, the different kinds of sentences can be linked (with appropriate tact in applying the insights) to the different temperaments: commands to the fiery cholerics who enjoy administering justice, exclamations to the airy sanguines who enjoy reacting to change, questions to the watery phlegmatics who like to chew things over and objective statements to the earthy melancholics who need outer reality to release them from themselves. In arithmetic, the 'four processes' (depending, I should add, on how they are actually pictured) also have their correspondences: the 'fair sharing' of division is a choleric process; the 'quick change' effect of multiplication is typically sanguine; the accumulative, 'slow and steady' process of addition suits the phlegmatics; and the sense of 'loss', coupled with the perspective in which losing can also be giving, appeals especially to the melancholic temperament. Red, yellow, green and blue seem to me to be natural colours to associate with the choleric, sanguine, phlegmatic and melancholic temperaments respectively, and are useful reference points in practical work.

In all of this and anything else to do with temperament, however, the teacher must avoid being simplistic, and above all avoid being *wrong*, in his temperamental 'diagnosis and prescription'. What matters most is that one's teaching should, overall, appeal in its different qualities to each one of the temperaments. This means working consciously on one's own temperamental disposition, and especially on one's speech, in order to ensure that one really can represent a 'rounded' experience to the children watching and listening. One might also, as part of a lesson, offer a range of different media, for example drawing materials, modelling materials, glue, card and scissors, perhaps costumes and props for acting purposes, which the children may use to recall an aspect of yesterday's lesson: this allows the children to 'suit themselves', not with regard to *what* they are learning but in respect of *how* they may integrate their learning into themselves via their temperamental disposition. (An approach to recall that Els Göttgens calls 'free rendering'.)

Dysfunction

This heading opens up something of a Pandora's Box. Many sub-headings immediately fly out: dyslexia, dysgraphia, dyspraxia, various aphasias, ADHD (Attention Deficit Hyperactivity Disorder), the autistic spectrum, Down's Syndrome. . . Some of these 'registered conditions' may have an organic basis, whether inherited at chromosome level or brought about by brain damage or other neurological disturbance caused by traumas of different kinds, e.g. accident, illness, vaccination, over- or under-stimulation of the senses. The different possibilities of dysfunction range from inherited to damaged to obstructed to disturbed; and different educational approaches may be appropriate in different cases, even where symptoms appear similar. In almost every case of real dysfunction, however, one is drawn to the threshold where 'normal' education ends and 'special' education begins. It is to be hoped that more and more normal schools will be able to deal humanly and effectively with more and more special children; to do this we shall need to develop both our objective expertise and our subjective willingness to make changes in what we have become comfortable with.

The specific relation of the full spectrum of dysfunction to questions of literacy gain focus from what Karl König, in his lectures *On Writing and Reading*,[55] describes as the 'four aphasias':

- Motor agraphia (the child can read but not write)
- Motor aphasia (the child can write but not read)
- Word deafness (the child knows individual letter sounds but cannot synthesise these into words)
- Word blindness (the child knows how to blend sounds but cannot retain links between sounds and letters and so is unable to analyse a written word into its phonetic segments)

König explores these aphasias in relation to what he calls the 'staff of uprightness' and the 'ring of attention'. Put very simply here, the 'staff of uprightness' refers to the complex of activity that becomes visible in a child's impulse to stand, walk and make other purposeful movements of the limbs. The 'ring of attention' is the complex of activities connected with the child's ability to form mental images and concepts. König associates the former with writing and the latter with reading, making an additional link between writing and listening, and between reading and looking. He makes the point that not all children naturally make these last links themselves. They may need teaching to listen to what they are writing, and to look at what they are reading. (It is equally plausible to argue that they may need teaching to look at what they are writing and to listen to what they are reading, but König's exhortation goes deeper, to the 'root relationships' of literacy.)

Rudolf Steiner describes human language as a higher metamorphosis of human movement. König is confirming this in saying that writing without listening is movement unable to metamorphose into a true form of speech. Steiner also describes our sense of *thought* as a metamorphosis of our sense of *life*. König's characterisation of reading is drawn out of its etymological derivation (in German = lesen) from the image of gleaning, harvesting or 'berry-picking': the latter a process of stretching out, plucking and gathering lots of individual impressions that promise to nourish and give us life. When reading isn't properly linked to looking then the sense of the activity as a whole isn't realised: the berries don't get gathered in the basket; the letters don't get gathered into words and sentences. The ring of attention fails to circumscribe processes of perception and make them meaningful.

Lower and higher senses

Both the writing-listening and the reading-looking associations are bound up with a relation between life processes and consciousness. The basis for most if not all educational dysfunction lies in a breakdown of this relationship. By far the commonest reasons for such a breakdown relate to environmental influences in early life which disrupt the healthy development of the 'lower' perceptual organisation (see table below) and prevent it flowering properly into the higher faculties such as language, thought and awareness of the otherness of other people. Another one of Rudolf Steiner's contributions is especially relevant here, in which he elaborates the activities of twelve rather than five human senses and examines the specific connections between them. As with the four temperaments, only a summary of these insights can be given in this book – but the reader is strongly encouraged to read further about this (see Bibliography) as it provides a clear and practical basis for working with both curative (special needs) and ordinary education.

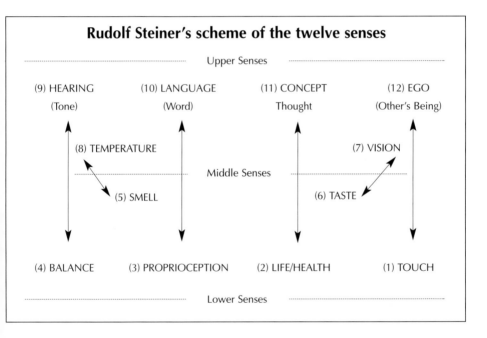

Rudolf Steiner's scheme of the twelve senses

----------------------------- Upper Senses -----------------------------

(9) HEARING	(10) LANGUAGE	(11) CONCEPT	(12) EGO
(Tone)	(Word)	Thought	(Other's Being)

(8) TEMPERATURE   (7) VISION

-------------- Middle Senses --------------

(5) SMELL   (6) TASTE

(4) BALANCE   (3) PROPRIOCEPTION   (2) LIFE/HEALTH   (1) TOUCH

----------------------------- Lower Senses -----------------------------

The numerical sequence given here to the senses has a basic relation to their chronological development; the arrows indicate inherent special connections between pairs of senses, the higher one being a metamorphosis of the lower. It should be clarified that

173

the lower senses involve perceptions of one's own bodily processes whilst the higher senses perceive things coming from outside one's body. Interestingly, just as the lower senses are pictured as transforming into higher ones, so all the senses together transform from vehicles of perception into vehicles of conscious knowledge. Through the process of *this* metamorphosis, the lower senses, which first allowed us to perceive the internal conditions of our body, now give us the basis for understanding the physical world outside ourselves; and the higher senses, through which we first received meaningful impressions of the world out there, above all through our experience of other human beings, now form the background to our inner experience of ourselves.

Delayed and precocious development

So to the last category of Else Göttgens's list. The '+1' status of the 'late developer' marks this learning difference as somewhat different from the others, and also one that needs to be thought about last rather than first. Because Steiner remarked that many late developers were in fact powerful individualities whose special qualities needed to 'mature in the vat', some Waldorf teachers have used the idea as a comforting label for children who needed rather more than that. I will certainly vouch from experience that some children really don't come into flower, particularly where literacy is concerned, until their twelfth year, and seem to have benefited from not being pushed to the limit to do so earlier. But not pushing to the limit has to be a conscious and careful decision, constantly monitored and tested by gentle probing of the more normal learning reflexes with normal classroom assignments. Many children are simply asking for a different approach.

As a final thought, I wonder if reality is asking us to consider a '5 + 2' schema? Is there a case for considering the '*precocious* developer' as possibly, sometimes, more than just the product of over-stimulation and over-anxiety? Is the 'Normal' template for human incarnation[56] and development perhaps itself in the throes of change? Do we need to work differently in our Waldorf kindergartens, where the traditional approaches don't always seem to work the way they did? Can we continue to rely on imitation in the way we always have? Do we need perhaps to intervene more in the child's incarnation process than hitherto, engaging him directly with remedial activities to promote, for example, the development of movement and the senses? Or do we need to give him more space to 'do his own thing'? Do we *know* what we need to do? Do we know what our children need us to do?

At the back of the book, in Appendix 3, there is another checklist, called 'Pointers to Learning Difficulties'. The reader is invited to consider whether the symptoms it indicates are uncommon or all too familiar.

Cultural difference

One highly significant learning difference still to be considered in this chapter is that of cultural difference. Culture is a big umbrella, and lots of things can be included under it. Basically, culture represents the sum total of the influences with which and through which a child has 'grown' up and been 'cultivated'. In the normal way of things it represents the context in which a child feels most completely at home. It affects how a child responds to the world and what he believes about the world; equally it affects the image he has of himself and his own worth. Education that isn't able to take account of such differences properly will run into difficulties and cause even more.

Everything set out in the Foundation Stage of England's green and pleasant National Curriculum about the importance of teachers having a living relation to children's social and cultural backgrounds can be mentioned again and applauded. There is a potential danger, nevertheless, that such exhortations pay mere lip-service to social awareness and multi-culturalism. I think this sometimes happens in the Waldorf world as well as mainstream, and often enough for understandable reasons: it is after all very difficult to break free of one's own cultural influences – including those represented by one's own educational tradition.

What the Waldorf tradition does have as a tremendous stimulus to cultural inclusiveness is the understanding derived from anthroposophy that all human culture expresses the different forms of development – different variations on a theme, to pursue the musical analogy – of a universal human archetype present in all of us. Everyone, in this picture, is equally human – and also equally less than *fully* human. The fullness of our humanity becomes appreciated only when we take all our variations together and gather them up in one basket. Although anthroposophy as such isn't taught in the Waldorf schools, the sense of a common stream of human development linking all times and all places certainly does form the heart of the education.

History as reflection of child development

In specific terms, Waldorf education offers a long and unbroken view of cultural evolution through its history curriculum. This begins, in fact, with pre-literate history: with the expressions of ancient oral traditions subsequently handed down and written down as the myths, legends and religious canons of different peoples. Steiner recommended that, when children are ten turning eleven, the teacher should tell stories and literature from Ancient India. The class is thus introduced to the spirit of the Vedas and, later, Buddhism, which is a spirit that sees the physical world as made up of *maya*, illusion. In the same year the journey should continue to Persia, Mesopotamia, Egypt and Greece. During this survey the emphasis will slowly shift from inner to outer history, and will reflect each culture's growing interest and engagement in the outer world. As part of this 'earthing' process the lesson will include a review of what contemporary culture has inherited from classical culture. This will be continued in the following school year with a study of Roman history and its legacies through to the end of the Middle Ages: a period that includes the birth and development of both Christianity and Islam, and also, focused especially amongst the Arab peoples, the rise of science. In the year after that the pupils will travel in every direction of the compass following the Italian, Portuguese, Spanish, English, Dutch and other adventurers to China, West Africa, the Americas, the Arctic and finally Australasia. For the ancient Indians the physical world was *maya*, an illusion: truth was to be found only with spiritual consciousness, which in the being of Krishna was shown to be something ever youthful and playful. For the great discoverers the physical world was a reality to be explored, mapped, conquered and inhabited. Children approaching their teenage years are on just such a journey themselves.

True, Waldorf education, like the Age of Discovery, was born in the heart of Europe, and its traditions have grown up having something of a Eurocentric slant. But the threads of Asian culture, African culture, American culture and Australasian culture are part of its fabric, and the sensitive teacher will draw what is appropriate from the *inner* characteristics of each region visited to address the *inner* disposition of the children in the class. The outer trappings of contemporary cultures will inevitably need to be acknowledged too – but these should be integrated into lessons in a lively and relevant way, not simply presented as information.

Spreading from the centre

The geography curriculum offers a complement to the history lessons in this respect. If Waldorf history begins with long ago and far away, its geography begins with the here and now. It actually begins with the classroom where the children are sitting. The first map is a drawing of this little world. Slowly the picture opens out, encompassing the school, the journey from home to school, the region, the country, the continent and ultimately the world as a whole. The purpose of the geography lessons, as with the history lessons, is to help the children feel at home in their world – which is one world for all of us. The wise teacher will acknowledge that today's children are generally far less rooted in the landscape and traditions of their own locality than those of 1919, when the first Waldorf school was founded, and will take account of this in the study of 'home surroundings', acknowledging the spread of family backgrounds in the class and the fact that many people today are in some degree migrants. But the aim will be to help all the children in the class feel at home where they are, not where they are not.

Complementary realities

The younger the child, the more the picture of the outer world is based on sense experience: what is real is what has been touched, tasted, seen and heard. It is a world of what William Blake called 'minute particulars'. The beginnings of our exploration of this world with children should be a process of focusing physical observations that each child has individually. The 'big picture', the global perspective, comes later. At the same time the coherence of the child's *inner* world is formed of universal imaginations: what is real here is what has been dreamed and believed and recounted the world over since time began. When we tell fairy tales we strengthen and develop the child's inner sense of belonging to the greater world of humanity. So also when we recount the ancient myths and the dramatic motifs of human history. The aim of education is to bring outer and inner worlds together, so that the minute particulars of sense experience come to acquire an increasingly universal significance, and the archetypes of humanity come to their flowering in individual human lives. If we prematurely attempt to abstract or generalise the outer world for the child we take something away from its reality, and we do the same for the child's inner world if we make him prematurely self-conscious.

Culture and media

One of the more recent phenomena in the sometimes desperate drive to motivate English boys to develop literacy is the involvement of famous footballers in the process. What we are looking at here is the influence of a new kind of culture. We could describe this as a hybrid of sport culture and celebrity culture – and its form and influence belong above all to the workings of television in modern life. There are other branches to the Tree of Celebrity too: music celebrities, film celebrities, TV celebrities. Today's children, in many cases, relate more strongly to these 'cultural icons' and the image world they inhabit than to any living culture with which they have personal contact. And this particular form of cultural identification does seem to be a successful motivator when it comes to developing literacy. However, we might then ask what *kind* of literacy it develops. The kind, perhaps, that feeds the circulation figures of *The Daily Star* in the UK – the only national daily apart from *The Independent* whose readership is growing rather than falling – and at an extraordinary rate too? The thing about *The Daily Star* is that it is a newspaper focused on television and celebrity news, not really on the real world at all.

I think there is a huge issue here. Are we happy with today's 'image culture'? Even if we are uncomfortable with it, do we accept it as the culture with which many if not most young people identify? Do the cartoons, soaps and celebrities, or the *kind* of reality they represent, together with contemporary music, pastimes and fashions, constitute appropriate working material for our lessons, as the things that enthuse and motivate our youngsters? Do we or don't we see our primary purpose as educators as giving children the special skills that are needed to fit into today's world so that they don't leave school at a disadvantage. If 'image culture' is so much a part of this reality, and if we can invoke it to help develop basic skills, why not write it into our curriculum?

Tact and authority

Suppose we have our reasons why not. How then do we deal with the influence of media culture, which we assuredly cannot deny? Do we let the children know that it doesn't belong in the classroom? If so, how do we do this? Can we do it in a way that doesn't develop in the children a consciousness of conflicting 'separate realities' whose claims to be real, relevant and interesting are at odds with one another? How would we respond, for example, to being called 'Steinerised'? How do we respond when a child proudly shows us a drawing he has spent ages doing, and it turns out to be a cartoon rather than the 'real' picture we asked for? How do we respond when a dyslexic child writes a lively historical narrative incorporating language and imagery drawn directly and inappropriately from television?

One thing a good teacher – and a good parent – will always need is tact. Tact means being in touch. Rudolf Steiner was insistent that Waldorf teachers remain in touch with contemporary realities. He wanted them to take sabbaticals every so often from their teaching and to get actively involved in different forms of work. He was also insistent, as already mentioned, that teachers be always in touch with the children they teach. Thus the truly tactful teacher will be in touch with the world into which his pupils are growing and in touch with the pupils who are growing into it – and will unite these two tacts into one.

The tactful teacher may or may not permit the drawing of cartoons or the writing of slang in a workbook. What matters is that the teacher's authority for making such decisions can establish itself as acceptable. If the good Doctor Steiner is right, then 'authority' is precisely what children in the heart of their childhood are looking for. They want a representative of 'how it is' – a guide, counsellor, interpreter and also protector – a person in whom they can fully trust. The basis for such trust is the twofold tact just described: being in touch with the world and being in touch with the individual. The vindication for such trust is when the teacher's authority continues to feel 'right' – even when it has been questioned and tested, as it inevitably will be. The children, deep down, will want it to be right; the teacher, whether committed to a class for one or eight years, must accept the responsibility for living up to this. The teacher who is truly trusted holds the key to the door between outer and inner realities – the door that television, above all, has flung open and left banging in the wind.

Completing the picture

In answer to the question of how to deal with the empty images of our image culture, I suggest that we begin by trying to see them as shadows of real and living images. For every cartoon character there is an archetype in our collective unconscious which has appeared in every mythology since the year dot. For every soap opera there is a real human drama, just as there is for every novel. When children respond to what they are seeing through their screens they are responding out of some form of inner resonance. What makes the process unhealthy is firstly that the children are being led into the image world through a process of passive rather than active imagination, and secondly that the images and sequences they experience are confused and fickle – like shadows thrown by a fire onto a cave wall, to use Plato's picture. This gives us two approaches to dealing with the situation.

Firstly, we must aim to get our children active. Physical activity will actually be a part of this, but beyond this we must try to lead activity into the realm of the imagination and also the realm of language. Children obsessed by images and sounds from the screen may appear to have an active imagination, but actually the way they spill out images and sounds and voices is more like being sick. Sorry to be so graphic. We need to distinguish between active and reactive. We need to help the children to take possession of what is possessing them, and to deal with it inwardly rather than outwardly. This does mean beginning with what is actually there, even if what is there is only a shadow.

Consider the boy who is incessantly drawing fighter planes shooting and bombing everything. Suppose we ask that boy to draw a follow-up picture where the aircraft is landing and going to its hanger? Suppose we then ask for a picture of people building back the houses and schools and hospitals that were destroyed in the first pictures? And a bit of writing to go with it? Through such a process we are involving the child in a metamorphosis of images initially received passively into images created more actively – not to mention giving them a more positive slant. Leading from one thing to another is different from supplanting one thing with another. This is not to say that there may not also be a case for turning a child's attention directly from a shadow image to a living image. A living image is by definition more real than a shadow; and if living images exist, as they do, these will engage children's attention through their own powers.

The truly tactful teacher needs to be in touch with the universal inner world as well as the contemporaneous outer world. He needs to know, for example, how to recognise the archetype of the Trickster, which is one casting especially captivating shadows onto today's screens. Loki is the Trickster in Norse mythology; Coyote in Native American folklore. Within both these environments the clever, shape-shifting, self-seeking character is ultimately contained and harmonised within the appropriate company of other archetypes. When the archetype reappears as the Joker in the Batman movies, his come-uppance has to be open-ended because of the sequels, but rather more disturbing is the fact that the agents of honesty and goodness who oppose him include a figure who identifies himself with a creature also identified with Count Dracula. The Mutant Ninja Hero Turtles also caught the imagination of the young and turned the normal heroic archetype inside out. True, there is an archetype for such transformations too: the Beast or Frog who is really a prince is known and understood by every child. But the fairy tales complete or resolve the picture, whereas not all the movies do.

We could look upon the task of teaching as 'completing the picture'. We cannot actually teach the child anything new; we can only work with what is there. Inwardly the child is all there: this we must try to raise to consciousness, to 'analyse' or unwrap into thoughts and imaginations that can be apprehended in a waking state. Outwardly the child sees only bits and pieces of a world: these we must try to help synthesise into a living whole, by relating them to each other and to the whole and living world within. When we condemn or belittle any part of a child's world we are being catabolic rather than anabolic, destructive rather than creative. If we begin by welcoming what the child brings with him we are then better able to say: 'Now let me show you this.' And if we then show the child something that is true and living and that resonates with his inner knowledge, he – or she, since of course the two sexes are different – will be able to take it in and actually grow with it.

Part Three: Closing the Book

12. The Three Persons of Literacy

We began this book with the prospect of a failed harvest in the realm of the human word. To get to the roots of the problem we first explored the nature of early language development, in the individual and also in human society, and followed these parallel strands through the metamorphosis of spoken into written language. In the second part of the book we applied these insights to assisting young people, sensitively and practically, to develop a valued and valuable form of literacy in the world today. It now remains to draw our wide-ranging considerations together and integrate them under the banner that ultimately declares literacy's highest purpose to the world: the fulfilment of literacy in all that has been written down and read as human literature. The writing and reading of books is a profoundly human and potentially miraculous affair. Properly understood, encouraged and enabled, it can bring the linguistic labour of ages to a golden harvest.

The present chapter offers a summary of all the insights we have clarified so far, united in a single, living image of the human being.

The key of three

The nature of literacy is bound up with the nature of language. Aristotle described language as having three elements: *logic, rhetoric* and *grammar*. Entering into this more deeply, he discovered the motif of threefoldness repeatedly recurring. Within logic he recognised the basic structure of *thesis, antithesis, synthesis*. Within rhetoric he distinguished *opsis, lexis* and *melos* – *lexis* being the words themselves, *opsis* being the visual imagery conjured up by language and *melos* referring to its musical qualities. The threefoldness of grammar is everywhere: in the sentence structure of subject-verb-object; in the three fundamental tenses of verbs – past, present and future; in the three persons of the verb – I or we, you, and he, she, it or they. Ultimately we may discover that what holds both language and literacy together is also what holds all art, science and religion together, and that this is most clearly represented in the unified image of the human being. The human being is indeed the world's most eloquent metaphor – nature's most open secret. Through the human *form*, that is, together with the different activities associated with it, we may read the Book of Life in its original language. There really isn't a better place to start the study of anything.

When we look at the physical body of a human being we see the picture of threefoldness as a living image.[57] Pursuing this further, we discover threefoldness in the processes and functions that unite the physical body with soul and spirit. The human being has a head, which is associated especially with the functions of the nervous system; a thorax, which is linked especially with the rhythmic processes of breathing and the circulation of the blood; and a set of limbs that enable a person to act upon the physical world and transform it, including the process of transformation involved in eating and digesting. This latter function effectively unites the limb system with the metabolic system as the third membership of the physical trinity. In psychological terms we associate the head with thinking, the trunk with feeling and the metabolic-limb system with will. We further link the head with wakeful consciousness, the metabolic-limb system with instinctive, unconscious processes, and the middle system – our feeling realm – with a mediating combination of the two.

A new-born child is most fully-formed in the head. Her awareness of the world, however, is centred in the unconscious processes of her metabolism and limbs. In terms of form, a child 'grows down'; in terms of consciousness, she 'wakes up'. Following the research of Rudolf Steiner and other educators, doctors and therapists who have worked further with his insights, this counter movement of physical growth and consciousness can be seen to extend through successive periods of seven years each, at the end of which time period something that began in the realm of the head has - unless genetic, environmental or psychological factors disrupt this process – come to rest in the realm of the limbs – and vice versa. At this point we can speak of a balanced interpenetration of life with consciousness and consciousness with life. Steiner describes the special fruition that belongs to the conclusion of the second seven-year period as 'earth maturity'. Sexual maturity, and the sexual consciousness that accompanies it, is only an aspect of this. The development of the lower jaw – the moving limb of the head – along with the limbs proper, indicates physically how a new quality of conscious personal will and capability is present in the 14-year-old. The adolescent's natural idealism is a complement to this, uniting her sense of self with a greater sense of the world.

From 'It' to 'I'

As head processes penetrate deeper and consciousness begins to flash upwards into the cerebral organ that can form and articulate it, the 'person' of consciousness changes. To begin with the child's awareness of both herself and the world is essentially couched in what is grammatically termed the 'third' person. This is the realm of 'he, she, it, they'. The characteristic 'primal' nature of this realm is actually best approached through the word 'it': the 'it' of 'It's raining' or 'It's alright, nothing got broken' – the realm of 'It'. Though quintessentially matter-of-fact, this world is, for the young child at least, a world that is flooded with life and being. To the extent that the child becomes aware of herself or other people in this condition it is typically by their actual names, not through the pronouns me or you. The child refers to herself by her name. All beings, including herself, have equal status within this condition. Piaget chooses the term 'egocentric' to describe this condition, but I prefer the term 'egoperipheral'.

In normal development the third person condition of being is followed by the second. This is the realm of 'You are'. In practice it is the realm of you and me, since 'you' give 'me' my meaning. It is the realm of conversation, a give and take that fluctuates between active and passive, receptive and expressive. It has everything to do with speech: in grammar, the second person is associated with the vocative case, which invokes the word for voice. In an older form of English the second person address was often introduced with the vowel sound 'O', as if to draw attention to the mouth itself. Through the medium of verbal exchange especially, the spiritual identity that lives behind the scenes in the objective world of 'It is' becomes embodied in the other person of a personal relationship. This person, so long as she is the subject of engaged attention, becomes the focus of the world. At the same time, the experience of being called 'You' by this same other being *we call* 'You' also bestows on us a personal identity that differentiates us from the world at large, that makes us feel special.

It is out of this social embrace that the experience of the first person will ultimately emerge in its own right. This normally happens for the first time somewhere towards the third year of life. The second person is pushed further and further away with the child's increasingly repeated 'No' and insistent 'Me'. And suddenly – because there are no half measures to such a birth – the word 'I' sounds forth for the first time from a child's awareness of self. 'I' is the only word no one else can say for us. This, however, is not yet a truly isolated experience of egohood; it subsists within a larger experience of the first person plural – of 'We'. Only when things are not as they should be does the experience of 'I' equate strongly with an experience of fundamental separation. And when it does, the first person singular cannot in fact develop properly.

Three literacies: it, you and I

So how is all this related to literacy? At one level literacy has to do with getting hold of the objective world, of grasping how things are. In this sense it is an extension of our metabolic-limb system. We speak here of 'functional' literacy, which has to do with a very practical, matter-of-fact relation to the physical world: it translates, as time goes on, into understanding instructions and labels and timetables and things like that, all of which have a bearing on survival, prosperity and range of opportunity, both for the individual and the species. This literacy is 'objective' and lawful, requiring accuracy and clarity of information. Its grammatical correlative is the third person, the realm of 'It is'.

At another level literacy is a social issue. Here it comes to involve particular *people* rather than objective principles and entities, and even though these people may be plural, the archetype of social literacy is the conversation between two single people who know each other or who wish to know each other. Just as we are still breathing the molecules of Julius Caesar's last living breath, so the way we share our lives with others through social literacy is a form of breathing. This is most clearly manifest in the to and fro of written correspondence.

The highest level of literacy has to do with our identity and, encompassing this, our destiny as human beings. When literacy speaks truly in the first person it speaks with the voice that distinguishes humanity from the animals on the one hand and the angels on the other. It is the voice of who we are as a species. Within this voice it is possible to hear and speak as 'all' people, as 'our' people, as 'my' people, or, lastly, as 'myself', and to do so in the faith that this understanding is grounded in a common human denominator. What makes cultural literacy possible is firstly that we share what Stephen Pinker has called the Language Instinct[58] – an inborn grammatical template for all human language, without which there would simply be too much to learn in a lifetime. Secondly, cultural literacy is possible because we talk to each other, and only thereby wake up to the fact that we have our linguistic identity in common. And thirdly, cultural literacy is possible because it continually recreates and preserves itself through cultural literature. Such literature is the signature of the human spirit and imagination that identifies us. In it we see our human face, just as through our instinctive grasp of universal grammar we experience an extension of our human limbs.

The three persons of literacy belong – of course – together. But they are not simply the same. Neither do they develop in the same way. Each depends on different initial conditions, different stimuli and different opportunities. Only by developing each single literacy in the right way and at the right time can a fully integrated, threefold, living literacy be achieved. The key for getting it right is the developing human being – the being that 'grows down' and 'wakes up' through three differing conditions, each with its own initiation rites and confirmations. A picture of the characteristic nature of these 'rites and confirmations' is given early in physical life, rather like the prologue to a play. The activities of walking, talking and associative thinking are anticipations of all that will continue to unfold from the realms of the limbs, heart and head – and are wonderful metaphors for our three literacies.

Walking, speaking, thinking

In order to walk we must first lift our head above our legs. This could be described as our first real act of under-standing. Only when a vertical orientation has been established can we begin to make conscious sense of the world into which we are born. Before this can happen we must learn the basic skill of how to liberate ourselves from horizontality. For this we need other people. Crawling and creeping may be instincts that unfold by themselves, but walking is not. It is a talent that we imitate from other human beings. We do *not*, of course, learn to walk by being told how to walk, or even by being deliberately shown how to walk. Nor do we learn to walk better through being 'helped' along the way by a device like a baby walker. We learn walking by tuning our own mobility to the mobility of those around us, and, through a sustained and remarkable act of will, being 'lifted' into uprightness by our impulse to 'do as others do'. Many times we try, many times we fail: the process requires countless repetitions, countless refinements, countless renewals of enthusiasm. Significantly, though adults will typically offer both physical and verbal encouragement to a child in her walking efforts, such encouragement is not in fact the key to success here in the way it is with talking. The key to children walking is adults and, often more strikingly, other children walking. Learning to turn this key once it is in the child's possession is a process of trial and error: this part of the story is wholly a case of learning through doing, and depends on the child's inner attention and strength of will.

The aspect of literacy that is like walking similarly cannot be taught directly through instruction, but only through a combination of example, a right set of circumstances, and trial and error. Like walking, this literacy is rooted in intentional movement. We may go so far as to say that only in an environment where human beings move purposefully can functional literacy be developed. Children will imitate all kinds of movements, including non-human and mechanical movements; but they will only fully master these movements when they are also able to imitate the condition of mastery. When movement is intentional, a young child will imitate the intention as well as the outer movement. An environment where purposeful writing and purposeful reading is taking place amongst other purposeful activities is the first condition for the development of functional literacy. The second condition is that a child is allowed to respond to this environment out of her own resources, and not be 'baby-walked' into premature reading and writing. The third condition is that the child is enabled to learn directly from experience, in a quite objective, 'It is' way. This means not being over-protective and sentimental with the child, nor moralising about shoulds and shouldn'ts, nor over-anxious and impatient; rather; it means being trusting and encouraging in a simple, matter-of-fact way, in the knowledge that life itself has always been the greatest of teachers, and that the human child is innately disposed to learn from it.

The fundamental difference between any form of literacy and the activity of walking is that literacy is essentially an activity of the head. Only the manipulations of handwriting are really a movement activity as such. Although, as we have discussed, these movements belong to the foundations of literacy, even when they are relegated simply to movements of the eyes, the developed skills of writing and reading are a metamorphosis of outer movements into movements of thought. If a child is also to learn these movements of thought in a way that compares with learning to walk, she must effectively be able to experience other people's movement of thought, and the intention behind them, through a direct process of intuition.

Children *do* intuit other people's thoughts and intentions. They do so because they are inherently 'sympathetic' beings – more so than the majority of adults, we might concede. Through this natural quality of sympathy a child is eminently predisposed to grasp what we really mean by our words and actions. And where the sympathy is mutual, the process of intuitive understanding is all the stronger. Many of you will have noticed, when sitting with a child to do some early reading, how she seems to be reading you as much as the book. Often, as you find yourself willing her to manage a word she does not immediately recognise, not even obviously mouthing it for her, out she comes with it. This process is a reality, and the key to living literacy. It can never be substituted by a literacy programme, however well-devised, and it can certainly never be reproduced by a computer. A computer program may *seem* to be responsive to a child's struggles, but this has nothing to do with sympathy and nothing to do with the development of living intuition. The great white hope of computer literacy is indeed already revealing itself to be a chimera: its processes are all disembodied, and can therefore never come to live in the heart, let alone the bones, in the way human interactions can. This is as much the case where learning difficulties are involved as in normal education:

Although much has been expected of computers in the education of the exceptional child, those expectations have not been realised. Research to date has failed to substantiate significant or even moderate gains in the academic areas. Furthermore, although some researchers have focused on the potential effects of computers on thinking and reasoning ability, research has failed to show significant gains. Thus the widespread hopes for educational uses of the computer remain to be realised.[59]

Computer expert(!) Clifford Stoll argues as follows:[60]

The computer changes the ecology of the classroom. Predictably, kids love the new computers and the kindergarten increasingly looks and sounds like a video arcade. Meanwhile, the machine becomes the centre of attention, pushing aside clay, crayon, and teacher. (...) All deliver long stretches of mental excitement with minimal muscular activity. Suppose we want to encourage attention deficit syndrome. I can't think of a better way than to point youngsters at fast animated video clips. (...) We naturally perceive other cultures the easy way: by watching them on TV or glimpsing them through a porthole of the Internet. This conveys images, not understanding. Rather than shrinking our globe, this shallow electronic information system makes foreign cultures more distant. (...) Social skills. Strength of character. Trust. Determination. Perseverance. Not traits downloadable from a web site. Quite the opposite: Every hour that you spend with your brain in cyberspace marks sixty minutes you aren't sharpening those skills that our world so desperately needs. The best way to create a community of loners is for each of us to escape into the welcoming arms of the Internet.

A similar distinction between human and technological learning can be made with regard to educational programmes on television. Researchers have found that what children learn from such programmes is hugely more significant if an adult sits with the child and draws attention to their interesting and relevant aspects: otherwise the content is passively absorbed, incompletely processed and insufficiently retained.[61]

What a well-devised programme, computer or otherwise, *can* do is identify the need for systematic *practising* of literacy skills. It also includes the possibility of measuring progress objectively, which the 'third person' of literacy requires, much as our limb system does in the trial-and-error process of learning new skills. We might even propose that a computer program develops initiative, since its operator must make the first move of the mouse before anything else happens. This, however, is not something I would wish to enthuse wildly about. What *is* worth overstating is that practice is an absolute and objective requirement of literacy. There isn't a literacy gene. We are not born reading and writing, any more than we are born walking and talking. The relevant instincts and predispositions that we do have must be integrated, developed and transformed through repeated application to the specific environment of literacy if they are to become an effective literacy faculty. In this realm there is no place for sentimentality, which is sympathy removed from reality. In this realm reality itself must be the teacher. Encouragement is certainly relevant, but the proof must remain in the pudding, and the child should taste this as her own success.

Progress is based on small steps. Even an aeroplane has to be entered on foot. Learning literacy is a matter of getting a few things right at a time, and of appreciating that one is nevertheless moving forward. Having declared that reality must be the teacher at this level, the human teacher may speak for reality and represent the reality of progress to a child who might otherwise miss the revelation. Here, in a sense, the teacher becomes like a mirror. Sometimes in the learning process the child must be like a mirror, sometimes it must be the teacher who reflects the child. Once again, this needs to be an objective not a sentimental affair. Such objectivity need not be – indeed should not be – unfeeling and clinical; it should be infused with love for the child as a developing human being. But it must be focused and consistent, and honest enough to reflect failure as the absence of something still to be achieved.

The ability of the teacher to shift between being an exemplar for, and a mirror of the child must be developed into the art of educating the will. The teacher must first *show* the child how something is done. Showing is more than telling, but need not always be the same as demonstrating. It may sometimes be communicated through pictorial imagination. For example, the fact that handwriting occupies three distinct levels – above, below and on the line – can be *told* to a child, which will affect her will very little; or *shown* to a child through a particular exercise, which will engage her will much more; or *pictured* to a child, perhaps by speaking of writing as being like a plant that spreads its leaves over the surface of the earth, that pushes its roots below the earth, and that blossoms up above the earth. This will impress her most deeply of all – as long as the imagination is intrinsically true, if this truth lives also in the teacher, and if the teacher links the image with the actual act of writing, including the child's own writing as this proceeds.

From function to relation

The relationship between teacher and child unfolds the third person into the second person of literacy. This does not actually mean that the second person wasn't there before: all three persons of literacy are there from the beginning. The shift is one of emphasis. The fact is that only once literacy is somewhat established at a functional level can a child begin to have a real two-way literate conversation. Before this (as I hope will have been clearly established by now) there needs to have been a culture of oral conversation and direct human communication within which the child has grown up. Second person consciousness is born the moment the umbilical cord is cut, and first becomes articulate through motherese and its complementary 'infantese'. But the transition between second person orality and second person literacy doesn't happen simply because there are two people involved in a writer-reader relationship. It doesn't even simply evolve because there are two parties in a teacher-child relationship. Only when the acquisition of literacy is wedded to an ongoing process of *real* communication can it hope to develop as a truly social skill.

The writing of letters is especially relevant in this context. Various forms of note, card and letter can be part of a child's writing and reading from the beginning. It is important, though, that literacy is associated with more than just idle chat. In fact the writing of letters can introduce a formality and clarity into communication that is not inherently less social that chatting, and may often be more so. Through the writing of different kinds of letter the child is learning different possibilities of human relationship. Where these are real letters written to real people the second person of literacy prospers most vitally of all. Even where the exercise is a little bit contrived because it is part of a lesson, the fact that letters can be a way of having a conversation, or of conveying and receiving messages, is a fact of literacy's life. What a child can learn through letter writing is something she may not learn from so-called 'creative' writing, which is that literacy is not an alternative to orality, but its complement. Neither is literacy an alternative to reality; and through the practical communications of letter writing a child may learn to keep her literacy in touch with other people and its feet on the ground. In the concluding chapter of the book we shall discuss the relation of letter writing to the forms of electronic communication favoured by so many of today's young.

Truth and fiction

As we come now to the first person of literacy we need to recall that literacy has the possibility of creating fictions. The ambivalence of the written word is that it conjures a world of images. These images may reveal, distort or deny the truth. They may do this in the name of the third person, second person and, most difficult of all to fathom, the first person. One of the most characteristic tricks of literacy, indeed, is that it can it can usurp the voice of one of its three persons and substitute another voice in its place. I have put a lot of my own thoughts and opinions into this book, but I have declared many of them in the third person. I have reported other people's thoughts and opinions in my own voice, as though they were my own. I have also involved you in the conspiracy, by creating the impression that you are actually there, still listening, still following, still part of the process.

When a child is told, 'You can write something out of yourself,' the genie is out of the bottle. The child can now do anything that is within the power of her literacy. She can create a world of her own imagination, characters of her own imagining, and she can create an image of her own self, in the way she would like to be, not necessarily at all as others would normally see her. There is indeed a sense in which all writing and reading is a first person experience, because it happens so much in the head. When, though, a piece of writing is consciously acknowledged to be a form of 'self-expression', it removes some of the constraints that are part of the third and second person packages. The danger that goes with this is that it can all the more easily become narcissistic, self-obsessed, reflecting only the writer's very personal inner world. Sometimes this world may be very wonderful; sometimes it may include much that is real about it; it may, nevertheless, prove ultimately to be a dead-end world, one that cannot develop and that doesn't lead anywhere else. For this not to be the case, three conditions must apply. Firstly, the writer must have a healthy relation to the world of the third person – the world of 'It is', known to most of us as the real world. Secondly, the writer must actually care about other people, and be able to draw inspiration from them as well as inspiring them. And thirdly, the writer must have access to the first person plural as well as the first person singular. These same preconditions, we might add, belong to a healthy readership too.

The first person plural is the voice used by human cultures, which may be either smaller or greater cultures. When the Queen of England says 'We,' she is identifying herself and her people as one being. Not everyone in England is a monarchist, but everyone knows at least something of what it means to be one. Some people are very fixed and limited in their relation to cultural identity – as fixated, one might say, as Narcissus on his personal identity. The tabloid newspapers tend to use the first person plural in their editorials and hook their readership into a sense of corporate identity that actually denies them individual freedom of thought. We must be honest about this and identify literacy itself, along with other mass communications media, for promoting nationalism and sectarianism as part of its shadow. But if we read the broadsheets as well as the tabloids, and books as well as the broadsheets, we shall widen our sense of 'we' and deepen it too. Let us follow this thought forward into a new chapter, the last but one of this book.

13. Harvesting the Word

Literacy to literature

The greatest gift that literacy has to offer anyone is literature. By literature I mean here the literature that we speak of as art. Artistic literature, imaginative literature, whether secular or sacred, is humanity's ongoing spiritual effort to unite the inner world of its own nature with the outer world of sense perceptions through the medium of language. As such, the picture that the body of world literature conveys is one of human evolution. We may read in it the epic story of our past, the drama of our present existence, and the urgent or fanciful imaginings of our future. The better we learn to read it, moreover, the more we come to appreciate how it not only gives voice to the three aspects of our being but unites them with increasing clarity in a single identity. The spirit that infuses human literature is what enables the different tongues in which literature is written to be understood by any one of us. The ability to understand all the different tongues of literature is the manifestation of global or spiritual literacy – the most living that literacy can be.

Aristotle, the first person to make a name for himself as a critic of literature as well as language, made a number of very relevant distinctions in his *Poetics*. He was, as we have noted, a 'threefolder'. In his words, the three dimensions of literature are *mythos, ethos* and *dianoia*. The dimension of *mythos* relates to actions and events – to the aspect that engages our will, namely the story or plot. Its characteristic literary form was (and still is) the epic. Linguistically, it has a special relation to grammar, the element that makes a sentence hang together in a consequential way. The dimension of *ethos* concerns human nature and the human situation; it engages us especially through our feelings and emerged historically as a literary form in the development of classical drama. Its linguistic focus is in the persuasive qualities of rhetoric. *Dianoia* means thought, and relates in literature to the element most easily described as 'theme'. Its classical literary form was the lyric, and linguistically it links itself with Aristotle's *logic* – the meaning that words can embody, but also the harmony they can create together (lyric comes from 'lyre', specifically the lyre of Orpheus).

The three literary forms or genres associated with *mythos, ethos* and *dianoia* developed successively in time and actually straddled the two worlds of orality and literacy. The original epics were live community events, participatory recitations that were always chanted aloud and frequently accompanied by choral refrains and physical movement. The original dramas were also community events, devised for performance rather than reading – though they did come to be written down more quickly than myths. One obvious distinction between drama and epic is that drama physically divides actors from audience, and then makes further divisions between its own characters (originally accented by the wearing of masks). Classical drama did, however, build a conversational bridge between actors and audience through the figure of the Prologue, who addresses the audience personally at the beginning and end of the play. It also included choral speaking to 'tell' the story as it went along. The audience was, in other words, invited to participate as much as possible without actually being on stage, and would indeed often join in verbally with passages learned by heart from repeated visits to the same plays. The clear distinction between author and audience marked the beginning of literature proper, and was first developed when the classical poets began to write lyrics. A lyric is composed as if the poet were thinking aloud. It is not a public address, nor a personal communication addressed to the reader as such, but a private musing to which the reader relates like an eavesdropper. The lyric poet's voice is the voice of an individual – an individual thinking his own thoughts.

Aristotle shuffled off his mortal coil before literature developed the genre we would simply call fiction, represented above all by the prose fiction of the novel. The interesting thing about narrative fiction is that it is not so much a completely new genre as a metamorphosis of the other three initially more poetic forms. A novel may actually be written in any one of three persons. (The second person is unusual, but I have a friend who has done it.) As mentioned, however, this nominal orientation may disguise other orientations, and the novel is par excellence a literary form that can be chronicle, biographical drama and personal confessional at once. In this it is the most literate of all literary forms.

Had Aristotle lived to see the day (and who knows, maybe his spirit still lingers on), he might have marvelled to see the way in which the future becomes a mirror of the past, with everything turned back to front and inside out. Within the realm of literary fiction – and what does that reflect? – history from classical times onwards has traced a process that moves from 'out there' and 'on high' to 'in here' and 'down below', and then on to a literary cosmos where 'in here' is equally 'out there' and 'down below' equally 'on high'. This process can be described in terms of changing literary 'modes', borrowing a scheme set out in a wonderful book called, rather unpromisingly, *Anatomy of Criticism*[62] by the Blake scholar Northrop Frye.

The descent of fiction

Frye characterises works of fiction as developing historically through five distinct modes. The first and highest of these is that of *myth*, whose settings and characters are what from our contemporary armchairs we would describe as supernatural, or perhaps as 'wholly imaginative', or perhaps as reflections of the inner world of the collective unconscious, depending on our persuasion – but whose stories are nevertheless told as objective realities in what could be classed a 'high' third person manner. In the second mode we meet settings and characters that are somewhat more down-to-earth and human, but which are still distinctly 'larger than life' and able to bend the ordinary rules of nature. This is the mode of *romance*, in which are written the legends of heroes and heroines, sorcerers and saints, talking animals and nature beings. The medieval period of Western literature is the great chapter for romance. Then comes the mode that closes the door on the 'other', supersensible world, and turns instead to what we might call the most ennobled form of this one, characteristically represented by royalty and the aristocracy, and historically highlighted in the Renaissance cult of prince and courtier. Frye describes this as the *high mimetic* mode. In the *low mimetic mode* we meet the kind of people and situations we know very well, and whose ordinariness charms us rather in the way a bathroom mirror does. The low mimetic mode dominated English literature from Defoe's time to the end of the nineteenth century, though it began about fifty years earlier in France. In the fifth mode, the *ironic* mode, we meet characters who are frequently 'low status', whose lives are dominated by adverse circumstances and an unsympathetic society around them, and whose struggles seem doomed to either failure or absurdity by their own shortcomings. The reader of ironic literature may often relate quite personally to its characters and their frustrations, but is led at the same time to look down on them from a position of detachment – rather (ironically) as if both reader and writer belonged to a conspiratorial league of deities. Thomas Hardy was a great early exemplar of this mode of fiction, and the bulk of twentieth century writing developed it as a specialism. The detachment of ironic fiction, significantly, is a freedom brought about by, and in the terms of, a developed literacy and literary imagination. It marks the turning point of literature's descent into realism and what I would call a 'culture of exile', and the beginning of its return to its origins.

In writers like Rushdie and Marquez we meet a development of the ironic mode into what is appropriately described as 'magical realism'. Here, what seem at first to be ordinary human characters with developed personalities living their lives in natural settings and circumstances (often limited and lowly) – these characters suddenly find themselves with magical powers, or alternatively that the world they live in has become magical – capable, for instance, of raining down showers of blossoms out of the sky, just like that. Magical realism as a literary genre is beginning to force open the crack between the worlds that closed with the ending of the epoch of high romance. It is beginning to dissolve the distinctions between all the various levels and conditions of being that would otherwise leave literature with nowhere left to go. It is restoring to the human imagination, the human spirit, the power to overcome the world of limitation and isolation. At the same time it is both acknowledging and celebrating the world of limitation as the shaper of individuality and the ultimate driving force behind the human need to be both I, you, it and we.

Children's literature: the magical child

So many of today's books are about thresholds. In children's literature this has actually been the case for rather longer: indeed, children's literature always has one foot in literature's developmental past, which included and integrated other realms. The wardrobe that leads to Narnia and the in-between platform from which Harry Potter catches the Hogwarts Express are two of the best known amongst many examples of threshold imagery. While 'harking back' is characteristic of children's fiction generally, a distinguishing feature of many children's books today is that they capture the imagination through their realism as much as their magic. Another distinguishing feature of the best modern children's books is that they are read by adults. Indeed, one senses that they are written as much *for* adults as children. Tolkien may have begun *The Hobbit* as a bedtime story for his own children but he didn't win through to *The Silmarilion* without knowing that he had become a storyteller of the epic tradition, a voice for all his people.

The Lord of the Rings has its roots in old Norse mythology but it grows up out of the 'Shire', which is clearly Tolkien's own world, and spreads its branches upwards and outwards into the future. The fact that it is now a blockbuster movie says something for its prophetic character. Like much of the so-called fantasy writing that has burgeoned in our latter-day culture, *The Lord of the Rings* is not so much a harking back as a hearkening forward. The elves may return to the world of once upon a time, but hobbits and mortals may not. They must go through the gates of Mordor – the gates into the world of ultimate isolation – and dissolve the ring of the spell that binds them to their own tower of egohood, their own unblinking eye of single vision, so that the world may be reunited as a conscious community of different peoples, and tried and tested individuals.

Tolkien, C.S.Lewis and the company of 'really magical' fantasy writers who have followed them have done more for children's literacy than most. They have given children a reason to read that reaches beyond usefulness and social expectations and touches something deep within the soul. The Harry Potter phenomenon is perhaps especially remarkable in this realm because it seemingly single-handedly turned the tide of falling children's book sales, in the UK at least, and became a literacy cult even before it hit the screen. This isn't just because J.K. Rowling writes ripping good yarns – although that is certainly part of it. It is also because she is so good at making the ordinary world of childhood into a magical world, and the ordinary child into a magical child.

All the effort that goes into educating the 'functional' child and the 'social' child becomes like dust in the wind when it fails to awaken and nourish the magical child. A magical child has the power to overcome her circumstances, work wonders, give body to her dreams and realise her deepest intentions. This may begin as something in her own mind, but it is a real power. In order to develop this power, however, the truly magical child must undergo an apprenticeship, like Harry at Hogwarts or Ged, the future Wizard of Earthsea, on the island of Roke. Apprenticeship is a socialising process; it requires and teaches trust, faith and humility. The magical child is aware that magic can be deceptive and may itself quickly become the enemy of trust. Good magic must never deceive its own practitioner, nor those who are servants of the good. For the magical child to *know* this, however, she must be left alone to work it out for herself. The trials of power and trust are followed by the trial of destiny. Like a traveller at a crossroads, the magical child may – indeed must – choose the direction that she wishes her life to take. This freedom will then be answered by the consequences of her choice. It may lead either to isolation and darkness or to fellowship and the light of day. All this is a secret hidden in the soul of every child. When she opens the right door, or the right book, the secret lights up.

Three archetypes of the book

The reading of books begins with the reading of the Book of Nature. The child in her first seven years has the task, time and opportunity to become livingly engaged and literate in the reading of this book, to engage fully with it with all her senses. All other literacies will emerge from this one, even as they are already hidden within it. This is harder for the city child, but hopefully there will still be manifold opportunities for her to experience stones, plants and creatures at – literally – first hand. The Book of Nature is described in Genesis as the Book of Life. God wrote it, so we are told.

The second in the trilogy of archetypal books is the Book of Other People. The child can first begin to make sense of this book in the middle of her first seven year period, but the task, time and opportunity to become really literate in Book 2 comes with the second seven years, which is the middle period of the three great periods of growing up. This middle period of growing up is the heart of childhood, and the Book of Other People is where the life of nature becomes identified with the life of knowledge. Adam and Eve came to conscious awareness by seeing each other naked – that is, by recognising each other's living differences – and even though this required them to leave the garden, the fact that they left it hand-in-hand promised the possibility that their ultimate gain would be greater than their original loss. The Book of Other People is a book to be shared like an apple. When we tell each other stories we have the Book of Other People open between us. The more that the shared, spoken word can be part of the experience of literature for a child up to the age of fourteen, the more deeply the second kind of literacy may be established. Obviously a child will read books alone before this time, but this may still be a shared experience when the books are talked about in the right way, and when the books themselves are appropriate both to the child's emotional and functional literacy.

The third book of the series, the Book of Knowledge, might also be called the Book of the Spirit. It is anticipated in the growing consciousness of earlier childhood, but really comes of age in the period from fourteen to twenty-one. In fact this book has as much to do with nature as spirit. Earlier we said that 'growing down' and 'waking up' are contrary directions that reach each other's place of origin at the end of each developmental period – and this is what the Book of Knowledge is all about. It reflects the natural world like a mirror and illumines it with the sun of consciousness. It is a book to be read and understood in the head – and then translated and rewritten through the limbs as deeds of life. If the Book of Knowledge stays only in the head then both nature and nurture have failed in their purpose, and the individual who cannot relate knowing the truth to doing the good has become trapped in a biographical and spiritual dead end. Equally, if the Book of Knowledge cannot be read in the head because consciousness has got itself too tangled up in the limbs, then this is the mirror version of the same dead end. We could describe the first failure as a form of motor agraphia, where a person can read but not properly write, and the second as a form of motor aphasia, where the person can write but not properly read. This is to be understood metaphorically rather than literally, where 'writing' has to do with all forms of self-expression and 'reading' with all forms of understanding.

This book, the one you are reading now, opened with an image of young people suffering the experience of being trapped in a dead end. Soon it will be time to close this book. The young people will still be there. Their graffiti will adorn the dead brick walls. Their private conversation will continue under the cover of the 'hood' – the neighbourhood – that defines and circumscribes their personal and 'tribal' identity. Much of this conversation will consist of formulaic phrases and hand signs. Some of it will be continued in a strange new form of literacy coming to be known as 'textese' – the thumb-written shorthand of the mobile phone. Maybe a small amount of conversation will be about films or television programs, but none of it will be about books. These young people, of course, are the extreme cases. I will venture to suggest that we cannot and should not expect to go into their alleys and 'rescue' them from their condition. What we may do is acknowledge them and learn from them. One thing we may learn is that it is 'we' who have a problem, not simply them. We may also learn that this is a problem with no quick fix – and that the quick fixes being attempted are doomed to come apart again. Finally, it is possible that what we are looking at as a dead end is not a dead end at all, but a way to get beyond the dead end that 'we' are in. There may be something 'out there', in other words, that can save us from what has happened 'in here'.

14. The Future

All the best stories begin with some form of separation and end with some form of reunion. The separation may take the form of leaving home, family, community or even one's senses. The union may be a homecoming, a marriage, some broader form of social reconciliation or even, as is the case in *The Wizard of Earthsea*, a union with one's own shadow. In the Bible, which William Blake succinctly calls the 'Great Code of Art', the ultimate separation is depicted as simultaneously a separation between Man and God, man and woman and everything represented by higher and lower nature. The ultimate union is represented as simultaneously a homecoming, a marriage and the establishment of a holy city. The New Jerusalem is both a community of redeemed ('bought back' and reunited) human souls, the Bride of Christ and a cultural regeneration of the Garden of Eden. It stands as the resolution of the original falling out that happened in the garden and marks the transformation of knowledge into love, and of instinctive communion into conscious community. The city, in this picture, is seen to be the divine-human form of a redeemed condition of general nature, right down to the mineral realm, which now appears in the shape of precious stones – 'lively stones', as the Book of Revelation describes them.

The Book of Revelation speaks of another city too. This city is named Babylon. It is the shadow image of Jerusalem. In place of a conscious community of individual souls it represents a sorry collection – perhaps we could call it an 'excommunication' – of lost souls. Where Jerusalem appears as the Bride of Christ, Babylon is identified as Satan's harlot. And where Jerusalem signifies the redemption of the Fall, Babylon's great beast or dragon is a terrifying reincarnation of Eden's serpent. Its mineralised scales are the antithesis of Jerusalem's lively stones.

Towers and temples

The internal imagery of the Bible makes it clear that the foundations of Babylon were laid way back in the beginning, in the chapter of the Fall, with the building of the Tower of Babel and human beings' misguided attempt to abandon earth and climb back to heaven the quick way. That effort was shown to lead to the confounding of human language and the breakdown of its spirit of community. The paradox of Babylon is that its founding impulse could be given the same mission statement as that of Jerusalem, namely the endeavour to break free of lower nature and get back on equal terms with the higher. The difference between the two cities is symbolised in their two representative works of architecture: the tower and the temple. The tower is an archetypal image of pride and self-centredness; the temple is where the collective lower nature bows before the higher and implores the higher to reach down and raise it up again through an act of grace.

Every city on earth today is both a city of towers and a city of temples. Both Babylon and Jerusalem are prefigured wherever humans gather in one place, regardless of their nominal persuasions and conscious intentions. However, Babylon and Jerusalem are not so easily distinguished in reality as they are in the imagery of the Bible. Outwardly there may seem to be a clear

213

antithesis between tower and temple. Simply by substituting the word mosque for temple and focusing on two towers instead of one we find apocalyptic imagery writ large in contemporary reality. It really doesn't take much imagination to see the skyline of Manhattan as a silhouette of biblically proportioned hubris, nor the domes of the mosques as hives of collective righteous indignation. But this is all much too simplistic. When the Twin Towers did come crashing down, the citizens of New York responded in the moment with an extraordinary display of civilisation. They went out of their way for each other; they reconfirmed their collective identity through caring about each other; their cultural and religious idealism was rekindled like the torch of Lady Liberty from the ashes of a globally proportioned economic self-absorption, however much the smell of oil may have stuck to it later. And while, across the street, America's religious adversaries may have been united for a moment in feeling that the Hand of God was on the joysticks of the highjacked aircraft, the reality of Islam, like the reality of *all* religious persuasions, is one of internal and interminable differences of opinion – a living picture of the original Tower of Babel.

Literacy's loss – orality's gain?

The breakdown of literacy, or the failure to achieve literacy, is a phenomenon above all of the inner life of our cities. The easy explanation for illiteracy in a situation where there is also universal education – and a 'developed' city has schools for every neighbourhood – goes like this: the one who does not see literacy as a key to economic success has no economic motivation to develop it; the one whose social environment is either illiterate or one that barely or rarely reads is socially uninspired to read and write; and the one who does not recognise his own culture in the literature on offer from the local bookshelves is likely to look elsewhere for cultural fulfilment. If a city represents the form of our highest cultural, social and economic ideals, it also starkly mirrors the reality of our failure to achieve and share these ideals. It is an environment of intensified double vision. I venture to suggest, however, that describing this as a polarisation between the 'haves' and the 'have-nots' is again being too simplistic. While both cities and literacy are commonly associated with the fruits of a civilising process, and 'rurality' and illiteracy with a lack of civilisation, the reality is much more ambiguous. Let's look at this ambiguity in terms of white and black. Many of the world's non-literates are black. Many of the world's so-called underdeveloped nations with their primitive rural economies are black nations. Much of the 'underclass' in white society is black. Many of the inmates in white people's jails are black. Many bad things in white people's language are black. But many black people have a great deal to teach many white people. It is the voice of black people we hear speaking the words 'brotherhood' and 'sisterhood'. It is Martin Luther King and Nelson Mandela we think of when we think of social justice. It is black people's music we hear when we listen to blues, jazz, reggae, rap and a whole lot of other sub-genres of popular music, and black people's street talk and gesture that we see the white kids drawn to emulate, however little they might wish to acknowledge it. Black culture is alive and kicking; it is articulate, persuasive and progressive – and all of this in spite of the fact that it is still significantly *not* a culture of literacy. Its special ability (yes, of course this is an unsafe generalisation) is to communicate *life* and *feeling*; and where it prefers other forms than the written word to express itself, this is perhaps partly at least because it is precisely these two elements that it finds missing in so many black letters on white pages.

We have been looking at literacy as a process where higher levels of consciousness are liberated from their primal 'bondage' to sense impressions and other physical constraints. We have pictured this as a process of standing upright, where the vertical orientation of consciousness distinguishes itself from the horizontal orientation of 'nature' that spreads outwards around our feet. Now we may also observe that this 'staff of uprightness' upon which literacy inevitably leans is actually a form of tower; and the imagery should alert us to the shadow side of literacy's promise. Put simply, the nature of literacy includes an inherent potential to overreach itself. When it does this, and begins to leave its 'earth nature' behind, it starts to dry up, grow rickety and start babbling like a creature in its dotage. Its own higher purpose becomes confounded by its divorce from actual life, and it crumbles into a legion of divided literacies, each with its own tongue and set of private meanings with no common dictionary to translate them. For the staff of uprightness to stand as an image of *living* literacy it must take the form of the staff of Hermes, where the vertical staff, winged though it is and drawn always towards the higher world, is interwoven and encircled by the image of two serpents raising themselves around it, heads held high but with their tails still on the ground.

Living with new media

Hermes was a communicator, a uniter of separate realities. Originally, when he worked for Zeus, he carried messages orally. Later, when he moved over to Egypt and appeared as Hermes Trismegistus, he communicated in arcane symbols and became the god of literacy. Today he has been claimed by a telecommunications company. Shall we brush this latter fact aside, or is there after all something not only integrally 'hermetic' about electronic communications, but also something that carries with it the future of both orality and literacy?

Who doesn't have a mobile phone? Who doesn't know how to use e-mail or the internet? Who doesn't accept that these are the things that the world is increasingly using to keep in touch with itself – at both lower and higher levels? I know that many people, including myself, are highly suspicious of electronic information and communications technology. We see electronic messages, much as many once saw printed books, as manifestations of a huge cerebral illusion – an image of reality substituting itself for the real thing. But is that *all* there is to it? For the lonely soul living out a fantasy existence in internet chat-rooms, maybe that *is* just about all there is. But what actually drives the communications industry is the underlying desire of human beings to rediscover and keep contact with one another. The huge overnight success of the *Friends Reunited* internet site which enabled people to get back in touch with old school mates was surely a testament to the significance of such technology as a way *through* the image world and back into the world of real life and real people. The prolific burgeoning of 'reality TV' might be seen in a similar light – though it can also be argued that such 'celebrations of the ordinary' don't actually lead back into real life in quite the same way.

Electronic communications can accommodate the forms of both orality and literacy. The mobile phone can be for talking or for texting, and these days may include a digital camera to include visual imagery as well. Most internet communication is done through text, but may also include the audio-visual dimension. It can hardly escape notice that where text is used, the normal conventions of written English are typically abandoned for something at the same time more shorthand and more idiosyncratic and 'personalised'. Basically, texting is leaving the established conventions of the written word and returning to those of the spoken word. Aspects of this new electronic oracy are certainly cliquish and what cultured people might call regressive; but in another way it has become a great leveller. For a start, you don't need to be able to spell or punctuate well in order to be able to communicate with it. For another, you can communicate via an alias and so project a self-image that you choose to project rather than one that is thrust upon you, while still feeling as if you are communicating. You may live in a high-rise in Jerusalem or a basement in Baghdad and no-one need know the difference.

Electronic communication isn't just about chatting. Scientific journals are published on the internet and live or near live debate and research can be conducted in this way by the global scientific community. Similarly with the proceedings of economic interest groups. Similarly, in fact, with the proceedings of all walks of life, from the most material to the most spiritual. Reaching way beyond the possibilities of books, this new incarnation of Hermes must surely be greeted as a phenomenon of the utmost significance for the future of the world. Remembering that Hermes himself was always a bit of a trickster may help warn us that illusion will always be a part of his activities. But his motto – 'as above, so below' – may further remind us that an illusion need not be so much an untruth as a dangerous half-truth – a displaced reflection of what is really there. If the reality of the world is that we are spiritually predisposed to become a global community, our global communications technology may appear as an image of this same progressive community spirit. It *may* do so, moreover, more 'livingly' than a library of books.

By applying the motto of Hermes to time rather than space we get the proposition 'as before, so hereafter', where (as I would like to interpret it) the future appears as a metamorphosis of the past, and the past, stretching the credibility of Darwinism, as a prefiguring of the future. We have looked at such an idea already in this book using the biological imagery of ontogeny and phylogeny, and also as a principle of education relating to the recapitulations and metamorphoses that take place through successive seven-year stages in a biography. We should further consider now that the notion of developmental motifs has the possibility of being biased – in one of two directions. One form of developmental bias is weighted towards the past, another towards the future. The former gives birth to nostalgia, the latter to ambition. In education, the 'ambitious' principle addresses itself continually to the 'next possibility', and works with the image of the child as a little adult. The 'nostalgic' principle is concerned to preserve the 'goodness' of the past, whether this be a quality of innocence or a developed set of traditional values and customs. Ambition has the tendency to overleap itself, and nostalgia to get stuck in the mud.

Trying to teach a child to run before he can walk would be a clear example of an ambitious approach to education. We may just as easily confirm that teaching a child ICT skills before ordinary literacy skills is as daft as teaching literacy skills before the basic elements of orality. That way leads to the Tower of Babel. However, once we acknowledge that ICT culture is unquestionably a part of our human future – and only an out-and-out nostalgic conservatism would attempt to deny this – we cannot ignore it or tell it to go away. Somehow we must recognise an image of this future in the unfolding reality of the present, and weave it into the fabric of our efforts to raise new human beings and introduce them into the world. This means more than just acknowledging that 'the time will come when our children will have to become ICT literate'; it means noticing that our children actually have a predisposition towards ICT literacy that really wasn't there in the same way during our own childhood. It has variously been observed that when a single creature within a species learns a new skill, this is often followed by the same skill being acquired by other members of the species in a different geographical location. The word 'synchronicity' is sometimes applied to such apparent coincidence. What this phenomenon suggests is that 'things happen when the time is right'. So how might this apply to the remarkable ability of young people to pick up computer skills – to be so 'at home' in the technological world?

When we ask ourselves what *lives* in ICT culture rather than what dies in it, we see many things that are appearing also in the culture of the street – both the back alleys of the ghettos and equally in the bookshops of the high streets. The common denominator in these different manifestations is that they all involve some kind of resurrection of the past. In the New Age we are witnessing a tendency to return to the Old Ways. Computer literacy, for example, hinges as much on interpreting icons – pictorial images – as understanding alphabetical text.[63] Getting what you want out of a computer is as much a matter of pointing (with an arrow using a mouse) as spelling things out. The way young people especially learn about computers is by playing with them, not by being told about them or reading about them. All of which is in itself a more primitive form of literacy than writing and reading. The parallel to this 'nostalgia' in street culture is the use of ritualistic body language and formulaic phrases rather than sophisticated sentence structures to communicate meaning and intention, together with the adoption of other signs and symbols to indicate one's identity within a particular 'tribal' community. (The computer does this by telling us through logo and label that we are all safely identified, say, within the Microsoft community.) Black street culture has further extended its exploration of more archaic linguistic forms in the development of 'rap', whose relentless driving of rhythm, rhyme and repetition is an evocation of ritual chant and primitive epic. Ritual chant and primitive epic are available also from all the best bookshops, and many of the quirkier ones too. Even the very cultured people who read *The Guardian* know a lot about the Old Ways. American supermarkets have whole sections devoted to the culture of the arcane and Aquarian 'alternative'. Blockbuster movies and popular TV shows are full of encounters with the Old Powers, frequently combining them with apocalyptic imaginations of the future. Demons are part of the imagery too. One of the first internet service providers called itself 'demon'; Batman has already been mentioned; the whole 'Gothic' impulse brought the demonic strongly into popular youth culture.

Barry Sanders, in his powerful study of the contemporary breakdown of literacy in *A is for Ox: the Collapse of Literacy and the Rise of Violence in an Electronic Age*, writes of 'ghosts and angels':

A door has been flung wide open to the 'other side,' and swarms of invisible spectres – ghosts and angels – have rushed in to take over the popular imagination. Watch a movie, or read a novel, or just pick up one of the slicker magazines – the world seems to be haunted.[64]

For Sanders, along with Neil Postman and other alert observers,[65] the electronic age is threatening the life and soul of the human imagination and all that goes with it. As the imagination becomes aware of this, Sanders suggests, it begins to picture its own demise:

The list of ghosts and ghostlike presences saturating popular culture could be extended indefinitely. It is true that ghosts often preoccupy cultures at the turn of calendrical centuries, but the end of the century won't fully explain why they hang around these days in such numbers and with such pervasiveness. Today, they refuse to leave. Today, we have more on our hands than just the end of the century. God is dead. The author has passed away. The written page is being deconstructed. Word processors have turned everyone into ghostwriters, so that technology, like a hard-wired vampire, has sucked the very essence out of life. Look around. Young people prowl the streets as if in mourning. They dress entirely in black, like spectators waiting at any moment to be summoned to a funeral.[66]

However, in his next sentence Sanders writes, 'There is a bright side to all this, a reason to feel hopeful.' He explains:

Today, when most things have been drained of their invisible presence, ghosts and angels in popular culture manifest a longing for a fully animated life, a spirited existence... Like pictures on a screen, the spectral images of recent popular culture allow people to look at their own condition more closely, and to reflect on it. The screen can act as mirror. This is the true meaning of vis-à-vis, to come face-to-face, vision-to-vision, with our visual echo. Like an echo, our beings reverberate meaning beyond our flesh-and-blood existence, beyond life even – each person a holy ghost. That ghostly image cannot be destroyed. To come to see that other is to 'reflect' on ourselves. In a world that emphasises the visual – television, video, and films – a survival mechanism has kicked in. We need to recover the art of seeing, vis-à-vis ghosts and angels. We yearn for true insight.[67]

The distinction between a ghost and an angel is ultimately a matter of life and death:

In some ways they meet as polar opposites – death and hope, the earthly and the heavenly, the frightening and the reassuring. Ghosts come to spook, angels to help; ghosts come to torment, angels to rescue. Ghosts hang out in the darkness of creaky, old houses, angels are dramatically present in the light of the Annunciation, and at the birth of Christ. One is secular, the other religious. Ghosts begin life on this side and cross over, shedding most of their particularity. Angels, on the other side, develop a holy individuality. But they work well together in our schizophrenic, modern time. From their separate worlds, they come trailing meaning.[68]

Ghosts, we might add, have a bias towards the past, and angels towards the future. Ghosts are the after-images of life, angels are living images of what is striving to come into being. The distinction between the two is a critical one, but a confusion between them is also understandable, especially in times of transition. And what makes this ambivalence especially meaningful is that a ghost may indeed *become* an angel, or at any rate a redeemed human soul, just as an angel may become a fallen angel – a demon or spectre. (So we are told by everyone who tells us about these things.) In times of transition – and surely we are living in one now – we get the impression of time contracting, of past and future becoming superimposed in a simultaneous present. Whilst this can give rise to some extraordinary errors of judgement, it also creates the opportunity for remarkable acts of redemption.

In most stories about dragons the dragon ends up getting killed by a hero. In some stories the hero comes to an understanding with the dragon, because the dragon knows things that the hero needs to know for his personal or social purposes, and the dragon is allowed to live on in return for divulging its wisdom. In yet other stories the dragon is actually tamed and reintegrated into human society – more often through the mediation of a female rather than male figure. Such acts of redemption are pictured also in the 'Great Code of Art': in the image of the wolf lying down with the lamb; in the forgiveness by Jesus of the harlot Mary Magdalene; in the resurrection of the fallen stones of Babel into the lively stones of Jerusalem. What *are* these images? They are indeed just that: images. But they are living images. They are the product of an imagination that sees life in the lifeless, love in the loveless, trust in the treacherous. Far from being sentimental and fanciful, this 'apocalyptic' imagination (for so it should be called) is very clear – absolutely clear – about the distinction between the contraries of existence; but having distinguished them, it then proceeds to redeem and reunite them.

The long journey home

If all the best stories begin with a separation and end with a reunion, the bit in between is what makes them good stories. This bit is the adventure or journey: the exploration of the 'otherness' that is created through separation, the evaluation of what means and matters most and the conscious attempt to realise these considered ideals as facts of life. The motif of union-separation-exploration-evaluation-reintegration is in everything we do and everything we are. It plays itself out in larger time scales and smaller ones. Like an octave in music, it is a playing of two halves, the second a kind of mirroring of the first at a higher level. What this recapitulation turns upon is what gives the process its heart: I have called it 'exploration' in the five-fold motif indicated above – the end of which, as T.S. Eliot beautifully describes in *The Four Quartets*, should be 'to arrive where we started And know the place for the first time.' This should be the end of all our exploring – but it is based on the assumption that we don't get lost, that we don't misread the signs that face us in the 'evaluation' stage of the journey. Where the assumption turns out to be misplaced then comedy (the story with a happy ending) turns to tragedy. King Lear misreads the relationship between his daughter Cordelia and himself – the relationship that should have led to a renewal and reintegration of his kingdom – and just about everyone ends up dead.

Lear's tragedy was typical: he was too full of himself, and as a result he sacrificed the part of his being represented by Cordelia, whose name echoes the word for heart. Through misreading his own heart he further lost control of his head and his limbs (imaged as the yielding up of his title as head of state and of his men-at-arms to his two other daughters). In the end Lear really does lose everything: his home, his family, his kingdom, his relation to God and nature, and finally his senses. It is Shakespeare's darkest play, and yet in the moment of Lear's own death we are given the briefest and most poignant image of a redemptive imagination at work. Cordelia, briefly reunited with her father at the end, is dead; the dying Lear, purged through tragedy of his own egotism, holds a mirror to her lips and believes in his final moment of consciousness that he sees the mist of breath upon the glass. Where, at the beginning of the play, he looked to his three daughters for an enhancement of his own self-image, now his last remaining hope lies in seeing this vanity dissolved by the ghostly wraith of his own true heart and soul upon the lifeless glass.

The mirror is a thing of images, and is itself an image of what this book has been about. What, let's ask again, is literacy? It is a way of interpreting images – of sounds, words, things, ideas. The characters of any human script are images of something else. They are ghosts of a meaning that once lived in the mind of their author. Or they are angelic spirits of prophecy announcing a meaning to be born again in the mind of their reader. Either way, they are only ever images. What releases them into life is at the same time an act of willing imagination and a misty breath upon the glass. This misty breath comes always from the other side of our separate reality, and always also from our own heart and soul. It is the sign and seal of the presence and the love of life.

Some say that to be born on earth is to die in the spirit. But the infant's first cry is the sign and seal of the presence of the spirit. The mother's first kiss is the sign and seal of the spirit. The child's first word is the sign and seal of the spirit. Wherever the breath draws life from the world, there is the sign of the spirit. Wherever the breath gives back to the world, there is the seal of the spirit. There is spirit in song, spirit in laughter, spirit in tears, spirit in the conversation of friends. Everywhere there is spirit. But the black letters on their white pages are only footprints of the spirit. The lucid images upon their silver screens are only silhouettes of the spirit. The electronic transmissions that hum within the mantle of the air are only echoes of the spirit. And sometimes – all too often – the footprints are too faint to follow, the silhouettes too vague to discern, the echoes too distant to catch.

Can we learn from other cultures?

What young person sitting a written test at school or college, or filling in an application form for a job, course or benefit, has any sense of the presence of spirit in that challenge? It was different before, when a rite of passage was above all else the means of confirming a young person's relationship with the spiritual world in general, and a personal 'guardian' spirit in particular. It is sometimes still different today, in cultures where what is spoken and what is 'signed and sealed' in any other form of communication continues to honour the sense of the sacred. When we look around us for places where literacy is relatively speaking alive and well – where it isn't perceived as a generic problem within a society or associated with a plethora of special learning difficulties – we find ourselves on a journey to the East. In China, Japan, Korea, Mongolia and other parts of East Asia, literacy levels are well above the world average, and the incidence of dyslexia seems barely worth recording. Why should this be?

The fact that the written scripts of these cultures is more pictorial, and their spoken language more musical than our western forms may well have something to do with it. If we take the case of Japan, however, only about 30% of the written language uses pictographic characters; the rest is written using two separate alphabets, or syllabaries as they should be called, since each character represents a phonic syllable rather than a single phoneme. There are 1,850 ideographic characters and 71 syllables that can be written with either of the two syllabaries – so becoming literate in Japanese would seem to be no joke, however pictorial-musical the experience. And yet children continue to manage it with remarkable consistency. Perhaps the answer to these oriental riddles lies less in the actual forms of the oral and written languages involved, and more in the cultural and educational traditions that go with them.

Oriental cultures, speaking generally, have preserved a more pervasive sense of spirituality in their daily life for much longer than we in the West. Spirituality is woven into the whole fabric of their culture, as much in the manner of how people do things as in the matter of their particular beliefs. The sacredness of custom and ceremony, the sense of reverence, honour and duty, the willingness to make personal sacrifices for the sake of one's community and people – all these are indications of a deeply established relation to values that are more than material. At the heart of these cultures we find a very strongly developed sense of family – not merely as a group of people who look after each other's interests, but as a microcosm of the whole society. Within the family, the task of bringing up children according to cultural traditions is seen as a paramount responsibility of parents. Education, in the broadest sense of developing ideals and abilities that are basic to community life, begins at home, and is taken very seriously. The role models that children are given to imitate, and the expectations that are laid down for them to live up to, have, until very recently at least, been clear and unequivocal, and backed up with total commitment.

A feature that must necessarily be associated with East Asia alongside its long-standing spiritual-cultural traditions is the influence of communism. While communism is clearly not an impulse that would call itself spiritual, it does attach itself to the word cultural. In the story of Ou Dede we met the activities of the Chinese communist government in the 'cultural preservation' programme that required him to pass on his bardic heritage as a matter of political duty – even when this meant breaking the traditional rules of bardic succession. The same government was responsible for bringing a schoolteacher to Ou Dede's village and the possibility of literacy and numeracy for his children. The same government continues to extol the virtues of family, community and honest labour, ostensibly at least in very much the same vein as the traditional cultures it grafted itself onto. Whatever else we may think about the relation of communism to the inner life of the spirit, it has invested its efforts in a combined cultural-social-economic enterprise that has certainly reaped a visible harvest from the lands and peoples it has stewarded. In the basic literacy stakes, communism performs better overall than capitalism. Where the tide of its influence has withdrawn from Eastern Europe, literacy levels have fallen rapidly and markedly.

The most obvious common denominator shared by communism and the cultures that spawned it (for it was never simply imposed from without) is that of a basic socialism. If communism gives this a materialist slant, it nevertheless continues to perpetuate a culture that is, and always was, rooted in community values, suppressing or inhibiting the emergence of individual freedom and the whole ethic of individualism as a desirable cultural outcome. In factories, fields and classrooms alike, the sense of 'we're all doing it together' is raised from being simply a way of life to being the practice of a conscious ideal. Even in the cities, which so easily isolate people within their apartments and workstations, the collective 'earthy' effort is conscientiously celebrated. Today, for example, my daughter has e-mailed from Hanoi, telling amongst other things how the latest yields from the rice harvests get broadcast over the city's tannoy system. Everyone's business is everyone's business.

Our trip to the Far East was focused initially on Japan. Japan is of course not a communist country; indeed, it ranks amongst the foremost capitalist economies of the world. Until very recently, however, this first amongst the economic 'tigers' of the East was as strongly rooted in the general ethos of communality as its communist neighbours. The Japanese corporation, like the Chinese commune, has always claimed to be larger than the individual, and the national identity to be larger than both. Only maybe from the 1990s onwards has the 'private' version of enterprise begun to supplant the collective ideal in a shaky period of transition for Japanese life generally. Along with this shift of emphasis in the business world there has been a marked change in Japanese lifestyles at a personal level, with the focus for mothers on going out to work beginning to take precedence over staying at home with the children, and a growing tendency to devolve the ongoing responsibility for bringing up children from families to professional carers and educators. It seems highly likely that the pressure of this particular transition is going to have long-term and difficult consequences for the younger generations. Already the incidence of childhood depression and even child suicide is soaring. If Japan doesn't join the club of developed nations with a major literacy problem in five or ten years time I shall be very surprised.

What am I saying here? That traditional spirituality is the answer to our literacy and other associated educational and social problems? That communism is the answer? That becoming a developed capitalist nation must inevitably lead to a decline in educational standards and attainments? No, no and no. Solutions to present difficulties can never, in my opinion, simply be found through turning the clock back. Nor are present difficulties ever the end of the story. What I am suggesting is that every human culture, wherever and whenever it has appeared, has something good, attractive and right about it – and that it may well be possible to imagine (if rather less easy to realise) a culture that is multicultural in the fullest and most creative sense: a culture that combines the best of all that humanity has yet come up with, in a way that fits together naturally and harmoniously and without imposition.

Cycles of history and seasons of biography

In developing this imagination we may remind ourselves (for the last time before this book ends) that within the recognition that 'for everything there is a season, and a time for every purpose under heaven', comes the deeper recognition that seasons come not once but many times, and in many settings, from the great epochs of history to the individual lives of you and me. And further: what was good, attractive and right about a period of history or development of culture lights up again within the corresponding period and developmental stage of a single biography. So: from pre-literate cultures we may take much that belongs naturally with the first period of childhood. From the many and various manifestations of the impulse of socialism we may take much that belongs especially with the heart of childhood and the practical idealism of youth. From the developed cultures of individualism we may take much to nourish our sense of freedom and calling as adults. But all this must be accomplished in the context of our own time and circumstances, which means reshaping the cultural models in a way that is fitting. This does not merely require us to acknowledge that our own time and circumstances have developed a culture of individualism, and that this culture permeates the air that a baby sucks in with his first breath; it also needs us to see beyond our current stage, and to take our own steps towards what is still waiting to be realised. If I understand it rightly, the only steps that go forward from here are those that also lead back the way we have come, though now in a more intentional way and without loss of that hard-won, worldly-wise awareness.

Such a global and temporal multiculturalism is surely more possible now than it has ever been. We have the world at our fingertips; we can see it in a grain of silicon, meet it in our city streets, fly to its farthest corners like birds. Shall we not welcome its offerings with open arms? Shall we not ask, 'What lives in you?' rather than always 'What ails you?' May we not learn to read the world and the times in a new way, and incorporate this into a renewal of all literacy? And are we ready to discover, if the depths of our exploration have led us at last to a deepest or furthest point, at which we turn again in answer to the tug of home, that perhaps now it must be the younger ones who lead the way, and we who follow gladly where they lead?

Appendix 1. School Readiness

The view we are putting forward in this book is that the way children learn is part of the overall way children develop. The times when children are ready to learn in new ways are, equally, nodal points in their general development. Child development is certainly not a mechanical affair, but neither is it arbitrary. It is the reflection of fundamental processes that are inherently consistent and predictable. Developmental differences between children are significant, but they do not imply that there are different developmental laws.

The most important fact about child development is that it is holistic. Physical, emotional, and intellectual aspects of a child's nature are profoundly linked, reflecting and affecting each other in ways that can be, and are being, established scientifically. Whilst this scientific confirmation is especially important in the face of current misconceptions, it is important to realize that developmental realities may also be confirmed by daily observation and common sense.

The following 'developmental check-list' is drawn largely from guidelines in use in Steiner Waldorf schools to help form the picture of a child's readiness to move from kindergarten to class 1 – generally between age 6 and 7. The check-list belongs to a tried and tested educational practice, one closer to the 'Central European' than the 'English' model, although it has distinctive features of its own. *It is important to emphasise that neither the author nor the Steiner Waldorf schools wish this list to be seen as a score sheet adding up to a definite decision about a child's school readiness.* It is used in the schools as a set of notes to support a genuine and open discussion between parents and teachers as to what is really right for a particular child.

Developmental principles are a reality. So is individuality.

A checklist for school readiness

Physical development

Certain anatomical features show that overall physical growth and development are normal for the age. A certain physiological readiness in terms of co-ordination, fine and gross motor skills, and balance is necessary if children are to start with formal literacy. Indications that the child has difficulties in areas of motor co-ordination are important to note. If all other indications point to the fact that the child is otherwise ready, then some remedial support can be given to strengthen motor skills and co-ordination. The anatomical features are general indicators of physical maturity.

The school-ready child normally shows:

- visible knuckle joints and kneecaps in place of dimples;
- arch in the foot;
- individualised facial features instead of baby features;
- S-curve in spine;
- evidence that second dentition has begun;

and can typically

- touch top of ear by reaching over top of head with opposite arm;
- walk forward on a beam, log, or line;
- catch and throw a large ball;

- hop on either foot;
- bunny hop (both feet together);
- habitually walk in cross pattern (i.e. swing opposite arm when stepping out with one foot);
- climb (but not necessarily descend) stairs with alternating feet on each stair;
- tie knots or, sometimes, bows; button/zip own clothing;
- use fingers dextrously (sew, finger-knit, play finger games etc.);
- demonstrate established dominance (especially eye/hand laterality) – although in some cases this may not be apparent before around 9 years; and
- shake hands with thumb separated from fingers, rather than offering the whole hand.

Social/emotional development

As indicators of typical developmental progress the following summary may be helpful.

The pre-school stages are characterised by:

- *Age 3*: not really social with other children; wants to possess things and try them out; reactive, transitory feelings, quick mood changes;
- *Age 3-4*: begins to discover the 'other person', but still essentially self-centred;
- *Age 5*: real need for social experience; beginning of give-and-take, sharing; some beginnings of joint planning in play.

The school-ready child develops (or with encouragement can develop):

- a feeling for others' needs;
- the beginnings of deeper friendships;

- a growing awareness of the principle of authority, e.g. as evidenced in games of animals and their owners;
- the ability to visualise objects or suggested situations;
- the ability to be more inwardly self-contained;
- the ability to join in offered activities;
- the ability to look after her own eating, drinking, washing, and toileting needs;
- the ability to share a teacher's or parent's attention and wait for a turn;
- the ability to follow instructions and carry through a task or activity; and
- the ability not to be unduly dependent on a 'security item' (thumb, blanket etc.).

Drawing and painting

Children's drawings and paintings reveal their developmental progression. The pre-school stages can be characterised as follows:

- *1st STAGE*: all about movement and process – forms and motifs appearing out of movement but are not the child's focus in the activity;
- *2nd STAGE*: the emergence of fantasy and imagination – the child begins to identify objects as they appear in the process of drawing rather than deliberately setting out to draw or paint them; also happy simply to play with the flow of colour;
- *3rd STAGE*: evolution of complete human form, including the use of the triangle; more interest in colouring in.

The school-ready child:

- will produce two-fold symmetries in free drawing, indicating the establishment of the brain's hemispheric functioning;

- draws 'change of teeth' pictures, containing horizontal repetitions such as birds flying, rows of mountains, castle crenellations, etc., reminiscent of rows of teeth;
- distinguishes strips of earth and sky, showing awareness of 'above and below' in contrast to the young child's feeling of wholeness;
- use of diagonal (related to perspective) – this is frequently seen in the triangle form of a roof or in drawing of stairs; and
- people, houses, trees, etc., rest on the grass or ground near the bottom of the page.

Development of intention

The child's will development can be characterised as follows. The school-ready child:

- shows conscious goals in her activity;
- shows growing awareness of (and often frustration at) the distinction between inner intention and outer result – 'I can't do it';
- shows signs of being dissatisfied, not knowing what to do with herself – often expressed as 'I'm bored'; and
- enjoys vigorous limb activities; likes to run errands (showing both goal consciousness and a new sense of authority).

Development of inner feeling

The school-ready child:

- shows signs of being able to manage her own feelings;
- likes to wrap objects as gifts for specific people;
- loves humour, limericks, rhymes, plays on words, silly words, naughty words, showing a new consciousness for language and its power;
- shows conscious awareness of rhythm;

- likes to whisper and have secrets (distinction between inner and outer); and
- may like to tell of dreams.

Development of thinking

The school-ready child:

- has begun to develop simple causal thinking in relation to concrete situations ('if', 'because', 'therefore'. For example: 'If I tie these strings together, they will reach that door');
- enjoys literally tying things together with string etc.;
- shows better use of verb tenses, e.g. 'I stood', not 'I standed';
- enjoys cunning, planning, scheming;
- enjoys riddles;
- shows an ability to access memories consciously on request;
- speaks clearly and fluently when relaxed;
- can concentrate on a chosen task for 10-15 minutes;
- can visualise things inwardly on request and can describe them; and
- begins to ask 'real' questions (not the typical younger child's constant 'why' for the sake of asking it).

Please note: It is generally the case that at this stage of development boys are about 6 months behind the girls.

'Children's Learning Suffers if They Start School Too Soon'
– headline of an article by Judith Judd, Education Editor, *The Independent on Sunday*, 25 January 1999.

*****

'Children should not start formal lessons until the age of seven, teachers said today. Members of the Association of Teachers and Lecturers called for classes in the three Rs to be delayed up to two years in schools, with children left largely to play instead of starting at five as at present. Delegates claimed children were being damaged by the Government's insistence on formal instruction in writing, reading and basic sums in nurseries and reception classes. Many pupils – particularly boys – who develop more slowly than girls – are incapable of coping with English and maths at five and feel 'failures' when they can't keep up, it was suggested. They are put under intolerable pressure by 'pushy' parents who 'cram' them with information and hire tutors to ensure they pass national tests, it was claimed. Early success for children had become a 'status symbol' among many middle class parents.'

Tony Haplin
Education correspondent, *Daily Mail*, Thursday 1 April 1999

'What we can say is that a later start appears not to be a disadvantage to children's progress (although it is important not to forget the important contribution made by children's experiences at home and in pre-school). Certainly, there would appear to be no compelling educational rationale for a statutory school age of five or for the practice of admitting four-year-olds to school reception classes.'

Caroline Sharp, paper prepared at Ofsted's request for the NFER's (National Foundation for Educational Research) Annual Conference, October 1998

Appendix 2. Checklist for Preparing a Child Study

Physical characteristics and abilities

- Size and physical development in relation to the child's peers (height, weight, build)
- Colour and quality of hair, eyes, skin
- Size and shape of head
- Length of limbs in relation to the trunk
- Stage of dentition
- Facial expressions and gaze (pulls faces, sticks tongue out when concentrating, focused gaze, nervous twitches etc.)
- Composure (can stand still, or is fidgety)
- Co-ordination
- Body image (knows and can touch the different body parts, including left and right)
- Lateral dominance: eye, hand, foot
- Balance
- Warmth of hands and firmness of handshake
- Movement: how does the child stand, sit, walk, run, skip, jump, throw and catch?
- Hearing and sight
- Fine motor skills (manual dexterity, pencil grip etc.)
- Vocal abilities: volume, pitch, modulation, flow (stammering, speaks only parts of sentences), pronunciation and articulation (e.g. cannot speak th, or f sounds)
- Habits, e.g. nail-biting, bed-wetting, sleep-walking
- Medical conditions and general health

Language, cognitive abilities, disposition

- Range of vocabulary, ability to express thoughts in age-appropriate ways
- Memory qualities
- Spatial awareness
- Sense of form, as shown in form-drawing, modelling etc.
- Ability to organise work and possessions
- Sense of time
- Ability to listen to teachers, other pupils, parents etc.
- Ability to form mental pictures (describe something not visible, reproduce with a sketch something not present)
- Imagination (expressed in verbal, written or other ways)
- Artistic/aesthetic qualities
- Literacy skills
- Numeracy skills
- Practical intelligence – can learn practical skills and solve practical (age appropriate) problems
- Concentration span
- Likes and dislikes in everyday matters (food, dress, subjects at school)

Social, personal and moral qualities

- Awareness of surroundings and ability to care for environment
- Social awareness (age appropriate) of other people
- Willingness to play/participate with other children
- Capacity to play/be with others
- Willingness to learn, enthusiasm
- Confidence: in school (subjects, activities), with friends, at home, in unfamiliar situations
- Motivation
- Emotional balance/imbalance
- Ability to see a task through, without support, alone

- Initiative
- Relationship to the truth (tells lies, what kind, to whom, admits to wrongdoing readily/reluctantly)

General biographical background

- Family status, siblings, bereavements etc.
- Does child live with both parents, one parent, see both parents regularly? Has he always lived in one place, how many moves, where?
- Medical history (major illnesses, accidents, traumatic birth etc.)
- Previous schools, reports

Appendix 3. Pointers to Learning Difficulties

- Poor balance
- Poor co-ordination
- Clumsiness
- Jerky movements
- Difficulty in throwing / catching ball (with one hand)
- Mixed dominance
- Can't stand / sit straight
- Poor pencil hold
- Poor letter formation
- Unable to write in a straight line on lined (or marked out) paper
- Does not place the descending 'tails' of letters below the line
- Does not place the ascending 'tails' of letters above the line
- Mixes capitals and lower case letters
- Reverses / inverts letters and / or numbers b/d/p/q, u/n, s, 2, 3, 5, 7, 6, 9)
- Puts too many (or not enough) legs on the letters n, m
- Is bright, but has real difficulty with writing / spelling / reading (or one of them)
- Unclear speech
- Does not know the days / weeks / months
- Has a poor memory
- Does not learn what has been taught
- Cannot tie her shoe laces
- Messy appearance, shirt hanging out, laces undone etc.
- Is intuitive

- Is imaginative
- Looks young (baby face)
- Has parents or siblings with special learning difficulties

Obviously an imaginative, young-looking boy isn't necessarily to be assumed to have learning difficulties. The normal checklist warning applies!

Appendix 4. Common Words

The hundred most commonly used words in English

(Cobuild, *The Bank of English*, November 1995)

(1) 20.45%	(2) 5.95%	(3) 4.26%	(4) 2.90%	(5) 2.37%
the	was	by	's**	which
of	on	but	had	all
to	he	have	we	been
and	with	are	an	were
a	's*	they	there	she
in	you	from	or	who
that	as	his	one	so
it	I	this	said	would
is	be	not	will	up
for	at	has	their	her

(6) 1.96%	(7) 1.50%	(8) 1.33%	(9) 1.17%	(10) 0.98%
if	do	Mr.	him	very
about	new	my	well	years
what	people	after	your	most
more	like	just	know	think
when	now	year	then	get
out	some	first	I'm	may
can	time	over	last	back
no	them	only	also	says
two	than	other	me	any
its	into	could	because	our

's* (possessive)
's** (contraction)

Appendix 5. A Curative Story

The following story was composed by Anca Torsan, a kindergarten teacher at York Steiner School, for a 5-year-old boy who had been disturbed by the death of a grandparent. The boy's parents were also involved in the preparation of the story, and later confirmed how deeply and positively their son had been affected by hearing it told.

The Star People

Once upon a time there was a little boy called Peter. He lived with his mother and father in a house on the edge of the forest. Peter 's grandparents passed away when he was very little – too little to remember them well. He often wondered what they were like. He tried to remember them and often longed to see their faces or hear their gentle voices.

One early morning Peter was walking in the forest nearby. He looked thoughtful. Suddenly he heard a bird's song. It was clear and so beautiful that Peter listened to it enchanted, hardly daring to breathe or make any move, lest it would be gone. It was a skylark who sang as the sun rose higher and higher in the sky. Then the song stopped. The skylark saw Peter and spoke to him . 'Why do you look so thoughtful, dear boy?'

'Oh...I was thinking of my grandparents. They passed away when I was very little and sometimes I miss them dearly...'

'I see...' said the bird. 'Maybe I can be of some help. Please, follow me.' And saying this, the skylark flew from tree to tree, always turning his little head and making sure that Peter was keeping up.

After a little while they came to a clearing where an old woman was resting under an oak tree. She had white hair under her bonnet and was wrapped in a brown, warm cloak. Her face was lit with kindness and beside her, on the grass, lay a basket full of freshly picked herbs.

It was the wise woman who lived in that forest.

'Good morning Peter,' said she, smiling. 'Good morning Skylark. I was waiting for you two... The trees whispered to me that you would come.'

'Here,' she said, smiling to Peter, taking from her basket a small branch, 'this is a gift for you, my child. It is a branch of silver birch... Take it and put it under your pillow tonight, when you go to sleep. Be patient and brave and you shall see what you shall see...'

Peter took the small branch and stowed it carefully in his pocket and thanked her... then the skylark guided him back home.

That night when he went to bed Peter put the branch of silver birch gently under his pillow. He looked out of his bedroom window. The sky was clear and many stars were shining. Then he saw a starry cross of light. Peter knew that they were the stars that always guide the sailors when they are at sea.

He lay on his bed, snugly under his blanket and fell deep asleep. In the middle of the night it seemed to Peter that a shining golden light filled his bedroom. And by his bed – lo and behold! – there stood a white eagle with gentle eyes. The eagle spoke with human voice: 'If you are brave enough I shall take you on a special journey. Climb onto my back and hold tightly to my feathers.' At first Peter hesitated, but his heart told him to follow and he climbed fearlessly onto the eagle's back.

And they flew like the thoughts and the wind, up in the sky, passing stars and planets until they reached a green meadow. There the eagle stopped and the little boy was admiring the flowers which grew all around. He looked in wonder and there, hidden in the trees, was a house. Coming nearer Peter saw that the door had a golden handle. How very strange... who could be living inside?

Then the door opened and two old people, a man and a woman, smiled at him. They welcomed him and make him sit around the table. The old woman had a soft wrinkly face and curly white hair. Her hands were plump and curled, too. She wore a woollen shawl round her shoulders and her eyes were sparkling like tiny stars. The old man was taller and had white hair too. He wore a clean waistcoat which suited him well. They spoke to him with gentle voices: 'We are the Star people. Once we lived on Earth, just like you. We walked in the forest and enjoyed every single sunrise. And we were busy always... until one day we knew it was time to come back to our home here, in the stars. We are glad you made it and came to see us here...'

Looking into their kind faces and listening to the music of their voices Peter felt his heart overjoyed. Then the old man said, 'You will not go empty handed from our house. Take this little silk bag and treasure it with care...' Then their faces disappeared in a misty cloud and, still hearing their voices ringing in his ears, Peter opened his eyes and found himself in his own bedroom, all snugly nestled under his blanket.

By now it was early morning – the sun was rising and the song of the skylark was clear and sweet. And lo! near his pillow there was a little bag of silk. He opened it full of curiosity and inside he saw seven tiny seeds. He worked hard that day, planting the seeds in the best places.

They sprouted and their beautiful flowers grew. And whenever Peter looked at them he was happy because he remembered the Star People.

Endnotes

1   Barry Saunders, *A is for Ox* (Vintage Books, 1995) p.134.
2   Source: *The Guardian*, March and April 2000.
3   Sacks, D., *The Alphabet* (Hutchinson 2003).
4   Pinker, S., *The Language Instinct* (Penguin, 1995), p.265.
5   Salter, J., *The Incarnating Child* (Hawthorn Press, 1987).
6   Doctors Bruce D. Perry and Ronnie Pollard found that children raised in severely isolated communities, where they had minimal exposure to language, touch and social interaction, developed brains 20% to 30% smaller than normal for their age. See Perry, B. D., and Pollard, R.: 'Altered brain development following global neglect in early childhood', *Society for Neuroscience: Proceedings from Annual Meeting* (New Orleans, 1997).
7   See Condon, W.S. and Ogston, W.D., 'Speech and Body Motion Synchrony of the Speaker-Hearer' in D.H. Horton and J.J. Jenkins (eds): *Perception of Language* (Columbus, Ohio, 1971), pp.150-73.
8   See Chapter 13 for further explanation of this idea.
9   See, for example, Lansdown and Walker, *Your Child's Development from birth to adolescence* (Frances Lincoln 1996), p.132.
10   Cited in Dworetzky, J. P, *Introduction to Child Development*, (St. Paul: West Publishing Company, 1981), p.82.
11   Steiner's descriptions of these three 'soul forces' was very detailed and specific. See Steiner, R., *The Education of the Child in the Light of Anthroposophy* (Rudolf Steiner Press, London, 1975) for a full exposition of these terms.

12 See particularly Steiner, R., *The Education of the Child in the Light of Anthroposophy* (publ. details above).

13 Hillman J., *The Soul's Code* (Bantam, 1997).

14 Colette, *Earthly Paradise: an Autobiography* (Farrar, Strauss and Giroux, 1966) p.77.

15 See Stephen Pinker, *The Language Instinct* (Penguin 1995) p.264.

16 See Mills, D. and C., *Lessons Britain Won't Learn* (Mills Productions Ltd., 2000) mimeograph.

17 Libby Purvis and Dorothy Selleck, *Tuning in to Children,* BBC Radio 4 1998.

18 Father and baby aged 1 month, *Tuning in to Children* BBC Radio 4, 1998.

19 Mother's side of conversation with baby aged 3 months, *Tuning in to Children* BBC Radio 4, 1998

20 Pinker, S., *The Language Instinct* (Penguin, 1995). See also Chomsky, N., *Reflections on Language* (Pantheon, 1975).

21 Colwyn Trevarthen, *Tuning in to Children* BBC Radio 4, 1998

22 Knierim, J., *Songs in the Mood of the Fifth (Quintenlieder)* (Rudolf Steiner College Press, California).

23 Kim Plunkett, Oxford University, *Tuning in to Children* BBC Radio 4, 1998.

24 Peter Bryant, Oxford University, *Tuning in to Children* BBC Radio 4, 1998.

25 See www.edu-cyberpg.com/Culdesac/ReadingModule/Munro.html

26 Another predictor of later pre-reading skill found in a group of 3-year-olds was their knowledge of nursery rhymes as such: a feature of memory as well as sensitivity to rhyme and rhythm. See Maclean, M., Bryant, P., and Bradley, L., 'Rhymes, nursery rhymes, and reading in early childhood,' *Merrill-Palmer Quarterly*, vol. 33, pp.255-281, cited in K. E. Stanovich, 'Learning disabilities in broader context,' *Journal of Learning Disabilities*, May 1989, vol. 22(5), pp.287-297.

27 See Chapter 12 for more on these senses.

28 Strauss, M., *Understanding Children's Drawings* (Rudolf Steiner Press, 1978).

29 McAllen, A. E., *The Extra Lesson*, Fifth Edition (Rudolf Steiner College Press, 1999).

30 As Francis Spufford notes in *The Child That Books Built* (Faber and Faber, 2002) p.51, some animal illustrations seem to capture the *archetype* of the animal, and seem to imprint themselves into the child's memory more deeply than many living animals.

31 Rawson, M. and Rose, M., *Ready to Learn: From Birth to School Readiness* (Hawthorn Press, 2006).

32 See School Readiness checklist in Appendix 1.

33 de Quiros, J. B. and Schrager, O. L., *Neuropsychological Fundamentals in Learning Disabilities* (Academic Therapy Publications, 1988).

34 Ibid, p.27.

35 'Think about what to write ahead of writing.' National Literacy Strategy guidelines for literacy in Reception year. Yet figures such as Philip Pullman, for instance, who are intimately aware of the creative writing process, have emphasised the value of the opposite approach: finding out what you want to say *through* writing, and pursuing threads that arise from the unconscious which you cannot anticipate in over-conscious thought. See also note 36.

36 Cf. Phillip Pullman on National Literacy Strategy: 'Something has gone wrong with education. Somehow, over the past quarter of a century we have seen confidence leaking away, and something else slowly seeping in to take its place. I think this something else is poisonous, and I think we ought to get rid of it at once. Take the glowing, radioactive core at the heart of the whole thing: the national curriculum and the literacy strategy and the SATs. This is what the Qualifications and Curriculum Authority says about the

reading part of the English tests at key stage 2 – that means, in human language, at age 11. It thinks that reading consists of using a range of strategies to decode, selecting, retrieving, deducing, inferring, interpreting, identifying and commenting on the writer's purposes and viewpoints, relating texts to the social, cultural and historical contexts. That's it. nothing else. That's what it wants children of 11 to do when they read.' (Extract from the Isis Lecture give at the *Sunday Times* Literary Festival 2003).

37 See bibliography.

38 See bibliography.

39 See *The Extra Lesson* for specific indications on hand-eye co-ordination and issues of dominance.

40 Taken from Niederhäuser H. R. and Frohlich, M., *Form Drawing* (Rudolf Steiner School, New York, 1974).

41 See Goethe, W., *Scientific Studies*, trans. Douglas Miller (Suhrkamp Publishers, New York, 1988).

42 See Steiner, R., *The Renewal of Education* (Basel, 1920, published by Kolisko Archive Publications for Rudolf Steiner Fellowship Publications, 1981) p.128.

43 Steiner, R., *Practical Advice to Teachers* (Rudolf Steiner Press, London, 1976) p.78.

44 This use of 'lower' does not, of course, mean of lesser importance.

45 See Appendix 4.

46 McAllen, Audrey E., *The Extra Lesson*, Fifth edition, Rudolf Steiner College Press, 1999.

47 Insights into the relation between red and blue and the respective functions of the right and left eye are also interesting, particularly in the context of recent research into the effect of different colour filters on some dyslexics' reading.

48 Steiner tells us that 'accurate listening supports accurate visual memory.' *The Renewal of Education* (Steiner Schools Fellowship Publications, 1981) p.184.

49 The descriptions are taken from the website for LDA

Newsbriefs Education Committee, Learning Disabilities Association of America, Newsbriefs, March/April 1998.

50 Steiner, R., *Creative Speech* (Rudolf Steiner Press 1999). MacAllen, A., *The Listening Ear* (Hawthorn Press 1989).

51 MacAllen, A., *Teaching Children Handwriting* (Rudolf Steiner College Press 2002).

52 Steiner, R., *The Renewal of Education* (Steiner Books 2001).

53 Matthew, P., *Sing Me the Creation* (Hawthorn Press 1994).

54 Jaffke, C., *Guides for English Teachers* (Pädagogische Forschungsstelle beim Bund der Freien Waldorfschulen, Stuttgart).

55 König, K., *On Reading and Writing: Towards a phenomenology and pathology of literacy: Karl König: with a contribution by Hans Heinrich Engel* (Camphill Books, 2002).

56 This term refers to the manner in which children do not just 'grow up' but also, in a real sense, 'grow down' into their bodies, learning to 'play' the physical instrument in a more and more accomplished and conscious way until they stand fully on the earth at adolescence. The concept also necessarily views the child as a being of spirit descending into matter, rather than as a creature of earth alone. See also Chapter 12.

57 The picture of the threefold human being that I am elaborating here was first proposed by Rudolf Steiner in 1908 in *The Education of the Child in the Light of Anthroposophy*.

58 Pinker, S., *The Language Instinct* (Penguin, 1995).

59 Hresko, W. P., and Parmar, R. S., 'The educational perspective,' in *A Cognitive Approach to Learning Disabilities* (McGraw Hill 1981) pp.3-44.

60 Clifford Stoll, *High-Tech Heretic. Why Computers Don't belong in Classroom* (Random House 2000).

61 Lean, A. E., and Eaton, W. E., *Education or Catastrophe?* (Wolfeboro: Longwood Academic, 1990), p.78.

62 Frye, Northrop, *Anatomy of Criticism* (Princeton University Press, 1973).

63 In addition to providing a means of selecting options and giving commands on a PC, icons have been incorporated into the language of 'textese' as an alphabet of 'emoticons' – visual symbols that can be selected to substitute for many of the commonplaces of ordinary informal conversation.

64 Sanders, Barry, *A is for Ox: the Collapse of Literacy and the Rise of Violence in an Electronic Age* (First Vintage Books Edition, 1995) p.148.

65 See Bibliography.

66 Sanders, Barry, *A is for Ox: the Collapse of Literacy and the Rise of Violence in an Electronic Age* (First Vintage Books Edition, 1995) pp.150-51.

67 Ibid, pp.152-3.

68 Ibid, pp.153-4.

Bibliography

'The Temperaments' in Davy G. and Voors B. (eds.), *Lifeways* (Hawthorn Press, 1983).

Aeppli W., *The Care and Development of the Human Senses* (Steiner Schools Fellowship, 1993).

Akaret R., *Family Tales, Family Wisdom: How to Gather the Stories of a Lifetime and Share them with your Family* (William Morrow & Co., 1991).

Anschütz M., *Children and Their Temperaments* (Rudolf Steiner College Bookstore, 2005).

Arnold J. C., *Endangered: Your Child in a Hostile World* (Plough Publishing, 2000).

Aulie J. and Meyerkort M., *Spindrift: Poems, Songs and Stories* (Wynstones Press, 1999).

Axline, V. M., *Dibs in Search of Self* (Mass Market Paperback, 1990).

Ayres A. J., *Sensory Integration and the Child* (Rudolf Steiner College Bookstore 1979).

Baldwin Dancy R., *You Are Your Child's First Teacher: What parents can do with and for their children from birth to age six* (Celestial Arts, 1989, Hawthorn Press 2006).

Baltuck N., *Multicultural Folk Tales about Stories and Storytellers* (Linner, 1995).

Barfield O., *Romanticism Comes of Age* (Wesleyan University Press, 1986).

Biddulph S., *Raising Boys* (Thorsons, 1977).

Brooking-Payne K., *Games Children Play* (Hawthorn Press 1996).

Bryson B., *Mother Tongue* (Penguin, 1990).

Buzzell K., *The Children of Cyclops: The Influence of Television Viewing on the Developing Human Brain* (AWSNA Publications, 1998).

Carey D. and Large J., *Festivals, Family and Food* (Hawthorn Press, 1982).

Caroll L. and Tober J., *The Indigo Children: The New Kids Have Arrived* (Hay House, 1999).

Childs G., *Understand Your Temperament! A Guide to the Four Temperaments* (Rudolf Steiner Press, 1995).

Clouder C. and Rawson M., *Waldorf Education* (Floris Books, 1998).

Coles R., *The Moral Intelligence of Children* (Plume, 1997).

Cordes C. and Miller E. (eds.), *Fools' Gold: A Critical Look at Computers in Childhood* (Alliance for Childhood, 2000).

Cromer R. F., *Language and Thought in Normal and Handicapped Children* (Blackwell, 1990).

Davis D., *Telling Your Own Stories* (August House, 1993).

de Quiros J. B. and Schrager O. L., *Neuropsychological Fundamentals in Learning Disabilities* (Academic Therapy Publications, 1988).

Dworetzky J. P., *Introduction to Child Development* (St. Paul: West Publishing Company, 1981).

Edmunds F., *Rudolf Steiner Education – The Waldorf Schools* (Rudolf Steiner Press, revised, 2004).

Eisenstein E. L., *The Printing Press as an Agent of Change* (Cambridge University Press, New York, 1979).

Eliot A., *The Universal Myths* (Penguin, 1976).

Elkind D., *The Hurried Child: Growing Up Too Fast Too Soon* (Addison-Wesley, 1981).

Engel S., *The Stories Children Tell: Making Sense of the Narratives of Childhood* (WH Freeman & Co., 1995).

Fenner P. and Rivers K., *Waldorf Education: A Family Guide* (Michaelmas Press, 1992).

Fenner P. J. and Rivers K. L., *Waldorf Student Reading List* (Michaelmas Press, 1995)

Frye N., *Anatomy of Criticism* (Princeton University Press, 1973).

Gladich J. and Sassi P. A., T*he Write Approach, Form Drawing for Better Handwriting – Books I and II* (Rudolf Steiner College Press, 1991).

Guroian V., *Tending the Heart of Virtue: How Classic Stories Awaken a Child's Moral Imagination* (Oxford University Press, 1998).

Haller I., *How Children Play* (Floris Books, 1991).

Harwood A. C., *The Recovery of Man in Childhood* (Anthroposophic Press, 1958).

Healy J. M., *Endangered Minds: Why Children Don't Think – and What We Can Do About It* (Simon and Schuster, 1996).

Healy J. M., *Failure to Connect: How Computers Affect our Children's Minds – for Better or Worse* (Simon and Schuster, 1999).

Heuscher J., *A Psychiatric Study of Myth and Fairy Tales: Their Origin, Meaning and Usefulness* (Charles Thomas, 1974).

Horton D. H. and Jenkins J. J. (eds.), *Perception of Language* (Columbus, Ohio, 1971).

Hunt J. and Nash-Wortham M., *Take Time* (The Robinswood Press, 1994).

Jaffke F., *Work and Play in Early Childhood* (Floris Books, 2000).

Jenkinson S., *The Genius of Play* (Hawthorn Press, 2001).

Johnson S., *Strangers in our Homes: TV and our Children's Minds* (a pamphlet published by Kimberton Waldorf School, 1999).

Kirchner H., *Dynamic Drawing, Its Therapeutic Aspect* (Mercury Press, 1977).

König K., *The First Three Years of the Child* (Anthroposophic Press, 1969).

König K., *On Reading and Writing: Towards a phenomenology and pathology of literacy: Karl König: with a contribution by Hans Heinrich Engel* (Camphill Books, 2002).

Kuhlwind G., *From Normal to Healthy: Paths to the Liberation of Consciousness* (Lindesfarne, 1998).

Kutzli R., *Creative Form Drawing, Workbook 1,2 and 3* (Hawthorn Press, 1985).

Large M., *Set Free Childhood – coping with computers and TV* (Hawthorn Press, 2003).

Lean A. E and Eaton W. E., *Education or Catastrophe?* (Academic, 1990).

Lievegoed B. C. J., *Phases of Childhood* (Floris Books, 1997).

Livo N. J., *Who's Afraid? Facing Children's Fears With Folktales* (Englewood, 1994).

MacAllen A. E., *The Extra Lesson*, Fifth Edition (Rudolf Steiner College Press, 1999).

MacDonald M. R., *The Parents' Guide to Storytelling: How to Make Up New Stories and Retell Old Favourites* (Harper Collins, 1995).

Maguire J., *Creative Storytelling: Choosing, Inventing and Sharing Tales for Children* (Yellow Moon, 1985).

Mander J., *Four Arguments for the Elimination of Television* (William Morrow, 1979).

Mary Ellen Willby ME (ed.), *Learning Difficulties – a Guide for Teachers* (Rudolf Steiner College Press, 1999).

Matthews P., *Sing Me The Creation* (Hawthorn Press, 1994).

McAllen A., *Teaching Children Handwriting* (Rudolf Steiner College Press, 1999).

McLuhan M., *The Gutenberg Galaxy: The Making of Typographical Man* (Toronto, 1962).

Medved M. and Medved D., *Saving Childhood: Protecting Our Children from the National Assault on Innocence* (Harper Collins, 1998).

Mellon N., *Storytelling with Children* (Hawthorn Press, 2000).

Meyer R., *The Wisdom of Fairy Tales* (Floris Books, 1988).

Mills D. and C., *Lessons Britain Won't Learn* (Mills Productions Ltd., 2000), mimeograph.

Nash-Wortham M., *Phonic Rhyme Time* (The Robinswood Press, 1994).

Niederhaüser H. R. and Frohlich M., *Form Drawing* (Mercury Press, 1974).

Opie I. and P., *The Oxford Nursery Rhyme Book* (Oxford University Press, 1992).

Patterson B. and Bradley P., *Beyond the Rainbow Bridge: Nurturing our Children from Birth to Seven* (Michaelmas Press, 2000).

Pearce J. C., *Evolution's End: Claiming the Potential of our Intelligence* (Harper, 1992).

Pearce J. C., *The Magical Child* (Dutton, 1977).

Pinker S., *The Language Instinct* (Penguin, 1994)

Pinker S., *Words and Rules* (Penguin, 1999).

Postman N., *Amusing Ourselves to Death* (Penguin Viking, 1985).

Postman N., *Technopoly: The Surrender of Culture to Technology* (New York, Vintage Books, 1987).

Postman N., *The Disappearance of Childhood* (Delacorte, 1982).

Poulsson E., *Finger Plays for Nursery and Kindergarten* (Dover 1971).

Purvis L. and Selleck D., *Tuning into Children – Understanding a Child's Development from Birth to Five Years* (BBC Education, 1999).

Rawson M. and Lutzker P., *Language and Learning* (Paideia Books, Steiner Schools Fellowship Publications, 2002).

Rawson M. and Richter T., *The Educational Task and Content of the Steiner Waldorf Curriculum* (SWSF Publications, 2000).

Rawson M. and Rose M., *Ready to Learn: From Birth to School Readiness* (Hawthorn Press, 2002).

Rawson M., *Free Your Child's True Potential* (Hodder & Stoughton, 2001).

Sacks, D., *The Alphabet* (Hutchinson 2003).

Salter J., *The Incarnating Child* (Hawthorn Press, 1987).

Sanders B., *A is for Ox: The Collapse of Literacy and the Rise of Violence in an Electronic Age* (Vintage Books, 1994).

Sawyer R., *The Way of the Storyteller* (Viking, 1962).

Sinclair A., *The Puppetry Handbook* (Richard Lee, 1995).

Soesman A., *Our Twelve Senses: How Healthy Senses Refresh the Soul* (Hawthorn Press, 1999).

Spufford F., *The Child That Books Built* (Faber and Faber, 2002).

Steiner R., *A Modern Art of Education* (Rudolf Steiner Press, 1954).

Steiner R., *Balance in Teaching* (Spring Valley, 1982).

Steiner R., *Deeper Insights in Education: The Waldorf Approach* (Anthroposophic Press, 1983).

Steiner R., *Discussions with Teachers* (Rudolf Steiner Press, 1967).

Steiner R., *Education as a Social Problem* (Anthroposophic Press, 1969).

Steiner R., *Education as an Art* (Blauvelt, 1970).

Steiner R., *Essentials of Education* (Rudolf Steiner Press, 1968).

Steiner R., *Human Values in Education* (Rudolf Steiner Press, 1971).

Steiner R., *The Education of the Child in the Light of Anthroposophy* (Rudolf Steiner Press, 1975).

Steiner R., *The Foundations of Human Experience* (Anthroposophic Press, 1996).

Steiner R., *The Four Temperaments* (Anthroposophic Press, 1976).

Steiner R., *The Kingdom of Childhood* (Rudolf Steiner Press, 1964).

Steiner R., *The Renewal of Education* (Kolisko Archive, for Steiner Schools Fellowship, 1981).

Steiner R., *The Roots of Education* (Rudolf Steiner Press, 1968).

Steiner R., *Waldorf Education for Adolescents* (Kolisko Archive, for Steiner Schools Fellowship, 1980).

Strauss M., *Understanding Children's Drawings* (Rudolf Steiner Press, 1978).

Thompson J. B. (ed.), *Natural Childhood: A Practical Guide to the First Seven Years* (Gaia, 1994).

Tolkien J. R. R., 'On Fairy Stories' in *Tree and Leaf* (George Allen & Unwin, 1964).

Tyre C. and Young., *Dyslexia or Illiteracy?* (Open University Press, 1983).

von Franz M., *Interpretation of Fairy Tales* (Spring Publications, 1982).

Wasserman J., *Caspar Hauser*, trans. Michael Hulse (Bantam Books, 1992).

Wilkinson R., *The Temperaments in Education* (Rudolf Steiner College Bookstore, 1983).

Wills C., *Children of Prometheus: The Accelerating Pace of Human Evolution* (Penguin, 1998).

Winn M., *Unplugging the Plug-in-Drug* (Penguin Viking, 1985).

Wisby A., *Learn to Sing, Learn to Read* (BBC Publications, 1982).

Zipes J., *Creative Storytelling: Building Community, Changing Lives* (Routledge, 1995).

Resources

Worldwide Web resources

The **Steiner Waldorf Schools Fellowship** (UK) Has its web site at
www.steinerwaldorf.org.uk
(e-mail: mail@waldorf.compulink.co.uk)
The **Alliance for Childhood** (UK) web site is at
www.allianceforchildhood.org.uk
(e-mail: alliance@waldorf.compulink.co.uk)
The **Alliance for Childhood** (USA) web site is at
www.allianceforchildhood.org   (e-mail: jalmon@erols.com)
Building Peace Through Play has its website at
www.media-awareness.ca/eng/med/home/advoc/bptplay.htm
The **Fair Play for Children** web site is at
www.arunet.co.uk/fairplay/relate.htm
(e-mail: fairplay@arunet.co.uk)
The **International Association for the Child's Right to Play** web site is
at www.ncsu.edu/ipa (e-mail: ncsu.edu/ipa)
The **Let the Children Play** web site is at   www.letthechildrenplay.org.uk
(e-mail: info@letthechildrenplay.org.uk)
The **Lion and the Lamb Project** web site is at www.lionlamb.org
(e-mail: lionlamb.org)
The **National Children's Bureau and Children's Play Council** has its
web site at www.ncb.org.uk
The **Parentline Plus** web site is at www.parentlineplus.org.uk
(e-mail: centraloffice@parentlineplus.org.uk)
The **Save the Children** web site is at www.savethechildren.org
The **School of Storytelling** web site is at www.emerson.org.uk
(e-mail: mail@emerson.org.uk)
'**How Television Affects Your Child**':
www.kidshealth.org/parent/positive/family/tv_affects_child_prt.htm
TV-Turnoff Network has its web site at www.tvturnoff.org
(e-mail: email@tvturnoff.org)

The following online (all American) 'resource sites' bring together Steiner Waldorf and home schooling, and include links to similar sites:
* www.bobnancy.com
* www.waldorfresources.com
* www.live-education.com w
* ww.oakmeadow.com

Contacts list

Steiner Waldorf and anthroposophical publishers

For names and addresses of publishers specializing in Anthroposophical and Steiner Waldorf education literature, and information on the activities of the Anthroposophical Society, contact:

General Anthroposophical Society
Postfach 134, CH-4143 Dornach,   Switzerland
Tel: (+41) 61 706 42 42 Fax (+41) 61 706 43 14
E-mail: sekretariat@goetheanum.ch

Waldorf Early Childhood Associations and training courses

For addresses of national Steiner Waldorf early childhood associations, Waldorf early childhood teacher training courses and Waldorf early childhood centres world-wide, contact:

International Waldorf Kindergarten Association
11 Heubergstrasse, D-70188, Stuttgart, Germany

Australia
Contact: Dr Renate Long-Breipohl
44 Manor Road, Hornsby NSW 2077
Tel: (+61) 02 9476 6222 Fax: (+61) 02 9476 6227
E-mail: breipohl@smartchat.net.au

Germany
International Waldorf Kindergarten Association
D-70188 Stuttgart, Heubergstrasse 18, Germany
Tel: (+49) 711 925 740 Fax: (+49) 711 925 747
E-mail: inter.waldorf@t-online.de

New Zealand
Contact: Marjorie Theyer,
c/o Kindergarten Training Course, Taruna College
Havelock North, Hawkes Bay, 33 Te Matu Peak Road
Tel: (+64) 06 8777 174 Fax: (+64) 06 8777 014

South Africa
   Contact: Peter van Alphen
   c/o Centre for Creative Education, PO Box 280, Plumstead 7801
   Tel: (+27) 21 7976 802 Fax: (+27) 21 7977 095
United Kingdom
   Steiner Waldorf Schools Fellowship
   Kidbrooke Park, Forest Row, East Sussex
   RH18 5JA, United Kingdom
   Tel: (+44) 01342 822115 Fax: (+44) 01342 826004
USA
   Waldorf Early Childhood Association of North America
   285 Hungry Hollow Road, Chestnut Ridge, NY 10977
   Tel: (+1) 845 352 1690
USA and Canada
   Joan Almon
   7303 Dartmouth Ave., College Park, MD 20740, USA
   Tel: (+1) 301 699 9058 Fax (+1) 301 779 3272
   E-mail: jalmon@erols.com

For a complete list of all Waldorf training courses and Waldorf schools
world-wide, contact:
Pädagogische Sektion am Goetheanum
   Postfach 81, CH-4143 Dornach, Switzerland
   Tel/Fax (+41) 61 706 4314

Other useful addresses

Alliance for Childhood
Australia
   Alliance for Childhood   E-mail breipohl@smartchat.net.au
Belgium
   Michiel Matthes   E-mail michiel.matthes@tiscali.be
   Web www.ecologyofthechild.org
Brazil
   Alianca pela Infancia
   E-mail Ute Craemer: utecraemer@monteazul.org.br
   Adriana Friedmann adriafried@globo.com
   Web www.aliancapelainfancia.org.br

Croatia
   Sonia Barac-Rudynski   E-mail soniarudynski@yahoo.co.uk
Denmark
   Sammenslutningen af Rudolf Steiner Boernehaver
   Web www.steinerboernehaver.dk
France
   Alliance for Childhood   E-mail je.arcenciel@free.fr
Japan
   The Alliance for Childhood in Japan
   Web www.forum3.com/projects/afc/index.htm
Sierra Leone
   Shannoh A. Kandoh, Programme Coordinator, ACP-SL
   E-mail shannohk@yahoo.com / waldorfsl@yahoo.com
South Africa
   Rain Martin   E-mail mmmstars@iafrica.com
Spain
   Web www.pangea.org/alianzainfancia/index.html
Sweden
   Alliance for Childhood   E-mail sekretariatet@waldorf.se
Tanzania
   Alliance for Childhood   E-mail pamelabhanji@yahoo.co.uk
USA
   Alliance for Childhood   E-mail info@allianceforchildhood.net
   Web http://www.allianceforchildhood.com
United Kingdom
   Alliance for Childhood   Kidbrooke Park, Forest Row, RH18 5JA
   Telephone (+44) 01342 827792   Fax (+44) 1342 826004
   E-Mail info@allianceforchildhood.org.uk
   Web http://www.allianceforchildhood.org.uk

Building Peace Through Play
   Ruth Taronno, Coordinator
   745 Westminster Ave., Winnipeg, Manitoba R3G 1A5
   Tel/Fax: (+1) 204 7758178

Fair Play for Children
   35 Lyon Street, Bognor Regis, West Sussex PO 21 1BW
   Tel/Fax: (+44) 01243 869922

Human Scale Education
96 Carlingcott, Bath BA2 8AW
Tel: (+44) 01275-332 516

International Association for the Child's Right to Play
Dr Marcy Guddemi, Dept of Education and Research, Kindercare,
2400 President's Drive, PO Box 2151, Montgomery, AL 36116
2151, USA
Tel: (+1) 334 2775090

International Save the Children Alliance
275-281 King Street, London, W6 9LZ
Tel: (+44) 020 87482554 Fax: (+44) 020 82378000
E-mail: info@save-children-alliance.org

Let the Children Play
Hillview, Portway Hill, Lamyatt, Shepton Mallet, Somerset BA4 6NJ
Tel: (+44) 01749-813 260 or 01749-813 971

Montessori Society AMI UK
26 Lyndhurst Garden, London NW3 5NW;
Tel: (+44) 020 7435 7874 Fax: (+44) 020 7431 8096

The National Children's Bureau and Children's Play Council
8 Wakley Street, London EC1V 7QE
Tel: (+44) 020 78436000 Fax: (+44) 020 72789512

National Playing Fields Association
Stanley House, St. Chad's Place, London WC1X 9HH
Tel: (+44) 020 78335360 Fax: (+44) 020 78335365
E-mail: npfa.co.uk

Parentline Plus
520 Highgate Studios, 53-59 Highgate Road,
Kentish Town, London NW5 1TL
Tel: (+44) 020 7204 5500 Fax: (+44) 020 7284 5501
Helpline: (+44) 0808 800 2222

School of Storytelling
Emerson College, Forest Row, East Sussex RH18 5JX
Tel: (+44) 01342-822 238

The Lion and the Lamb Project
4300 Montgomery Avenue – Suite 104,
Bethesda, Maryland 20814, USA
Tel: (+1) 301 654 3091 Fax: (+1) 301 654 2921

The Early Years Trainers Anti Racist Network
PO Box 28, Wallasey CH45 9NP
Tel/Fax: (+44) 01516 396136

The Working Group Against Racism in Children's Resources
460 Wandsworth Road, London SW8 3LK
Tel: (+44) 020 76274594

TV-Turnoff Network
1601 Connecticut Avenue, NW 303, Washington, DC 20009 USA
Tel: (+1) 202 5185556 Fax: (+1) 202 5185560

World list of Rudolf Steiner Waldorf School associations

The full list of kindergartens, schools and training courses, together with information for countries not listed below (running to some 80 pages in all), can be obtained from the Pedagogical Section of the School of Spiritual Science, Goetheanum, CH-4143 Dornach, Switzerland. Full title: 'World List of Rudolf Steiner (Waldorf) Schools and Teacher Training Centers, Stand Februar 2000', Herausgegeben vom Bund der Freien Waldorfschulen e.V., Heidehofstrasse 32, D-70184, Stuttgart (Tel. ++49 (0)711-21042-0; e-mail bund@waldorfschule.de)
With thanks to the publisher for permission to reproduce this (abbreviated) list; and to the editor of the journal Steiner Education, Dr Brien Masters, for permission to use that journal's list summary.

Australia
    Association of Rudolf Steiner Schools in Australia
    213 Wonga Road, Warranwood, Victoria, Australia, 3134
Austria
    Österreichische   Vereinigung   freier   Bildungsstätten   auf
    anthroposophischer Grundlage, Endresstrasse 100, A-1230 Wien
Belgium
    Federatie van Rudolf Steinerscholen in Vlaanderen,
    Kasteellaan 54, B-9000 Gent
Canada
    Association of Waldorf Schools of North America, c/o David Alsop,
    3911 Bannister Road, Fair Oaks, CA 95628, USA;
    Ontario: Waldorf School Association of Ontario,
    9100 Bathurst Street, Thornhill, Ontario L4J 8CF, Canada
Denmark
    Sammenslatningen af Rudolf Steiner Skoler i Denmark,
    Strandvejen 102, DK-8000 Arhus
Estonia
    Eesti Waldorfkoolide Uhendus, 14 Koidula Tanav, EE2100,
    Rakvere, Estonia
Finland
    Steinerpedagogiikan seura ry-Foreningen- for Steinerpedagogik rf,
    c/o Lea Blafield, Jyvaskylan Rudolf-Steiner-koulu, Honka harjuntie
    6, FIN 40600 Jyvaskyla
France
    Féderation des Écoles Rudolf Steiner en France, 11 rue de Villaines,
    F-091370 Verrières-le-Buisson
Germany
    Bund der Freien Waldorfschulen e.V., D-70184 Stuttgart,
    Heidehofstrasse 32
Ireland
    Irish Steiner Waldorf Education Association, Raheen Road,
    Tuamgraney, County Clare
Italy
    Associazone Amici Scuola, via Clerici 12, 1-22030 Camnage Volta
    (COMO)

Latvia
Lettishe Assoziation fur Waldorf-padagogik, Pirma iela 26a,
Rigarajons, LV 2164
Luxembourg
Verain fir Waldorfpadagogik Letzebuerg, 45 Rue de l'Avenir,
L 1147 Luxembourg
Netherlands
Bond van Vrije Scholen, Hoofdstraat 14 B, NL-3972 LA Driebergen
New Zealand
Federation of Rudolf Steiner Schools, PO Box 888,
Hastings, Hawke's Bay
Norway
Steinerskolene i Norge, Prof. Dahlsgt. 30, N-0260 Oslo
Romania
Federatia Waldorf din Romania, Bd.Marasti nr.59, sector 1,
RO-71331 Bucuresti
Slovenia
Drustvo prijateljev, waldorfike sole, Rodiceva 2,61000 Ljubljana,
Slovenia
South Africa
Southern African Federation of Waldorf Schools, PO Box 67587,
Bryanston, Transvaal, 2021 Johannesburg
Sweden
Waldorfskolefederationen, Fridhemsgatan 17, S-12240 Stockholm
Switzerland
Koordinationsstelle der Rudolf Steiner Schulen in der Schweiz,
Robert Thomas, Carmenstrasse 49, CH-8032 Zürich
United Kingdom
Steiner Waldorf Schools Fellowship, Kidbrooke Park, Forest Row,
East Sussex RH18 5JA
USA
Association of Waldorf Schools of North America, Chairman, 3911
Bannister Road, Fair Oaks, CA 95628

Index

Michael Rose completed a BA in English Literature at York University. Wanting a balance to academic work he learnt to make shoes and was a self-employed shoe-maker for a couple of years. Through an involvement with a Camphill community Michael got to know about Steiner Waldorf education and became part of an initiative group to found a school in York. This led him to complete a teacher training course in Waldorf Education and to becoming a founding teacher of the York Steiner School. Michael has taught there as a class teacher ever since, and has also been a tutor on the North of England Steiner Teacher Training Course (NESTT) for over ten years.

Other Books from Hawthorn Press

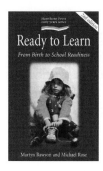

Ready to Learn
From birth to school readiness

MARTYN RAWSON AND MICHAEL ROSE

Ready to Learn will help you to decide when your child is ready to take the step from kindergarten to school proper. The key is an imaginative grasp of how children learn to play, speak, think and relate between birth and six years of age.

**224pp; 216 x 138mm; 978-1-903458-66-2; pb
(new edition)**

You Are Your Child's First Teacher
What parents can do with and for their children from birth to age six

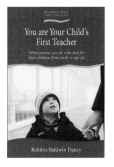

RAHIMA BALDWIN DANCY

This clear, practical book will guide you through the maze of key parenting concerns in the early years and help you find solutions that work for your own family situation. Discover how to create your own family rituals, nourish your child's imagination, and use imitation, repetition and setting limits to promote positive discipline.

400pp; 234 x 156mm; 978-1-903458-65-5; pb

The Parent and Child Group Handbook
A Steiner/Waldorf approach

DOT MALE

Dot Male's lively, accessible guide to running a thriving parent and child group expains how to: create a calm, harmonious space; use rhythm and ritual to structure a session; devise appropriate toys, crafts, games and outdoor play; celebrate seasonal festivals and the cycle of the year; fulfil key health, safety and legal requirements.

256pp; 246 x 189mm; 978-1-903458-46-4; pb

Getting in touch with Hawthorn Press

What are your pressing questions about the early years?
The Hawthorn Early Years Series arises from parents' and educators' pressing questions and concerns – so please contact us with your questions. These will help spark new books, workshops or festivals if there is sufficient interest. We will be delighted to hear your views on our Early Years books, how they can be improved, and what your needs are.

Visit our website for details of the Early Years Series and forthcoming books and events:
http://www.hawthornpress.com

Ordering books

If you have difficulties ordering Hawthorn Press books from a bookshop, you can order direct from:
United Kingdom
Booksource
50 Cambuslang Road, Cambuslang, Glasgow
G32 8NB
Tel: 0845 370 0063
Fax: 0845 370 0064
E-mail: orders@booksource.net

USA/North America
Steiner Books
PO Box 960, Herndon
VA 20172-0960
Tel: (800) 856 8664
Fax: (703) 661 1501
E-mail: service@steinerbooks.org